SWORD AND MASQUE

Julius Palffy Alpar M. Phys. Ed. Maître d'Armes.

SWORD
AND
MASQUE

JULIUS PALFFY-ALPAR

Maitre d'Armes
Master of Physical Education

F. A. DAVIS COMPANY

PHILADELPHIA

DEDICATION

I dedicate this book to my wife Eva who accompanied me with love and understanding in my wanderings through seven countries —from Budapest to San Francisco—while teaching young and old, unknown and famous, the secrets of fencing.

She always was the friend of the family of fencers who gathered around me to learn and understand the conversation of the blades and acquire knightly manners in "the sport of Kings and Cavaliers."

THE MASTER

to Julius
Aspar
Meyt Fencing Master
in Frue dedication
and Friend
always Yours
MARCEL
80

Foreword

I consider fencing to be a great art which raises men to *Knights* in their thoughts and behavior. Fencing is a school of humility and develops speed, perfect control of the body, balance, beauty, and strong grace. It should be recommended to all men wanting to master their feelings and actions during their lifetime. Through this art they will think clearly and act always with style in their decisions.

As a mime actor I should say that fencing in our profession is an important factor for mental and physical development. The fencer is an acrobat, a constant actor in action, a dancer, and a performer sensing timing, speed, intensity, and pulsation. All these dramatic effects are the basis of real theater.

I thank Julius Alpar, whose pupil I still remain, for bringing the love for fencing to my soul. Julius Alpar is not only a great fencing master, but a man of stature whose warm personality and pedagogic knowledge I will always remember. I recommend those who want to practice this noble art to receive their first lessons from an artist like Julius Alpar. He makes me remember the moment when Cyrano de Bergerac said before he fought his duel *a l'hotel de Bourgogne* against Valvert:

> Elégant comme Céladon,
> Agile comme Scaramouche,
> Je vous préviens, cher Mirmydon,
> Qu'à la fin de l'envoi je touche.

I treasure those lines because Cyrano knew that he could touch his *adversaire* at any time he wanted, which is the supreme proof that the most important feeling in life is self-command. This is the only way to lead men to rule over their passion and reach the most precious aim in life: liberty.

Marcel Marceau

Foreword

Julius Alpar, in *Sword and Masque,* has made a unique contribution to the literature of fencing. This is the most comprehensive and authoritative book, available today, dealing with this sport.

For its preparation, he has drawn from his extensive, varied, and eminently successful experience as a coach of Olympic fencers, a university instructor in beginning, intermediate, and advanced (competitive) fencing, and an instructor in dramatic fencing.

During the years he has served on the Berkeley Campus of the University of California, enrollments in fencing in the voluntary basic instruction program of physical education have increased markedly, and his students have won numerous awards in intercollegiate competition.

This welcome publication will be of value to instructors, actors, and historians interested in fencing.

CARL L. NORDLY
Professor Emeritus
Department of Physical Education
University of California, Berkeley

Contents

AUTOBIOGRAPHY xv

Section I: HISTORY OF FENCING. 1

    Early Fencing   2
    Early Middle Ages   4
    Fifteenth Century   7
    Sixteenth Century   9
    Seventeenth Century   14
    Eighteenth Century   16
    Nineteenth Century   18
    Twentieth Century   20
    The Swordsmith's Craft   24
    The Sword   25
    Special Terms Used in the Description of the Weapons   26
    Dimensions of the Weapons   27
    Costumes   29
    Salutations   31
    Manners   33
    Historical Perspective   37

Section II: THEORY AND GENERAL ADVICE 39

    Analysis of Movement   39
    Reflex Testing and Selective Responses   43
    Psychology of Fencing   47
    Training   51
    Physical Condition   54
    Competition   57
    Diet   58
    Manners   60

Section III: COMPETITIVE FENCING 63

General Background   63
The Teaching of Fencing   65
Weapons   66
Styles   66
Equipment and Its Proper Use   67
Preparatory and Other Exercises   69

Chapter 1: THE FOIL 71

The Grip   71
Positions of the Body   74
Foot Movements   75
The Target   79
The Salute   80
The Positions of the Weapon   81
Fundamental Movements and Definitions   86
Simple Actions   88
Defense   89
Compound Attacks   101
Composite Parries   106
Compound Ripostes   107
Renewed Attacks   108
Actions in Time   109
The False Attacks (Fausse Attaques, Attacco Simulato)   115
Disarmament (Desarmo, Sforzo)   115
Free Play   116
Electrical Fencing   117

Chapter 2: THE ÉPÉE 119

The On Guard Position   120
The Footwork   120
The Hit   121
The Parries and Ripostes   121
Other Actions   122

Chapter 3: THE SABER 127

The Grip   127
Position of the Body   129
Foot Movements   131

The Moulinets   136
The Target   137
The Salute   137
The Positions of the Saber   138
Simple Actions   141
Compound Actions   155
Composite Parries   158
Compound Ripostes   159
Dual Feints   160
Renewed Attacks   161
Actions in Time (Tempo)   162

Section IV: THEATRICAL FENCING 171

Introduction   171
Ancient Combat   173
Middle Ages   175
Early Modern Period   182
Modern Period   187
Exercises Useful for Stage Movements   189
The Fencing Scene in Hamlet   195
Molière's Don Juan   202
Romeo and Juliet   204
King Lear   208

APPENDIX 215

Summary of the Olympic and World Championship
    Winners According to Nations   215
Grand Total of Olympic and World Championship Gold
    Medals in Fencing   231
Summary of the Olympic Gold Medals in Fencing   231
Summary of the World Championship Gold Medals in
    Fencing   232
Summary of Olympic Championships in Fencing   233
Summary of World Championships in Fencing   234
References   236

INDEX 237

Autobiography

I was born in 1908 in Hunyad-Kristyor, Transylvania, which at that time was part of Hungary. My father was a descendant of German settlers, and my mother was a member of the ancient "Pálffy" family which gave many prominent noblemen to Hungary. In 1927 I received my diploma of senior matriculation at the high school in Békés-Gyula and then spent three years at Békés-Csaba with the Army.

In 1930, there was a need for Army Sports Instructors. Since I had placed second in the national interterritorial competition in the 400 and 800 meter runs and had ranked third academically in the Officer's School, I felt that I could qualify for this profession. I entered the Toldi Miklos Royal Hungarian Sports Institute and graduated at the top of my class. After three years as an Assistant Instructor at the school I received my Master's degree and Diploma as Maitre d'Armes and Sports Instructor.

At the Sports Institute, besides fencing, I studied almost all the known sports. During my years there, I won the individual ski championship for the Army three times and was a member of the champion Ski Biathlon Team for five years. For two winters I was sent to Austria by the government for Alpine and glacier climbing exercises. As a member of the Modern Pentathlon Squad, I participated in horseback riding, shooting, fencing, running, and swimming competitions.

After graduation in 1935, I accepted a position on the teaching staff of the Ludovika Akademia (Hungarian Military Academy). I devoted myself to professional teaching until 1945 at which time I held the rank of Captain Professor at the Academy. I also was the Maitre d'Armes of the Hungarian Athletic Club and the Hungarian Officers' Club, and one of the coaches of the 1936 Olympic Champion Team. In 1943 I won the Three Weapon Championship for Army Fencing Masters.

Before 1945 I coached Adam Paul Kovacs, Olympic and World Saber Champion, and Tibor Bercelly and Ladislaus Rajcsanyi, members of the 1936 Olympic Champion Saber Team. In 1945 I became the Sports Manager for the top recreation center of the American Army in Europe, at Garmisch-Partenkirchen Winter Olympic Resort at Eibsee in Bavaria. There, besides teaching other sports, I learned and taught water skiing, adding this fast-growing sport to my knowledge.

In 1948 I spent one year in Coblenz with the 10th French Division where I had the opportunity to work with the French Master Epee Champion, Maitre d'Armes Devimeux. After I left Coblenz, I worked in Saarbrucken with German fencers, among them Otto

Certificate given by Cdt. Bontemps, former president of the Fédération Internationale D'Escrime and Federation Francaise D'Escrime.

Adam—the German Saber Champion and President of the German Fencing Association.

In 1948 I left for Paris where I taught at the Racing Club de France with Maitre Bourdon and Maitre Spinozi. This time was very valuable to me not only because of the amiability of all my French colleagues, but because I had a chance to observe the French foil fencing in its native country and compare it with the Italian style we learned in Hungary. When I left Paris in 1949, the French Association, in appreciation of my work, gave me a certificate which I value very much.

From 1949 to 1960 I was the Maitre d'Armes of the University of Toronto, Canada, the largest university in the British Commonwealth. In 1949 I won the trick riding event at the Canadian Waterskiing Championships.

In 1960 I was invited to come to the San Francisco Sports Academy, where I was the Chief Instructor until 1962. I then became a faculty member of the Physical Education Department of the University of California in Berkeley.

In Budapest I was connected with the film world through my work as the fencing director of the Hungarian film "Mayfair." I gave lessons to Marcel Marceau, the world-famous French pantomime artist whose friendship encouraged my interest in theatrical work.° I taught theatrical fencing in the New Play Society, a theatrical school in Toronto, under the direction of the former English actress Dora Mavor Moore. During my stay in Toronto I gave fencing instructions to, among others, Robert Goulet, Hollywood and Broadway star. I am currently associated with the Department of Dramatic Art at the University of California, giving instruction in theatrical fencing.

JULIUS PALFFY-ALPAR

° The major operas and dramas for which I staged fencing and gymnastic movements included: Mozart's *Don Giovanni*, Gounod's *Faust*, Rostand's *Cyrano de Bergerac*, Molier's *Don Juan*, Oliver's *The Antifarce of John and Leporello*, and Shakespeare's *Henry IV*, *King Lear*, *Hamlet*, *Anthony and Cleopatra*, and *Romeo and Juliet*.

SWORD AND MASQUE

Section I

History of Fencing

In beginning the history of fencing, let us cite Molière's definition of fencing:

> Fencing is the art of giving cuts without receiving them. The necessity of touching the opponent but avoiding his cuts makes the art of fencing very difficult and complicated. The eyes which observe and prevent, the brain which considers and decides, the hand which carries the decision through must harmonize accuracy and speed to give the necessary life to the sword. (Quoted from I. E. Koch's Bühnenfechtkunst, page 10.)°

In both ancient times and during the Middle Ages, fencing was not only a means of combat, but was also a daily exercise for soldiers and men of the upper classes. Today it is a mental and physical exercise which helps improve and maintain health and fitness. Fencing has been taught in various places: gladiator schools, military institutes and salle d'armes and, at present, is offered in high schools, universities, clubs, theatrical schools, and dance and modelling schools by amateur and professional instructors.

Most historians date the beginning of modern fencing from the Battle of Crècy (1346). The use of fire-arms in combat brought about the abandonment of heavy armor and the improvement of proficiency with the sword in close combat. The use of the lighter weapons encouraged the development of modern techniques of fencing. If we call the use of the ancient sword primitive fencing, we must go back much further than 1346 to trace the origin of fencing.

°(The above quotation seems to be an amplification taken of Molière's *Le Bourgeois Gentilhomme* and other works.)

Early Fencing

When men first started to fight with beating or cutting weapons, they naturally had to practice attacks on the enemy and find some defenses against similar attacks. Archeologists have found stone and bone striking weapons with straight or leaf-shaped form, dating back to prehistoric times. Even prehistoric man had to exercise with offensive and defensive weapons to obtain food and protect himself and his family. As families joined into tribes, groups of guards were formed to protect the tribal territories. As tribes grew into nations, armies equipped with various weapons were formed for protection.

In Ancient China the sword was used as early as the twenty-second century B.C. In Ancient Egypt, during the twelfth and thirteenth centuries B.C., soldiers carried bows, spears, battle-axes, sickle-shaped, long daggers, and straight, narrow swords. For protection, they wore helmets, leather or gilded tunics, shields with eyeholes, and kerchiefs (for protection against the sun). The oldest written statement about fencing dates from 1190 B.C. and was found in the temple near Luxor. The hieroglyphics recording a fencer's speech say: "On guard and admire what my valiant hand shall do." The spectators' reply is: "Advance, advance, on excellent fighter, on meritorious fighter."

The credit for the invention of fencing is given by the Italian fencing master, Copoferro, to Ninus, the king of Assyris. From the Assyrian kingdom we have recovered descriptions of lightly and heavily armed warriors. The light arms included: metal helmets, round shields, long spears, and short swords (carried hanging from a double sword belt); the heavily armed warriors carried the same weapons but also wore a coat of mail.

The Hindus believe that Brahma taught the Brahmins to fence and in the *Mahabharata* both the thrust and the parry are mentioned:

> Brightly gleamed their lightning rapiers as they ranged the listed field.
> Brave and fierce is their action and their movement quick and light.
> Skilled and true the thrust and parry of their weapons flaming bright.

The use of iron weapons was introduced by the Hittites (1200 B.C.) and spread quickly to every country around the Mediterranean. We have very few written documents from Greece about fencing.

One of the first references to the use of any weapon by women has been found on a Greek vase picturing a Phrygian Amazon wearing a cap, hose, and lightly laced boots, and carrying a battle-axe and a small, round shield.

Fencing was not part of the Olympic Games. The sport called *oplomachia* was perhaps used only to train the warriors who needed the sword for battle. The sword used in ancient Greece was made of bronze, and was short, double-edged with a half-circle point, a hilt or crossbar, and was ridged from the point to the hilt. It was carried in a case, strapped very high to the belt, and hung almost vertically. The left leg and knee were covered with greaves and the right shoulder and elbow were armored. A round oval shield, about 39 inches (one meter) in diameter was carried with the left arm to protect the body. The head was covered by a metal helmet with a crest and a movable cheek guard. The spear was used for thrusting, and javelin-throwing was one of the Greek national sports. In battle, if a Greek soldier's spear broke or was thrown, he used the sword for close combat.

In Ancient Rome the soldiers wore leather tunics (often mounted with iron bands or scales), leather breeches, studded girdles, metal helmets, and carried round or rectangular shields. They used straight double-edged, pointed swords (gladius) and spears (pilum). The sword was attached to the left side of the body; a short dagger was carried on the right side. Both legs were covered with greaves and knee-guards, and the right arm and elbow covered with protectors.

The gladiators used lighter protection and were better trained than the average soldier. Of the different kinds of gladiators, the *Myrmillo* and the *Samnite* were the heavier armed with helmet, shield, left leg protection, and sword. The *Thracian* gladiators wore helmets, two greaves, and used a short dagger. The *Retiarius* fought with a net in one hand and a trident in the other, and wore only a girdle with loincloth, greaves with bands, and a bandaged left sleeve with metal shoulder plate. This type of gladiator was usually matched with a heavily armed opponent and fought either by throwing his net over his adversary and stabbing him or keeping him away with the trident. The sword, which in the beginning was a short, wide weapon, later was made about three feet long and thinner.

To satisfy the spectators the gladiators had to perform skillfully. Losing a fight usually meant death, unless the loser won the sympathy of the mob. The Latin proverbs show the seriousness of the games: "Ave Caesar morituri te salutant" (Hail Caesar, those who are about to die salute you); "Gladiators vincendum or moriendum erat" (The gladiators must conquer or die); "Vae victis" (Woe to the vanquished). These expressions allow us to guess the fate of the conquered.

The gladiators received their instructions in special schools, called *Ludi*, from the *Lanesta* or director of the school. The gladiators were classified according to skill and the Lanesta arranged the combats for them. The students learned the basic movements in groups by using wooden swords. They practiced first on a fencing post, and then with different partners. In the arena, before the real fights, the gladiators usually put on a mass demonstration with wooden swords. After this exhibition, the real fights started and were almost always fought to the death. If a gladiator was reluctant to fight, he was persuaded by whips and hot irons. When a participant was wounded or disarmed he turned with open arms to the emperor and the audience for mercy. As a sign of mercy, the spectators waved their handerchiefs; if the judgment was to be death, it was expressed with closed fist and thumb down. In the beginning, the gladiators were prisoners of war or slaves, and later, criminals condemned to death. Eventually, free citizens, patricians, and even women frequented the schools and fencing became fashionable. Unfortunately, no written documents are left to reveal the intricacies of the instruction in the gladiator schools; the excavation of ancient Roman cities give us the only ideas we have of their training. In spite of the popularity of fencing itself, the duel was considered barbarian by the Romans.

Early Middle Ages

From the fifth century on, the use of the sword was part of the military training of every man. The Western European nations, for the most part, used Roman armor and weapons. The barbaric tribes who flooded Europe used bows and arrows, spears, or battle-axes, but preferred long, wide, straight swords (spatha) for fighting.

Thyerry in *Histoire d'Attila* mentions that in the fifth century the Huns, on festive occasions, held tournaments using these weapons. The Lombards, Goths, and Franks were very skillful in using the long sword and shortly all the other nations adopted it. The duel became an acceptable way of solving differences between two people and the clergy permitted it as *trial by ordeal*.

After the Germanic tribes swarmed over and settled in Europe, the general level of civilization declined. During the ninth, tenth, and eleventh centuries, the tribes, city-states, and even private landlords engaged in constant *little wars* against invaders or each other. To protect themselves and to increase their own strength, the populace united in feudal contracts. The land was divided into *fiefs* and each fief had to support at least one armored mounted knight. The expense of good armor prevented the raising of large armies. It was better to have a small but well equipped force than a mass of poorly armed peasants who could easily be conquered by small bands of mounted knights. Fighting became the professional occupation of the upper classes. The lance, straight sword, battle-axe, and mace were the main offensive weapons. The sword used was wide, straight, double-edged, long, and pointed.

To defend themselves the early knights wore knee-length cloth or leather tunics, covered with iron rings or scales, iron caps, and shields. Parries were not attempted; the knights evaded blows or used their shields for defense. To gain the required strength, they had to practice with the heavy weapons every day for hours. Yet armor was vulnerable, and its weaknesses led to the further development of weapons and, in turn, to the improvement of armor.

When the ringed or scaled coat failed to give enough protection, it became necessary to use chain mail made of dense small links which gave a strong, flexible surface against cuts. During the middle of the twelfth century, knights wore a tunic over the coat of mail to protect it but this proved to be very warm in the heat of the sun. Eventually, a long narrow sword was developed for thrusting which passed through the links. The blade was three-or four-sided and very stiff. This *estoc* made it necessary to wear plate mail over the chain mail. The plates were fastened with straps to the chest, shoulders, elbows, knees, and thighs. This so-called gothic armor was developed about the fourteenth century (Fig. 1-1). The use of this armor again made cuts important and so the weight and size of the sword was increased. The dagger became useful since, at close quarters, it could be slipped between the plates of armor.

FIG. 1-1 *Gothic armor.*   FIG. 1-2 *Maximilian armor.*

Courtesy of The De Young Museum, San Francisco, California.

The increased use of metal plates led to the *Maximilian* type of armor used in the fifteenth century. This metal suit covered the entire body and consisted of a basin helmet with movable visor, shoulder, back, and breast plates, arm casings, elbow guards, iron gloves, loin plates, knee caps, greaves, iron shoes, and a coat of mail (Fig. 1-2). The protection was completed with a shield. A complete suit of armor sometimes consisted of 158 separate parts which weighed about 84 pounds (38 kg.). Powerful horses were developed to carry the fully dressed knight. The horse was also protected with a heavy coat of armor and was trained to take part in the fight by trampling the foot soldiers and biting and kicking the other horses.

The offensive weapons included the jousting lance, heavy sword, mace, axe, and dagger (Figs. 1-3, 1-4). The lance was carried over the right arm, the sword on the left side of the saddle, shield on the left arm, and the dagger on the right side of the body. If the knight had to fight on foot he wore only the upper part of the suit of armor so that he could move around freely. His shield was then used to protect his legs.

FIG. 1-3 *German swords of the fifteenth century.*

Courtesy of the Metropolitan Museum of Art, New York City.

In combat against the fully armored knight, opponent's found the two-hand sword effective. This weapon could knock the knight unconcious, cut through his armor, or kill the horse with one blow.

In peace time, jousts or tournaments were held to keep the

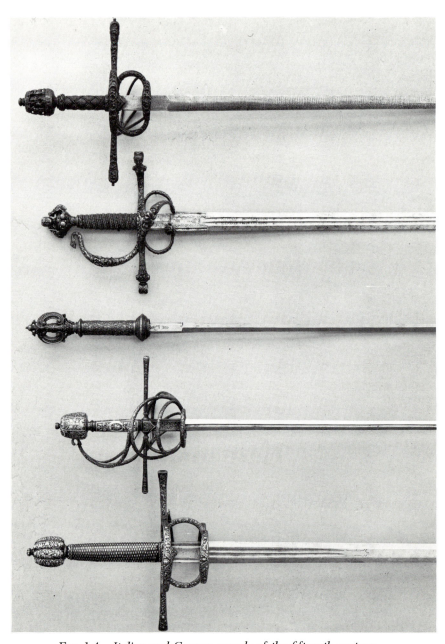

Fig. 1-4   *Italian and German swords of the fifteenth century.*

knight in combat condition. The tournaments were conducted by well-defined rules and were carried out with as great a ceremony as the one held when the knights were accepted into Knighthood.

The use of both heavy armor and heavy weapons allowed only simple movements, forcing the knight to concentrate on one blow at a time; the tournaments, therefore, had no direct influence on the development of fencing.

After the introduction of fire-arms (1346) forced the knights to regard heavy armor as useless, lighter weapons such as the long, slim, elastic blade (*la centille*) came into favor. The use of this type of blade led to the development of the sword-rapier which pointed the way to modern fencing. The rapier became a part of the everyday dress, and thereby increased the chance for dueling. The custom of dueling improved the technique of fencing, and led to the establishment of fencing schools all over Europe.

The Spanish established the first fencing schools and gave the blade a triangular shape which increased its rigidity. According to the Spanish, the first book on fencing was written by Diego de Valera in the second half of the fifteenth century.

A book called *Talhoffer's Fechtbuch* was produced in Germany in 1467 but contained only pictures and no text.

The Germans, who favored the long cutting sword even after the adoption of the rapier blade, maintained an old-fashioned style of sword play. Associations called the *Fecht Bruderschaft* were formed, the members of which received authorization and privileges from Frederick III to teach fencing. The oldest of these associations was the *Bürgerschaft von St. Marcus von Löwenberge*, founded in 1480, and its members were called *Marxbrüders*.

Sixteenth Century

Fencing spread from Spain to Italy in the beginning of the sixteenth century and one Italian school after the other was opened. The wide-spread rise of printing made it possible to publish more books about fencing. The first such book in Italy was *Opere di Scherma* written by Mozete in 1509. Marozzo also wrote a book in the first half of the fifteenth century but the fencing positions he described did not gain acceptance.

A more noteworthy book was written in the middle of the same century by Agrippa, an architect and engineer, title *Trattato di Scientia d'Arme*. The author explained the movements and positions of fencing. He gave four positions which are related to the positions used today: the *prima guardia* (similar to *prime*, close to *quinte*); *seconda* (high *seconde*, close to *tierce*); *terza* (low *tierce*); and *quarta* (low *quarte*, the point close to the ground). Parries are mentioned but not defined. Perhaps they were the same as the positions described but executed rather like the time-thrusts of today. Wearing a glove of mail on the left hand made it possible for the fencer to grasp the opponent's blade or use a buckler, dagger, or cloak for defense. The buckler was a small shield about 12 inches (30 cm.) in diameter, often with a spike in the center, used in close fighting.

The buckler was soon discarded in Italy in favor of the dagger, which was used to parry the opponent's thrust or was crossed with the rapier to stop head-cuts. The dagger often had strongly curved quillons to trap the opponent's blade and was used in close quarters for stabbing. Two guards are mentioned in the literature of the time, in the *stoccata guard*, the rapier hand was held near to the hip with the dagger point close to the rapier's point; in the *high guard*, the rapier was held in a high straight position and the dagger (with the point out), near the left hip. A cloak wrapped around the left arm was used as a defense against thrusts or could be thrown over the opponent's head or weapon to obstruct his use of it.

Grassi in his book, *Ragioni di Adoperar Sicuramente l'Arme*, published in 1570, mentioned the lunge and gave more importance to thrusts than to cuts. Viggiani described the lunge and gave examples of different thrusts as secret movements (*Botta Secretta*) in his book, *Trattato dello Schermo*, published at the end of the sixteenth century.

The next development in fencing was the guard, which gave more protection to the sword-hand. The shorter and lighter blade encouraged the use of the disengage and feints (Figs. 1-5, 1-6). In the on guard position the left foot was put forward when the dagger or other defensive weapon was used. If only the rapier was used, the right foot was put forward and the knees slightly bent with the weight of the body on the left foot to keep the head away from

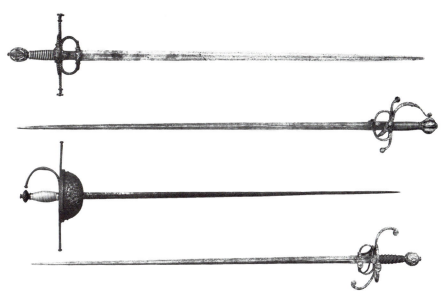

F<small>IG</small>. 1-5   *Rapiers of the sixteenth and seventeenth centuries. Top to bottom:*
Spanish, dress; French, dress; Italian, cup-hilted; Italian, dress.

Courtesy of The Metropolitan Museum of Art.

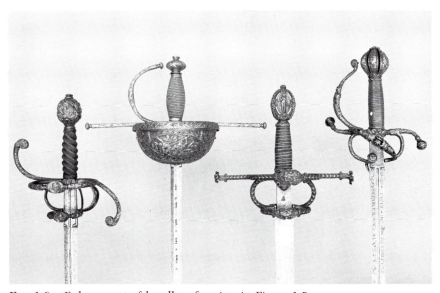

F<small>IG</small>. 1-6   *Enlargement of handles of rapiers in Figure 1-5.*

Courtesy of The Metropolitan Museum of Art.

the opponent. Passing (*passado*), stepping with one foot in front of the other, ducking, and displacing the body were practiced. For training sessions, real weapons were used, but they had blunted ends.

In France fencing was taught by Italian fencing masters. The first French schools were established after the middle of the sixteenth century. Around 1570 the Academie d'Armes, the first association of masters, was recognized by Henry III. In 1573, Sainct Didier wrote the first book in French about fencing, *Traicté Contenant les Secrets du Premier Livre sur L'espèe Soule, Mère de Toutes Armes*. The new French fencing masters tried to modify the Italian mode of fencing to the French nature, and, in doing so, created a new style.

In Germany the Marxbrüders controlled the teaching of fencing. Once a year, in Frankfurt, they held examinations for fencing master candidates, giving *letters of privilege* to those who were to be allowed to teach. The first book with German text was *Eingründung der ritterlicher Kunst der Fechterei* published by Paurnfeindt in 1516.

Hans Sachs, fencing master, shoe maker, and famous Meistersinger belonged to the Marxbrüders and wrote the first poem about fencing.

> Fechten macht wer as wohl kann
> hurtig und thätig einen jungen Mann
> geschickt und rund, leicht und gering
> gelenk, fertig zu allem Ding,
> gegen den Feind beherzt und unverzagt
> tapfer und keck; der's mannlich wagt
> kühn und groszmüthig in dem Krieg
> zu gewinnen lob, ehr, und sieg . . .

Translated into English:

> He who can do it fences
> an agile and active young man;
> skillful and balanced, moderate and modest
> adroit for everything,
> against enemies courageous and fearless
> brave and daring; he who does it manly,
> audacious and magnanimous in the war
> to win fame, honor and victory . . .

In 1570, Meyer published *Kunst der Fechtens* written with typical German profundity about the weapons of his time.

In England, in the first half of the sixteenth century, a guild, Masters of the Noble Science of Defense, was founded. This group controlled the grading of examinees. The applicants were graded as: beginner or scholar; junior or free scholar; assistant or provost. *Paying the prize* was the term used for the matriculation to earn the degree of master.

After the introduction of the rapier, the English upper classes studied the use of this weapon—either by going to France or by importing Italian fencing masters. One of the newcomers was Saviolo who published a book called *His Practice* in London in 1595. Silver published his book, *Paradoxes of Defense*, in 1599 in which he attacked the Italian masters who preferred the use of thrusting weapons to English type sword play. In spite of this criticism, the Italian schools flourished.

The use of the sword and buckler which spread from Italy, France, and Spain to England became popular with the lower classes, along with the *waster* or *singlestick* type of fencing which was employed as practice for backswording. Backswording was a military exercise with a basket-hilted, straight, pointless sword used with a simple technique. The singlestick was a wooden sword with cross hilt; people who fenced with it did not use padding and removed their coats.

While in Italy, France, Germany, and England fencing adhered to similiar principles, the Spanish masters evolved a strange way of fencing. Toward the end of the sixteenth century they brought philosophy and even mysterious mystical elements into fencing. Fencing in Spain became a mathematical and geometrical problem involving different line and diagrams drawn on the floor. Di Garranza is recognized as the father of this style. His book, *De la Filosofia de las Armas*, was published in Lisbon in 1569. This school was so artificial that it never found followers abroad and had no influence on the main stream of fencing.

From the middle of the sixteenth century, the popularity of dueling steadily increased all over Europe. The duel had long been considered a good way to settle grievances and in early times permission was readily given by the local rulers. However, dueling soon got out of hand. Quarrels with others were provoked without reason and gentlemen sometimes crossed swords just for the fun of it.

Henry II of France, after losing his favorite courtier, Chastaigneraie, in a duel in 1547, forbade dueling, but the royal decree had no effect. In fact, the situation got worse and even women became involved in dueling. In England, by order of Elizabeth I, jail sentences were given those caught dueling. Rebellion against such orders was considered a sign of courage, so duels went on.

At the end of the sixteenth century the square shaped blade (*the Flamberg*) came into use in Germany, France, and Italy; this weapon served as a transition between the rapier and the small sword. The broad sword became the military weapon in the West; the curved, light sword brought by the Turkish invasion to Europe was used in the East by Hungarian and Polish cavalrymen.

Seventeenth Century

The insecure political situation in Italy left its mark on the development of fencing in that country in that many of the masters emigrated to try their fortune elsewhere. Fabris, one of the most famous of these fencing masters, traveled to France and Denmark. His book, *Sienza e Practica d'Arme,* published in Coopenhagen in 1606, demonstrates a preference for the thrust over the cut.

Giganti mentions in *Teatro . . . di perare et di ferire di spada solo* the counter-parries and doubles which became possible with the shorter and lighter rapier. In 1610, Rodolfo Capo Ferro with his *Gran Simulacro Dell'Arte e Dell'Uso della Scherma* enriched the fencing literature. His *universal parry* was a sweeping move from tierce (passing quarte) to seconde, crossing all the lines.

At this time, the point (button) was invented for use in practice. The point, about the size of a golf ball, reduced the danger of putting out the opponent's eye or hurting his face.

The French school of fencing became dominant in this century. The education of fencing masters was regulated and encouraged by a royal order providing for the training of fencing masters in the army. With this act, Louis XIII laid down the foundation for the leadership of the military maitre d'armes in France.

This was the heroic and romantic age of the *Three Musketeers* on one hand and a time of dishonest and treacherous fighting on the other. Louis XIV regulated the teaching of fencing and allowed only maitre d'armes to open a salle d'armes or to teach fencing. This king also set up the *Guard of Honor* (a committee of high ranking people) to settle affairs peacefully, and he enforced the anti-dueling laws with some severity. To get around the law, people claimed to use the duel for self-defense.

In 1653, Besnard used the name *fleuret* for the thrusting weapon for the first time. He described the eight parries, feints, and attacks on the blade. De Lyancourt mentioned the *coupée* (a thrust passing around the point of the opponent's blade), which became one of the characteristics of the French school. De Lyancourt was active for more than fifty years in Paris and has been cited as one of the greatest among the French masters. Labat's book *L'Art en fait des Armes* (1696) contains a discussion of all the major movements still taught today.

From the middle of the seventeenth century, the full mask (with wire openings for the eyes) came into use for practice sessions. The rapier no longer had cutting edges, and the mail gloves were replaced by buff-gauntlets. The military cutting sword was replaced by the bayonet which was attached to the gun-barrel for fighting and was used in close combat by the infantry.

In Germany the fencing guilds lost much of their importance and the universities took over the leadership in the development of fencing. In the first part of the seventeenth century, Wilhelm Kreussler, master of fencing at the University of Jena for fifty years, was the most famous of the German fencing masters. Four of his sons became masters also and taught at different German Universities. At Jena, Kreussler was followed by one of his sons, Godfried, who was succeeded in turn by his son, Johann Wilhelm. The German style taught by these men was a mixture of the Italian and French methods.

In England, around the middle of the seventeenth century, the association of masters disintegrated and fencing suffered a serious decline. The so-called fencing masters performed on the stage competing for prizes. These displays were popular with the common people but were looked down upon by the aristocracy. The low moral standards of these fencing masters gave the occupation a very dubious reputation; as a result, even today, the English fencing teachers call themselves professors of fencing rather than masters.

This was the century in which the long rapier lost its popularity, and the small sword was recognized as an integral part of a gentleman's dress. Real fencing was maintained by the gentry, and the schools were frequented only by noblemen and cavaliers.

Toward the end of the century Sir William Hope wrote several books on fencing, of which the best known is *Scots Fencing Master*.

Eighteenth Century

In the eighteenth century the small sword replaced the rapier entirely. Fencing in most European countries became a sport rather than a preparation for dueling (Fig. 1-7).

The French and Italian styles became clearly different. The Italians based their fencing on the fundamentals of the use of the

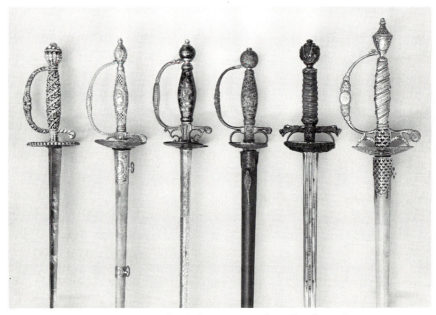

Fig. 1-7   *Court swords of the seventeenth and eighteenth centuries.*

Courtesy The Metropolitan Museum of Art.

16   SWORD AND MASQUE

rapier; the French developed a more flexible style with smoother movements. The French method of teaching was more unified and gained faster acceptance than the Italian, where each fencing master had his own view and felt that his school was the only good one. In France the small sword became the national weapon, and the use of the simple hilt led directly to modern fencing. Girard, at the beginning of the century, described, in a pamphlet, almost the same movements used today. (*Nouveau Traite . . . Sur le Fait des Armes*). La Boessière and St. George invented the modern mask which allowed the *on guard* to become the offensive-defensive position known today.

In 1766, De Danet, who was the president of the fencing academy, gave new names to the parries. This act evoked such violent opposition from the maitres d'armes that he had to abdicate his position. A picture in his book showed the Italian and French on guard position. The left hand of the Italian fencer was held overhead as we do today; the French fencer kept his hand in front of his chest indicating that the use of the left hand was still allowed in defense at that time.

In 1798, during the French revolution, the academy was dissolved and its last president, Rousseau, who was the private fencing master of the King, was guillotined.

In Germany, Jena, Halle, Leipzig, and Heidelberg were the centers of fencing, and the sport was compulsory in the military schools. Heinrich Wilhelm Kreussler (the grandson of Wilhelm Kreussler) became the most famous German master of this century. The tradition of fencing families was continued when three sons of Heinrich F. Roux, Kreussler's assistant, became teachers at different universities. Dueling flourished in the universities, and it was transformed into the *Mensura* or *Schlager* fencing which became a German specialty. The schlager involved a pointless blade and baskethilted guard. The blade was sharp, $\frac{7}{8}$ of an inch along the front edge and 2 inches along the back edge. The neck, wrist, armpit, and abdomen were protected with bandages and a leather apron; goggles were worn over the eyes and temples. The beginner was allowed to wear a protective cap. The on guard position with the weapon was the high tierce and the position of the feet was fixed (the duelist was not supposed to move). The fencer had to deliver a certain number of cuts within a certain time and a hit finished the fight.

In England backswording remained popular and was practiced with a stick (*cudgelling*) as a relatively safe form of fencing. In 1755 Italian master Angelo (pupil of Parisian master Teillagory) went to London where he later published the book, *Ecole des Armes* (1787).

In Spain the *Espada*, almost 5 feet long, was used in fencing. The bouts were still fought in circles with a diameter a little longer than the extended arm with sword. To attack the fencer leaned forward so that his front knee was bent and his back knee stretched; in defense he leaned backward with his front knee extended and the back knee bent. By the middle of the century, a small sword called the *Espadin* completely replaced the Espada which was in general use among the Spanish.

Nineteenth Century

After the end of the French occupation in Italy, it became obvious that the two conflicting styles (the Northern French-Italian and the Southern Spanish-Italian) should be united. Many schools were opened in an attempt to achieve this goal. Zanghery started to use the name *Fioretto* for the crossbarred Italian foil and the name soon gained general acceptance.

In 1868, three military schools were founded. The head of the cavalry school, Radaelli, in *Instruzione per la Scherma di Spada e di Sciabola* (1855) outlined the basics of Italian saber fencing. Barbasetti and Pini were famous members of this school. Barbasetti's book, *L'Escrime a Travers des Sciecles la Scherma per la Sciabola* (1898), was the best book of the time on saber fencing.

In Rome the Scuola Magistrale di Schirma was founded to train military fencing masters for the Italian army.

In France the elaborate way of fencing, incorporating suppleness, evasion, and deception gained full recognition and became known as the French style. Great names connected with this evolution were Jean-Louis and Bertrand in the first half of the century and Merignac, Prevost, the Loze family, and Bonnet in the second half.

In 1852, one of the most famous fencing schools was founded in Joinville le Pont and has been educating fencing masters in France since that time. In dueling, which was becoming rare, the *épée du combat* was used for thrusts only.

In England in the first half of the century fencing was neglected and only the upper classes practiced it in exclusive clubs. Around the middle of the century the French Salle Bertrand was opened. The London Sword Club was founded in 1848 and soon club after club developed which helped the revival of fencing.

In Germany the schlager fencing did not really contribute to the development of modern fencing. Around the end of the eighteenth century the Italian fencing master Sestini opened his school in Berlin which led to the acceptance of the new style.

Until the beginning of the century, Austria had followed the German footsteps and had only one school of modern fencing in Vienna which was run by the Frenchman, De Saint Martin. In 1852, however, a school for army fencing masters was founded at Wiener Neustadt with the Hungarian Igalffy as the head of the school. In 1894, the Italian fencing master Barbasetti was invited to teach at the school and many of the famous Austrian-Hungarian fencing masters of the twentieth century were taught by him.

In Hungary the saber was accepted as the national weapon, having been used in the constant wars against the Tartars, Turks, and other oppressors. The handling of the saber became second nature to the Hungarian noblemen and soldiers. In 1825, an exclusive club, the National Fencing Institute of Budapest, was founded with the Prussian Franz Friedrich as its first fencing master. Chappon's book *Theoretisch praktische Anleitung zur Fechtkunst*, the first of its kind in Hungary, was published in 1839.

In 1851, Keresztessy, the father of Hungarian saber fencing, opened his school to teach a very simple system of saber fencing. This Hungarian style involved wrist fencing which meant the use of short swings with circular motion of the wrist in cuts and parries. Another recognized fencing master was Halasz who taught fencing at the best Hungarian club, the Magyar Athletikai Club, at the end of the century.

In 1896, an international competition with 140 participants was held, and Santelli, winner of the Master's saber event, remained in Hungary.

Dueling was forbidden in theory, but was, in fact, many times overlooked by the civilian authorities and was accepted by the army, noblemen, and the upper classes of society. The dueling weapon was the saber and usually only cuts were allowed; the more dangerous thrusts were only rarely permitted. In extreme cases there were combined duels with pistols being used first and then sabers. Generally, the duel was considered a proof of responsibility and courage rather than a threat to the life of the duelists.

In the United States fencing made slower progress than in Europe. There was more interest shown by the 1870's. The first fencing school was opened in New York in 1874 by Senac. One of the first books on fencing published in the United States was Senac's *The Art of Fencing.* A few years later, Rondelle, who also taught in New York, wrote *Foil and Saber.* Corshesier, Gouspy, and Jacoby were other noted masters of this time.

In 1891 the Amateur Fencers' League of America was founded, and in 1894 the Intercollegiate Fencing Association. As immigrant fencers and fencing masters started to build interest in this sport, the New York Athletic Club and soon other clubs offered an opportunity to learn fencing.

Twentieth Century

By the beginning of the twentieth century, the French school of fencing had developed the foil and épée to approximately the same form and size we use today. The Italian Scuola Magistrale di Scherma chose the rapier as their model for the foil and épée and the *Pecoraro,* a light weapon with a perforated guard, as the model for the saber.

The twentieth century with its rapid means of travel and communication made possible an international community among sportsmen; from the beginning of the century, fencing Masters from France, Italy, and Hungary were invited to visit other countries. After World War II and the revolution of 1956, Hungarian masters and amateur fencers sought new homes to practice their skills.

In 1896, Olympic Games were held in Athens in which individual competitions of the men's foil and saber took place. In 1900, individual épée competitions were added; in 1904 men's foil and saber teams were formed, but the foil team was discontinued until

1920, and in 1908 épée teams entered the games. In 1924, there was a women's individual foil competition and in 1960 a women's foil team competition. From 1960 on, all the various individual and team competitions were a regular part of the Olympics.

From 1921, except for those years in which Olympic games were held, the European Championships were the top competitions. These became known as the World Championships in 1937.

During the twentieth century the great leaders of Italian fencing were Pini, Toricelli, Sassone, Greco, Nadi, and Mangiarotti. Pini wrote the first important fencing book of the century, *Scherma di Spada*, in 1904; this was followed by Greco's *La Spada e la sua Disciplina d'arte* in 1912. Barbasetti, after the outbreak of World War I, moved from Austria to Paris where he taught fencing until his death. His book *Das Sabelfechten* was published in the German language during his stay in Austria.

A few of the famous French masters of this period are Kirchoffer, Tagliapietra, Conte, Jeanty, Rabou, Jaquemard, Dodier, Coudurier, Catineau, Breton, Boulay, Clery, and Lacroix. Many of them received the *Legion d'Honneur*, making France the first among the nations who honored her fencing masters with a visible decoration.

It was in this century that Hungarian fencers began to rank among the leaders. The Hungarians combined the spectacular Italian saber style with the older Hungarian wrist-fencing, creating an economical, simple, and fast athletic, rational approach to fencing. Halasz, Lovas, Vizy, Arlow, and Rakossy were the outstanding masters at the beginning of the century. Rakossy's pupil Fuchs won the first Olympic title in saber fencing for Hungary in 1908, and repeated his feat in 1912. After World War I, Santelli, Borsody, Geller, Gerentsér, Gerevich, Schlotzer, and Tusnády were the top masters. The most remarkable of these men were Santelli and Borsody whose pupils long dominated saber fencing in the Olympics and World Championships. Santelli, the most distinguished of all masters, was adaptable enough to adjust his Italian style to the Hungarian temperament. He taught for almost fifty years in Budapest and was beloved by all with whom he came in contact. His service to Hungarian fencing was recognized with the award of knighthood. Borsody, the master of the Toldi Miklos Royal Hungarian Sportinstitute, was one of the founders of the Hungarian style. His ability to build an artistic composition from the simplest movements, his personal philosophy, and natural psychological approach caused him to be admired by his students. Once every year he pitted the master-candidates against each other with practice sabers, carefully disinfected to protect their nude torsos, and with only masks and gloves for protection. In this way, the participants could experience the physical and psychological feelings of the duelist. The drastically changing political ideas brought a pistol into Borsody's hand to put a tragic end to a precious life, rich in success and recognition. Unfortunately, he left no written material about fencing.

Geller, the master of the thrusting weapon at the same institute and a follower of the Italian school, was the author of a book with Tomanoczy in 1942 titled *Vivás Kézikönyve*. Gerentsér was fencing master of the Pázmány Péter University in Budapest. His book is one of the best about the rapidly developing Hungarian saber technique of the time, *Modern Kardvivás* (1944).

In the women's event at the 1924 Paris Olympics, Miss Gizella Tary ranked sixth and soon became a professional fencing teacher, one of the few women in the world to become a master.

In England, at the beginning of the century, the London Sword Club was the leading fencing club under the leadership of the French master Mimiague and the best known school was the Salle Bertrand. Bertrand's book *Cut and Thrust* was published in 1927.

In 1902 the Amateur Fencing Association was formed. The British Academy of Fencing reorganized in 1949 under the National Training Program gave a tremendous boost to the number of fencers. The Association, starting with only 300 members, today has an estimated several thousand in more than 400 separate clubs. From 1950 on, the British Empire Games brought together a great number of fencers from every corner of the Commonwealth.

In Russia, during the Czarist regime, fencing was primarily used as a training method for duels. French maitres d'armes Lougarre, Ternant, Luppi, Michoux, and Grisier were active in Russia before the revolution, but after the revolution Russian fencing declined. After World War II, the Russians made contact with Polish and Hungarian fencers. The Russian fencers studied the movements of the best Hungarian fencers, taking slow motion pictures of the bouts to help them analyze the actions. They have made unbelievable progress in the past 15 years moving from anonymity to world-wide recognition, contradicting all previous ideas of slow evolution. The secret of their success possibly rests on the fact that their appearance in international competitions coincided with the adaption of the electric scoring system. Their fencing is accomodated to the demands of such a scoring device in that it is simple, fast, expedient, aggressive, and powerful. In addition, their system of training the body is excellent.

In Germany Nerilac, Murero, and Schovannis are the notable masters of this period. Schovanni's pupil, Casmir, became one of the best fencers, and his nephew, E. Casmir, followed in his footsteps. Others like Gazzera, Tagliabo, and Melicher were among the leaders as fencing masters.

Poland is one of the fast advancing countries with a fast improving record in international fencing, having some very good fencers, especially those adept with the saber. As yet, they have won only one Olympic Gold Medal, but have already captured some World Championships.

In the United States, fencing started its upswing in the first third of the century. The best known fencing masters at this time were Costello, Nadi, and Greco; all of whom wrote books about fencing (Costello, *The Theory and Practice of Fencing;* Nadi, *On Fencing;* Greco, *Fundamentals of Modern Fencing*). At present, about 180 coaches are working at different clubs and schools. Many are professional fencing masters who have come from European countries. Some of these teachers received diplomas from the old masters, and some were amateurs who have become professionals.

As a matter of interest, it should be mentioned that two cities have erected statues to their great masters: Montpellier in France to Jean Louis, and Padua in Italy to Salvatore Fabris.

Because of the isolation of the Asian countries until quite recent times, the history of the development and use of the sword in Asia was not well known in the West. Most of these countries used the exercises with a sword only for the purpose of war and developed certain kinds of sword dances as training or entertainment. Except in Japan these exercises had no influence on the growth of fencing as a sport and have no connection with our modern fencing.

In Japan fencing can be traced back to the warrior class of the eighth century. The art of fencing was at that time practiced for the purpose of readying the warrior for combat. Specific rules of swordsmanship were established during the twelfth century. The samurai learned how to handle the spear, halberd, bow and arrow, and in addition had to become a judo expert. The training of the samurai was based on more than physical development; the philosophical and moral concepts of the individual, evolved from Buddhism, Shinto or Confucionism were greatly emphasized as indispensable elements in perfecting aggressive and defensive combat maneuvers. The invention of protective equipment in the seventeenth century paved the way for the development of *Kendo* fencing, better known today as *Japanese fencing*. This is a combat sport which utilizes bamboo sticks as weapons. Specific places on the opponent's body (based on the location of joints in the armor) must be struck in order to score a touch; cuts to the head, temples, wrists, and upper body, plus the thrust to the throat are used. Parries and ripostes were employed in defense. Due to the prohibition of sword carrying in 1876 and dueling in 1889 by Emperor Meiji, Kendo declined until 1895 when the *Buttokai* (Martial Arts Society) gained permission to resume teaching it. From the start of the present century Kendo has been taught in Japanese schools. After World War II, Kendo developed into a sport that teaches all the virtues we learn in our fencing. Modern Western style fencing became popular after 1945 and Japanese fencers now appear in international competitions. Recently, Maitre M. Pecheux from France began helping the Japanese fencers to improve themselves in modern fencing.

The Swordsmith's Craft

The man of the Stone Age made his short sword of the flint that he found in chalk or limestone. It was a very hard kind of quartz which was chipped into the desired shape for the purpose of killing. After learning about the malleability of bronze in fire, man tried making longer weapons, but found that this sword was easily bent or notched and was not good for thrusting. It is believed that the Egyptians eventually invented a method of tempering the bronze, but this technique has been lost.

Some time between 1500 and 1200 B.C., it was discovered that hot iron could be tempered by dipping it into water. Hammering and tempering the iron afterward gave durability and flexibility to the blade but proper tempering was a very difficult job. If the blade was too hard, it chipped easily; if too soft, it notched easily. It was found that the correctly tempered iron blade would take and keep a point suitable for thrusting. Great skill and experience was needed to obtain the right hardness. Tempering became a secret which often was passed from generation to generation in a family. After it reached a certain color in fire, the glowing iron was repeatedly dipped into water or oil and the blade was tested by beating a stone with the side of it and by using it to pierce a hole through an iron plate. A satisfactory blade could break or cut the opponent's blade in two. The hard work and the secret which went into tempering made the sword very valuable, and the outcome of a fight depended a great deal on the quality of the armor and weapon.

In the Middle Ages, a period filled with superstitious beliefs, the swordsmith's craft was made a mysterious occupation involving work with a magic metal, the *Electrum Magicum.* Under the influence of the stars the swordsmith was supposed to be able to give supernatural strength to the armor and sword. The Electrum Magicum was a metal composed of gold, silver, copper, and lead; it is no wonder that a good suit of armor cost so much and that only the wealthiest knights could afford to have one.

In some places the art of tempering became so special that the local steel made the cities famous. Swordsmiths from Toledo in Spain, Milan in Italy, Augsburg in Germany, and Damascus in Syria produced the best blades for centuries. Making good swords is an art, even with today's advanced metallurgy. Fencing blades manufactured by different companies differ in quality, flexibility, and durability. It is still difficult to produce steel suitable for all the requirements.

The Sword

The *sword* in general terms is an offensive-defensive weapon, usually metal, which varys in length. It has a straight or curved, wide or narrow, heavy or light, stiff or flexible, one-or two-edged, sharp or blunt, pointed or pointless, flat, triangular, or quadrangular blade. It is used from short or long distances for cutting, thrusting, and parrying in combat or friendly contests.

The *dagger* is a pointed, metal weapon varying in length, with a stiff, flat, triangular or cylinder shaped, edged or edgeless blade used offensively for cutting or stabbing in close quarters or for defense in connection with the rapier.

The generally known weapons are:
1. Weapons used from short or longer distance
   (a) Swords for cutting and thrusting
   (b) Rapiers primarily for thrusting
   (c) Small swords exclusively for thrusting
2. Weapons used in close quarters
   (a) Daggers and dirks for thrusting and cutting
   (b) Stilettos exclusively for thrusting
   (c) Bayonets and combat knives for thrusting and cutting
3. Modern fencing weapons
   (a) Foil exclusively for thrusting
   (b) Épée exclusively for thrusting
   (c) Saber for cutting and thrusting

Special Terms Used in the Description of the Weapons

Pommel: Light or heavy button on rear end of the weapon to fasten the blade to the guard.

Guard: Rings, shells, plates, cup, bowl, or basket for hand protection.

Tang: The continuation of the blade from the guard to the pommel.

Quillon: Crossbar traversing the guard for better grip and protection.

Knuckle-Bow: Curved bar from quillon to pommel or a narrow continuation of the guard to the pommel to protect the knuckles and the hand.

Hilt: The handle of the sword.

False guard: A short bar or widening of the blade in the front of the quillon.

Pas d'ane: One or two rings between the quillon and false guard for better grip and finger protection.

Ricasso: Part of the blade between the quillon and guard.

Foible of the blade: The thinnest part of the blade towards the point.

Forte of the blade: The thickest part of the blade towards the guard.

False edge: The short back edge of the single-edged sword.

Point d'arret: Tip with little sharp points or rings or a flat cone with edge to catch the material of the opponent's outfit.

Dimensions of the Weapons

Prehistoric swords: Straight or leaf-shaped bone, wooden, or stone weapons about $19\frac{5}{8}$ inches (50 cm.) long.

Ancient

> *Greek sword:* straight, double-edged, pointless, mostly bronze, $19\frac{5}{8}$ inches (50 cm.) long, $1\frac{5}{8}$ inches (4 cm.) wide, widening in front of grip or having a short crossbar.
>
> *Roman sword:* straight, double-edged, pointed, iron weapon, $19\frac{5}{8}$ to $27\frac{1}{2}$ inches (50 to 70 cm.) long, $1\frac{5}{8}$ inches (4 cm.) wide, with a short crossbar.

Medieval

> *Swords:* Up to the first half of the sixteenth century—straight, stiff, double-edged, wide, pointed weapons about $39\frac{3}{8}$ inches (100 cm.) long, $1\frac{1}{8}$ to $3\frac{1}{8}$ inches (3 to 8 cm.) wide. The early guard was a crossbar. Curved, single-edged swords about the same size were also used.
>
> *Two-hand sword:* wide, heavy sword with flat pointed blade, $61\frac{1}{8}$ to $78\frac{3}{4}$ inches (154 to 200 cm.) long, $1\frac{5}{8}$ to $2\frac{3}{8}$ inches (4 to 6 cm.) wide; the guard was a simple crossbar $15\frac{3}{4}$ inches (4 cm.) long. In the front of the crossbar were the false guards and *pas d'ane.* The *Estoc* was a two-hand sword, with stiff tri- or quadrangular blade used only for thrusts.
>
> *Lance and Halberd:* $78\frac{3}{4}$ to $98\frac{3}{8}$ inches (200 to 250 cm.) long; the first a pointed weapon; the second a pointed weapon with an axe attached. These do not belong to the weapons of the sword-class, but should be noted since theatrical productions may require their use.

Sixteenth Century

Rapiers: From the second half of the sixteenth century to the first quarter of the seventeenth, double-edged, slim, flexible blades 50 to 55⅛ inches (127 to 140 cm.) long, 1⅛ (3 cm.) wide were used chiefly for cuts; the handle was about 9⅞ inches (25 cm.). Towards the end of the sixteenth century the length was increased to 65⅛ inches (165 cm.) but later was reduced. The Spanish and Italian blades were ridged and used mainly for thrusting. During the course of the sixteenth century the guard was elaborated from plain quillon, knuckle-bow, and *pas d'ane* to the guard with rings, counterguards, shells, and *ricasso*. The quillon passed the guard on both sides. In Spain, a steel cup with pierced decorations was used. At the turn of the century, the shells were opened and the guard was simplified to quillon and small cup (the *Flamberg*).

Swords: Straight with double edge and a rapier-type guard or (in broadsword class) with basket guard. In England the backsword was straight, without point, but with a sharp front edge and a basket guard.

Daggers: Double-edged, 7⅞ to 12⅝ inches (20 to 32 cm.) long, with or without side rings or quillons. The Spanish dagger had a small cup and long straight quillons.

Seventeenth Century

Small sword: From the second quarter of the seventeenth century the dimensions were reduced. The blade was 31⅞ to 40⅛ inches (81 to 102 cm.) long, triangular in shape, with the guard made more like a complete cup. Used only for thrusting. In Spain and Italy the double-edged blade remained in existence.

Military sword: Narrower for the infantry, wider for cavalry and navy, with basket guard.

Daggers: Not used in the seventeenth century for fencing.

Eighteenth Century

Small sword: The blade gradually tapered towards the point. The guard became a complete cup.

Military sword: Blade became narrower and the basket smaller.

Nineteenth Century

Small sword: Used for practice or occasional duels. *Épée du com-*

bat, straight sword with triangular blade used in France. In Italy, it had a square-shaped blade, *pas d'ane,* and quillon. The *dueling saber* was a light blade approximately $\frac{1}{2}$ inch (14 mm.), blunt or pointed, with front and back edge.

Military sword: Very similar to that of the eighteenth century. For cavalry use, the light slightly curved Hungarian saber was adopted all over Europe. From the middle of the century, a blunt weapon (light Italian saber) was used in practice for sports.

Twentieth Century

Military sword: After the first decades of the century, the sword went out of general use. In several countries it has been retained as a decorative weapon used with full uniform or in parades.

Foil: Quadrangular shaped, flexible, light blade tapered to blunt point, or *point d'arret,* used for thrusting only. Total length not more than $43\frac{1}{4}$ inches (110 cm.). Length of the blade $35\frac{3}{8}$ inches (90 cm.); maximum diameter of the cup-guard less than $4\frac{3}{4}$ inches (12 cm.).

Épée: Triangular shaped, stiff blade tapered to the *point d'arret* used for thrusting only. Total length not more than $43\frac{1}{4}$ inches (110 cm.). Length of the blade $35\frac{3}{8}$ inches (90 cm.); maximum diameter of the cup less than $5\frac{1}{4}$ inches ($13\frac{1}{2}$ cm.); the depth of the guard $1\frac{1}{8}$ to $2\frac{1}{8}$ inches (3 to 5 cm.).

Saber: Quadrangular at the bottom, becoming triangular and tapering to a quadrangle towards the blunt point; it is used for cutting and thrusting. Not longer than $41\frac{3}{8}$ inches (105 cm.); the length of the blade $34\frac{5}{8}$ inches (88 cm.). The guard is a smooth metal basket or a slightly curved protective plate.

Costumes *

THE SWORD-BELT

The ancient warrior carried his sword suspended around his neck, hanging down in front of his chest or strapped across the

---

* Hansen, H. H.: Costumes and Styles, E. P. Dutton Company, New York, 1956; Payne, B.: History of Costume, Harper & Row Company, New York, 1965.

right shoulder to the left side of his body. In the eleventh century double straps worn crosswise were in use for sword and dagger. In the fifteenth century the sword strap was attached to the hip underneath the armor but above the jerkin. From the sixteenth century on the rapier was worn with a wide shoulder strap on the left side, while a second strap kept the sword in oblique position. Up to the seventeenth century, the heavy sword was worn with a shoulder strap coming down over the right shoulder to the left side. This strap was worn over the dress but under the cloak. Courtiers carried the sword belt strapped over their hip. In the eighteenth century, it became the fashion to wear the sword outside the coat pocket in such a manner that the guard was visible while the scabbard was hidden by the cloak.

THE CAPE AND CLOAK

The cape was hooked to the shoulders and worn either hanging down the back or over the left shoulder in warm weather or on parades. In rain or cold weather, however, the wings were pulled together in front of the chest. The cloak covered the whole body down to the heels. It could be hooked like the cape or fastened with a cord to the neck, covering both or only the left shoulder. If a wing were thrown back the hanging part could be carried slung over one arm or both wings could be picked up separately and carried hanging over both arms.

THE HAT

A big felt hat with broad brim was worn (seventeenth and eighteenth century) on the back of the head leaving the face exposed. The right hand part of the brim was usually turned down, the left hand part up. When lifting the hat, the right hand was placed at the left front side with the forearm above the brim, the thumb on top. After removing the hat, it was placed either in front of the chest or kept to the side of the body. The three cornered hat, worn in the eighteenth century, being stiff, could be lifted at the right corner and placed on the left forearm or in front of the chest with the brim leaning against the body.

When standing, the gentleman rested his cane near his foot; when walking, he placed the point a little to the side. With each step the tip of the cane was flung to one side.

Salutations

THE SPANISH SALUTATION

In the sixteenth and seventeenth centuries, Spanish etiquette was accepted at all European courts. Part of this etiquette was the Spanish salutation. This movement was a harmonious as well as a spectacular way of expressing reverence to others and could be executed from the standing position or while walking or backing up. The starting position is the third position of ballet or the initial fencing position. The right arm moves obliquely upwards to the front, and the left is taken down obliquely behind the body. Both arms are slightly relaxed. The standing salutation should be practiced with coordinated arm and leg movements in three sequential parts.

First: The right hand (with relaxed arm) is moved in a clockwise semicircle while the left hand is brought up from behind so that both hands meet back to back on the left side of the chest. In the meantime, the left foot is moved back about twelve and a half inches with slightly bent knee while the right leg remains straight, foot flat on the ground.

Second: The right hand continuously describes a counter-clockwise semicircle as the arm is stretched obliquely forward and down to the right. The left hand (with slightly stretched arm) describes a clockwise semicircle sidewards and backwards to the left. Simultaneously, the left knee is bent and the upper part of the body (including the head) bows.

Third: The right foot is brought back to meet the left foot into the original position and the arms are relaxed.

After these three movements have been perfected, the salutation should be executed in one movement, smoothly and harmoniously.

If a fencer desires to repeat the salutation, he should, instead of dropping his arms in the third movement (when upright), bring his hand back up to his chest again (the right hand will describe a counter-clockwise circle). The action is continued by stepping back and bending the knee into the second part of the salutation.

The repeated salutation with the backward jump is executed so that, instead of the third movement described above, the right leg crosses behind the left leg with a jump backward while the hands and arms execute the second movement, as given above.

In the standing salutation, the left hand rests on the guard of the sword held at the side while the right arm and feet execute the movements as described.

If the salutation is done with a hat, it begins the same as the standing salutation but the hat is removed during the initial movements.

The *small* salutation is done with the right hand only, describing two small circles in the front of the chest and towards it as the arm is stretched sidewards to the right.

THE FRENCH SALUTATION

By the end of the seventeenth century French etiquette dominated society, and the French salutation was favored by courtiers. The entire salutation was adapted to the minuet and could be executed to either side.

First: The first movement is begun in the initial fencing position (third position of ballet). Both arms, slightly bent, are lifted to shoulder level, palms up. Simultaneously, the right foot moves one step forward and to the right. The weight of the body is shifted to the right foot and the left heel is raised. The body is kept erect and the head turned upward.

Second: In the second movement, the left foot is placed behind the right with a circular motion. Both knees are bent; both hands meet in front of the body just below the knees. The body weight is equally distributed on both legs, the body being slightly bent forward.

Third: In the third movement, the body weight is shifted to the left foot while the right knee is stretched and the left is bent more.

The heels touch the floor, and the arms are raised to a position a little higher than the waist.

Fourth: This movement returns the fencer to the first position. The fencer stretches his left knee in order to distribute his weight equally to both legs. (If making two or more consecutive salutations with retreat, after the fourth movement the front foot should be brought back behind the other with a circular motion. Both hands should again meet in front below the knees.)

Fifth: In this movement, the right foot is brought back to the initial position.

If this salutation is made with a hat, during the first movement the hat is raised sidewards and up; in the second it is brought down to the knees; in the third, sidewards once more. After the salutation, the hat is put on or carried to the left side on top of the left forearm.

If done with cane in hand, the salutation is given only with the free arm while the other arm lifts the cane from the floor and keeps it about waist high.

Manners

Throughout history, men have been judged by their manners. A gentleman's conduct has always been regulated by the written and unwritten codes of his society.

The rules of conduct for the gentleman of Rome included courtesy, rhetorical speech, impeccable dress, and refined demeanor, both publicly and privately.

Although the gladiator fights were cruel and the spectators found excitement in bloodshed, skillful technique and clever tactics were very much appreciated.

In the early part of the Middle Ages the codes of society were crude, but finer manners developed with the rise of chivalry. In France in the eleventh century church synods defined rules of behavior; "That henceforth no man should break into a church, no one should molest or injure monks and their companions, that no one should dare to take a peasant or peasant woman or steal or kill domestic animals, that no one should attack merchants or pillage their wares."

Under feudalism, in order to receive support and protection, the vassal had to promise fidelity and obedience to his patron. This pledge was expressed in a simple manner. The vassal placed his clasped hands between the hands of his patron, symbolizing that he was at his lord's disposal. The covering hands of the patron acknowledged acceptance of this service and the promise of protection. The knight took an oath to be honest, to protect the weak, and to defend the existing order. He swore not to be cruel to a wounded enemy and to be merciful to conquered opponents. The young pages were trained in knightly manners and proper conduct. Strict rules were established for tournaments and the breech of these rules jeopardized a person's claim to knighthood and its privileges, and could even cost the offender his life.

The sword itself was highly respected, was not to be drawn without reason, and was only to be used honorably. The motto engraved on a Toledo blade was: "Do not draw me without cause, do not sheath me without honor." The point of the sword was not supposed to touch the ground. Before a fight the knight kissed the cross of his sword, and in tournaments he blew kisses with his sword to his lady in the gallery.

When taking his oath, the knight held his sword in his right hand, either with his arm obliquely up, or down, or in both hands in front of his right shoulder with the blade straight up. The award of knighthood was symbolized by the touch of the king's sword on the shoulder of the kneeling knight.

The blade was held on the open palms of the hands in a horizontal position when it was handed to another person. When presented to a superior, the knight knelt on one knee. The sword as a symbol of might was carried in victory marches and always in the presence of the king. To call the people to war, it was carried, blood stained, around the country.

For combat in tournaments, blunt swords and buttoned jousting lances were used to avoid fatal injuries. If one knight met another, it was a friendly gesture to raise the visor of his helmet, reveal his identity, and give a sign of peaceful intentions. In *trial by duel*, a jury supervised the weapons and enforced fair conduct.

With the abandonment of the heavy armor manners also changed, giving way to the freer manner of the cavalier.

By the fifteenth century adventures traveled from country to country looking for opportunities to prove their bravery by challenging the skill of others. Fights also occurred when one gentleman at a public place or inn would declare his lady to be the most beautiful in the world, thus forcing the others to draw their swords to defend the honor of their own ladies.

To touch the badge on the left arm of a gentleman or to pass a discourteous remark was sufficient provocation for a "friendly" fight, but if the badge were torn off or a more serious insult made, the duel might be a matter of life or death.

The sixteenth and seventeenth centuries were the great ages of the duel. Hutton relates several instances of gory duels in *Sword and the Centuries* (1901). Following are a few brief examples:

Peter of Corsica and John of Turin, two good friends, became involved in a bitter quarrel. Neither wished a reconciliation. Prince Cianno de'Medici had them locked in a hall and permitted them to duel. During the course of the fight Peter was wounded on the head, but John granted him time to dress his wound. Later John was disarmed and his opponent waited until he rearmed himself. They fought with such vigor that even when both lay on the floor, the duel continued. Finally, the Prince had to separate them by force.

The Captain of Piedmont fought a duel with his friend, wounding him in the fight. The fight was stopped, and the Captain smeared his own face and arm with blood to make it appear that both were wounded so the prestige of his friend would not suffer.

In another case, one of the duelist arrived at the place of combat on foot, the other on horseback. After the horseman seriously wounded his opponent, he carried him on the horse to the nearest doctor.

In many instances the duelists became friends after the duel was fought.

After some dishonest persons ambushed their opponents, the use of *seconds* was started, but only in the role of witnesses. Later, they also became involved in the fights, and duels developed into real clashes.

To be disarmed was considered even more disgraceful than defeat. Hutton points this out citing the *Three Musketeers:* "The last of the Cardinal's guards was surrounded by all four musketeers and forced to give up his sword without being wounded, the most disgraceful defeat according to the standards of the time."

In public places, weapons were generally carried, but at private social gatherings it was considered impolite to wear a sword or cloak. Only the dagger was permissible because of its use in dining. At Court the sword was not detached, but the helmet or hat was carried on the arm or in the hand. The guards on duty kept their helmets on.

Louis XIII of France introduced the Spanish court rules, but these were not in favor for long. Louis XIV elaborated the rules of behavior and forced the French court rules to extremes. Every move was prescribed by court convention, dress was regulated according to social standing, and etiquette was maintained by force. Courtesy and grace were the measure of the ladies and gentlemen. The walking cane became part of the dress for men and women and its formal handling was taught.

When, in the eighteenth century, the small sword replaced the rapier all over Europe, the rules and technique of the French fencing schools dominated fencing. Before the mask was invented and in order to avoid injuries to the face, the riposte was not permitted before the opponent returned to the on guard position from the lunge. Stop hits were not permitted, and the emphasis was on good style and form rather than on effectiveness. With the invention of the mask, fencing developed rapidly. Greater speed and variety of actions were possible with this new safety device. The removal of the mask at the end of the bout was required as a polite gesture towards the opponent and jury.

In Germany the student duels became part of the university life. The young men wanted to prove their boldness and contempt of fear, and they proudly bore any scar resulting from their duels.

Throughout Europe duels were conducted in accordance with the established rules. The challange was generally expressed by tossing a glove at the opponent's feet or by slapping his face. In a later period, the exchange of visiting cards was common. After the insult had taken place, each party asked two gentlemen to be their seconds. The four seconds met to judge the degree of the offense, and their decision became binding to the parties involved. If the outcome of the dispute was to be a duel, the seconds decided on the place, the weapon to be used, and regulated any other conditions.

The dueling weapon was usually the épée; in some countries the saber. Pistols were eventually accepted in every country as the international weapon.

The duel with swords was fought until the first blood was shed or until exhaustion. In saber duels the naked torso was protected by bandages placed at the neck, armpits, wrists, and stomach, in order to guard the arteries. The number of bandages was sometimes reduced according to the conditions or, in very serious cases, completely abandoned. In saber fencing cuts were allowed but thrusts were seldom permitted. In pistol dueling two or more exchanges took place after advance warning or at the time of a specific signal. The pistols were special smooth bore, muzzle-loading dueling weapons. Both men wore dark suits to avoid being an easy target. In spite of frightening descriptions in the literature, these duels were seldom dangerous; the objective was mainly to satisfy the demands of custom. If anyone refused to give satisfaction, he was disqualified and not accepted in certain circles of society.

To avoid possible interference from the police, duels were fought in military institutes or on university grounds. Most pistol duels took place in forests or in riding schools. If the duelists were caught, the prison term they had to serve did not lessen their reputation.

Historical Perspective

It is interesting to draw comparison between the development of fencing and arts, music, and manners. Every age imposed its characteristics on each of these aspects of society. The parallel development might not look obvious, but is certainly fascinating.

The *Early Middle Ages* was a time of massive, dark castles, inferior quality of arts, unharmonic music, primitive fencing, cruel fighting, and crude manners.

The *Middle Ages* was a time of Gothic-style architecture, a tendency towards naturalism in arts, melodious music of wandering troubadours, and more mercy in combat created by chivalrous manners.

The *Renaissance* was a time of gracious buildings, decorative beauty in arts, harmonious madrigals, and formal, precise manners. It was also the time of the rapier, and with this weapon more agility and variety in fencing actions developed.

The *Early Modern Period* was a time of beautiful palaces, operatic music, realistic representation in arts, and the period of the small sword. With this weapon, swordsmanship approached stylized perfection. The cavalier's manner and courtesy were dictated by an intricate code of manners.

The *Modern Period* has seen the introduction of practicality in architecture, departure from representational forms in arts, widespread knowledge of music through records and radio, and the endeavor for speed and simplicity in fencing. The use of electricity eliminated the boundaries of the different fencing styles. The sword, no longer used for combat, has been retained by gentlemen for use in sports. Unsophisticated, naturalistic behavior is the characteristic of our time; the fixed forms of social conduct of the past have been largely abandoned.

Section II

Theory and General Advice

The following discussion will cover some important related aspects of fencing. Exercises, actions, and the physiological and psychological background are areas of knowledge which should be examined and contemplated by both the serious competitive fencer and the fencer who regards the sport as fun and good exercise. The depth of the following discussion is somewhat superficial, yet informative enough for an instructor to teach his students the technique, tactics, and theory of fencing. Some of the physiological aspects discussed have not yet been completely proved, yet they have been used in the past with much success. Most of these aspects of fencing are applicable to all three weapons but material particularly pertinent to one weapon will be discussed separately.

Analysis of Movement

This is the separation of various actions into their component parts, e.g. beginning, progression, and completion of a particular movement.

The mechanics of footwork consists of coordination of the arms and legs, the movement of the front foot and the extension of the back knee in a lunge, and the progress and arrangement of both feet in the execution of a step, jump lunge, of flèche. The other major division of fencing movement concerns the hand and wrist. The correct execution of the thrust, cut, beat, parry, and the completion of different feints with finger play and wrist and arm movements are all vital in producing near-perfect fencing action.

The direction of the point and blade; the proper extension of the arm; the correct placing of the point with the thumb and forefinger; the pronation and supination of the hand in the various parry positions used in foil and épée; the rolling movement of the fingers, and the use of the wrist and arm in saber fencing are all separate actions which must be studied and practiced constantly in order to attain the necessary mechanical adeptness.

DYNAMICS

The dynamics are application and effective use of force, speed, and energy in a movement or action. For example, dynamic footwork can be seen in the energetic snap of the rear knee in the completion of a lunge, in the strong gripping action of both feet in a step or jump lunge, and in the thrusting force of both feet and legs in the flèche. Similarly, examples of the dynamics of hand movements can be seen in changing pressure and relaxation of the fingers on the grip of the weapon; the continued execution, acceleration, and energy used in the thrust or cut, and the execution, speed, and control of the parries. Speed will be discussed in more detail later.

PRECISION

Precision is made up of controlled hand and foot movements and technique. These movements should eventually be executed with a minimum amount of strength and exertion, yet must achieve the desired result. Precision can only be attained through a considerable amount of practice and training on the part of both the beginner and the experienced fencer.

A mirror is a definite aid to achieving precision. If the salle has a mirror available, a constant check on posture, hand positions, and fencing movements is a great aid.

SPEED

After the fencer has gained precision, he can work on his speed in order to increase his effectiveness. For attacks or stop-hits from middle or short distance, bursts of speed are required while a successively accelerated speed is necessary from the far distance. Regardless of distance, the final phase of a movement should be the fastest. Since the key to attaining speed is muscular elasticity, exercises which increase skill and flexibility of both hand and footwork are indispensable building blocks for the fencer.

BALANCE

Balance, a very important factor in fencing, must be under control at all times so that the fencer will not be slow in executing his movements or lose his control in the middle of an action. In the on guard position the center of gravity is generally midway between the feet. However, in certain movements the center of gravity must be shifted in a direction necessary for the execution of an action. If a fencer prepares for an attack, the center of gravity should imperceptibly be shifted to the front foot in order to allow the back leg and foot freedom for the shortest, fastest, and most explosive lunge or flèche. In preparing a parry, the center of gravity should be shifted slightly to the rear foot so that the distance is increased and more time is allowed for the parry and riposte movements (Fig. 2-1).

FIG. 2-1   *Balance.*

With the saber, it is impossible to complete the preventative arm-cut successfully without proper balance. The arm is completely extended during the initiation of the movement; almost simultaneously the weight of the body is shifted to the front foot while the back foot moves. This, in turn, prepares the fencer to draw his upper body away from the opponent, immediately following the cut. The backward movement of the body is initiated by a powerful push of the front foot followed by a jump backward or a series of small steps.

As can be readily seen, the fencer's center of gravity changes constantly, varying with his own actions and those of his opponent's. The on guard position must be taken, so that the feet are not too far nor too close together since good balance depends on proper weight distribution. Another important factor is that in the lunge the knees must be bent enough to lower the center of gravity, thereby giving enough leverage to the lower legs for effective, well-controlled movement.

DISTANCE

The maintenance of the proper fencing distance has a decisive effect on the outcome of fencing. There must be close synchronization between closing and opening distances and the various actions of the hand. In an attack, the point must just reach the opponent and in defense the fencer must be able to evade the attack or execute an appropriate parry. A fencer, if he initiates a movement, must try to close the distance and ready himself for an attack. However, he must close the distance so that he is also ready for a parry riposte. When the correct distance is attained, the attack should be carried through with an instantaneous burst of energy and speed. An attack should be aimed at the distance where the opponent will be when he realizes he will be attacked and not at the distance prior to the attack. In foil fencing the middle and far distance is usually kept. In saber and épée fencing the far distance is nearly always used because the target is extended to include the weapon arm which is much closer to the opponent than the torso.

SIMPLICITY

Paradoxically, simple movements can only be perfected through the practice of more complicated actions. Through complex maneuvers, the muscles become looser and capable of obeying smoothly, quickly, and with minimum effort. It takes a long time for a fencer to simplify his fencing to include only necessary movements. Once precision and timing have been acquired, simplicity is the next goal for a good fencer. He should never use more energy than is absolutely necessary in order to gain a touch. A novice fencer will start out by using simple movements because he does not know the more complex ones. As he progresses, he finds that these movements frequently do not result in touches, so he begins to use more complex movements. Eventually, he learns that a combination of simple and complex actions will bring him success.

PRACTICE

Each movement should be practiced often enough so that it becomes a conditioned reflex, allowing the brain to concentrate on the planning and completion of the action. The movements should be practiced slowly at first and then with more speed until perfect control of the arms and legs is attained. It is also important to remember to practice in such a way that the correct reflexive action is given in response to a definite movement by the opponent. A parry, attack, remise, etc. should become reflexive, yet remain adjustable enough that it can be adapted to the movement which is most suitable for each opponent.

Reflex Testing and Selective Responses

THE EYES

A person reacts to a quick motion towards his eyes by instinctively blinking. A fencer hit on the mask by a headcut will also automatically blink at the moment of the hit. The master should work with his students to overcome this instinctive reaction. At first, the master tells the student that he will not actually be hit, and instructs him to keep his eyes open throughout sudden feint movements at his eyes. Later, with the face protected by a mask, the student tries to keep the eyes open throughout the cut directed to his mask. With sufficient practice, the fencer should be able to keep his eyes open at all times. Otherwise, in close distances, the fast moving point can hit him at the instant when his eyes are shut. The opponent, if aware that the fencer closes his eyes when threatened, may provoke this reaction and utilize the moment of blindness for a hit.

THE PARRY

The fencer should remember to only use a parry against a real attack. The opponent's false attacks can be followed with half positions.

The master directs cuts or thrusts to different parts of the target. The student follows these movements but stops when the master stops, parrying only the real attacks. Next, the master makes the same threats, but the student does not follow with his blade. Again, the parry is taken only when the real cut or thrust comes. This procedure teaches the student to parry only at the last moment.

At a more advanced stage of the training period, the master attempts with exaggeratedly wide cuts, stamps of his feet, and perhaps even shouts to make the student react. The student, as before, endeavors to parry only the final attack.

RHYTHM

The sequence of movements in a composed attack, like the jump-step, jump-lunge, or a series of ripostes to all sections of the target after the same repeated parry, are rhythmical movements. The regular repetition of an advance and retreat or a false cut and return to position may be part of a preparation, and serve to impose a rhythm on the opponent. This gives the fencer a better choice of time or action.

Rhythmical movements have a certain soporific affect on the opponent if he allows himself to be led into the cadence. Conversely, the fencer must be careful to avoid being trapped by his own actions in preparation.

If the opponent wants to impose his own rhythm, the fencer should try to break the timing by making sudden changes with cuts or beats or by altering the distance. The best type of footwork to break the rhythm and interrupt the opponent's planning is the *check*. Naturally, the fencer who is able to impose his own rhythm on the bout has the advantage of being in control of the situation.

TIMING

The fencer soon discovers that an action, although technically perfect, can be frustrated by the opponent's preventive hits, which take the right of way over to the opponent's side. Therefore, it is essential to time the attack at exactly the right moment when the opponent cannot avoid being hit.

Timing in fencing means the ability to recognize the opportunity and seize the right moment for an action. The timing can be analyzed through its physical, physiological, and psychological aspects:

1. The hit may land when the opponent is in the midst of making a movement himself (during the course of a movement).

2. The hit may land in the fluctuating cyclic events of tension.

3. A hit may be made when the opponent is not paying attention, when his concentration flags, or when he is preoccupied with his own plans.

This perfect moment may be either seized instinctively or provoked consciously. The opponent may be induced to do something specific or to attack a given target (as in the case of a second intention attack on counter-time). The opportunity for a good time-hit in most cases lasts only for an instant. Good fencers must sense rather than perceive their chance to strike. During the course of a bout there are numerous opportunities for a time-hit, but no fencer, no matter how good, can catch them all. Therefore, those fencers who have a highly developed sense of timing have an advantage at all times.

VISION

The fencer must understand the distinction between central and peripheral vision.

Central vision means that the eyes and attention are fixed on one point. In peripheral vision, however, although the eyes are fixed on one point, the attention is expanded to a larger field. Central vision may be thought of as being sharp and clear, while peripheral vision is more diffuse.

Vision in the early time of an infant's life becomes stereoscopic. We appreciate the distance and the depth of the observed object (or objects) because of our binocular vision. In fencing, the point of the weapon, the hand, and the target are all in one line and are all simultaneously in the field of stereoscopic vision.

In fencing, stereoscopic-peripheral vision is used almost exclusively since, in the course of the bout, both fencers are nearly always moving.

When the beginner first puts on his mask, his vision is disturbed by the wire mesh. Later he accustoms his eyes to the presence of the mesh and learns to focus his attention outside the mask. At the very beginning the student tends to concentrate all his attention on the details of what he is learning and relies on central vision. The master helps the student learn to expand his attention over the entire area by making full use of his peripheral vision.

The following is a simple exercise to develop this type of vision. The master extends his index finger and instructs the student to concentrate on the point of the finger. He then brings the index finger of his other hand into the student's field of view and slowly describes letters and numerals with it. The student should be able to expand his attention sufficiently to recognize the figures without changing the focus of his eyes.

The field of vision is enlarged by distance and diminished at close range. Also, it is generally easier to follow the opponent's footwork than his point or hand, since the foot moves relatively slow compared to the more rapidly moving hand or point. Practice enables the fencer to comprehend even faster movements. To help the beginner gain this ability in the first few lessons, the master has the student watch the forte of his blade, and has him strive to make evasions against simple, circular, or changing engagements. Then, the master instructs the student to change the focus of his field of vision from the blade to the center of the field to be observed, about chest height. The student should, by this time, be able to make the same evasions using his peripheral vision to comprehend movements of the master's hand, blade, and feet simultaneously. This more comprehensive vision becomes the vision of fencing (Fig. 2-2).

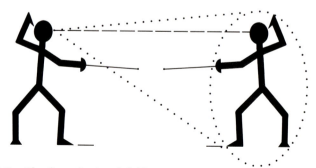

FIG. 2-2 *The fencer's visual field.*

While judging, the members of the jury must stand sufficiently far from the *piste* so that they are able to watch the target of each fencer. The president of the jury stands at a greater distance in order to see the space separating the fencers and both their targets. In this way, the judges have a smaller and the president a wider range of peripheral vision. The judges' attention is consequently more concentrated than that of the president's since he is required to follow the entire course of action, while the judges must see only the actual landing of the hits (Fig. 2-3).

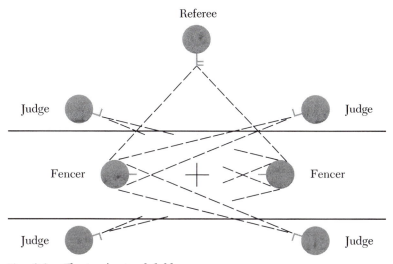

FIG. 2-3   *The jury's visual field.*

Psychology of Fencing

STRATEGY, TACTICS

Tactics are the brainwork of fencing; they are based upon observation and analysis of the opponent and upon intelligent choices of actions against him. The tactical approach consists of three parts: prelude or preliminary analysis, preparation, and execution.

The purpose of the prelude is to lay the foundation by scrutinizing the opponent's habits, virtues, and faults. The fencer should know whether his opponent is aggressive or defensive, whether he likes to make actions on time, and what his favorite attacks and parries are. Much of this can be learned by observing the other contestants while they fence one another and by watching the other fencers who are likely to qualify for the next round. But even after a fencer knows his opponent's game thoroughly (e.g. when the two have fought with each other) it is often necessary to devote some time at the beginning of the bout for an analysis. The reason is that a fencer's physical and mental condition varies from day to day and from bout to bout. He may be fresher on one day than on another; his reactions may be quicker or slower, and even in the same competition he may move differently if he is not sufficiently warmed up, is tired, or is in the process of getting his "second wind." The process of testing out the opponent's current reactions, his physical and mental condition, his disposition and spirit must be carried out with caution. The fencer should shorten and lengthen the distance and make use of false attacks that are persuasive enough to force the opponent to reveal the quality and speed of his parries. The prelude may be expected to take 30 to 60 seconds at the beginning of each bout. The rest of the time is used for preparation and execution.

Since actual execution of an attack, parry riposte or stop-hit, is a matter of only split seconds, there is ample time to prepare each scoring action. It is during the preparation of the action that each fencer looks for cues and tries to outwit his opponent. The variations are endless, but a few may be pointed out. For example, the fencer who plans to score on the attack has to take the initiative and keep control of the play. He attempts to mislead his opponent by sometimes making a false attack followed by a real attack to a different area or to the same target area. The lines and positions should be varied in order not to give the opponent a free moment in which to seize the initiative.

The preparation of the attack should be cautious, and the fencer must always be ready to parry if the opponent tries to make a sudden stop-hit or counter-attack. The *execution* of the real attack must be done with proper timing, quickly without break or hesitation. It must be a conscious, accelerated, determined, and decisive movement. Surprise is vital, and the fencer must believe in its successful outcome. Preparation of actions used to score on the parry riposte or stop-hit follow the same principles. The opponent must be lured into the attack at the exact moment desired by the defender, so that the latter may score on a short, determined parry riposte or an action in time.

If the opponent takes the initiative, the fencer must discourage him by constant threat of counter-attack, by short thrusts or cuts, by beating his blade, or by other legal means which will disturb his concentration.

The following is an example of a calculated phase in a bout, in which the attack, counter-attack, second intention, feint in time, and counter-time are used.

Fencer A executes a simple or composed attack. Fencer B replies with a simple counter-attack or parries the attack with a direct riposte. Fencer A knows that B will make a counter-attack or a parry riposte, he, therefore, attacks with second intention. Fencer B guesses A's plan and makes a feint into the second intention, a feint in time, or counter-riposte. Fencer A being aware of B's plan to make a feint in time or counter-riposte, steps forward, pretending to attack. He suddenly makes a preventive stop or blocking time-hit into B's action.

The above explanation is that of the Italian school of fencing. The French school would explain it as follows:

Fencer A makes a simple or composed attack. Fencer B makes a simple feint or feint counter-attack. Fencer A, pretending to attack, provokes the counter-attack, and puts his stop or time-hit into the counter-attack.

Naturally, complicated actions such as these are not learned through one exercise. They are the result of constant practice and are put into use instantly at the opportune moment. Only a very advanced fencer or a highly trained official can analyze, explain, or recall the foundation, calculation, and speculative guesswork which goes into creating the two visible terminal parts of the fencing process.

EXPERIENCE

When a fencer starts to free fence, he soon discovers that competition is different from lessons and exercises. He cannot make errors, take risks, or lose time without paying a high price for it. The opponent is not assisting any more; on the contrary, he tries to prevent any chance of scoring a hit. Actions which worked well during practice sessions do not always work, and the fencer feels lost for a while. The first competition is usually a frustrating one, but in time the fencer is able to find himself again. His experience can be enriched by fencing with as many individuals as possible, especially strong opponents. Even with a weaker opponent, a fencer can enjoy and profit from practice by equalizing the competitive factors through a limitation of his own actions. Also, a fencer can try out new, not always successful, maneuvers with a weaker opponent. In this way, he can build up confidence to attempt them with more proficient opponents. In time, he will be able to reduce the wide variety of situations he meets to a series of basic patterns or routines which will enable him to cope with them quickly and effectively. At the start a fencer may feel that he can learn everything very quickly, but after exploring all the variations of attacks and defenses his courage can falter, and he begins to feel that he will never be able to learn the art of fencing. While struggling through this period, a novice soon realizes that fencing is not an easy sport, but that it is possible to become proficient at it if determination and hard work are applied.

At first, the beginner is concerned only with the physical activity of the sport, but when the movements become automatic the importance of the fencer's mental ability begins to grow. If physical qualities between fencers are equal, intellectual superiority helps to achieve victory. Between equally intelligent fencers, mechanical and technical knowledge can be decisive.

Some points should be brought to the fencer's attention which will be very useful in later times. The master should point out that the fencer cannot use the same actions against every opponent. Against a calm, quiet fencer the feints must be longer; against a nervous fencer the feints shorter. With the calm fencer, one should remain calm; the nervous type should be agitated (while the fencer himself tries to remain calm).

Tall fencers usually are slower, but their long lunges are dangerous so it is essential to keep a safe distance.

Unconventional fencers use wide, sometimes unexpected, motions. Against such opponents the fencer must keep his distance and the parries should be taken at the very last moment. Unorthodox fencers usually use simple actions and almost always execute these in the same tempo. The attacks are made with wide movements, giving a chance for time or stop-hits. The loss of a bout against such an opponent frequently points to the fencer's inflexibility and his inability to adapt his style to the requirements of the moment.

Left-handed opponents cause the average fencer difficulties because of the reversed target, and because the left-handed fencer can easily parry the attack right-handed fencers customarily use against right-handed opponents. The left-handed fencer's arm often blocks or intercepts the attack. The fencer who uses his left hand has usually learned the quarte and counter-quarte parries very well. Therefore, the right-handed fencer should avoid finishing his attack in this line.

Usually left-handed fencers are vulnerable on the outside (in sixte) or on the flank. Many times, attacks aimed below their quarte (*tagliatta*) are successful. If an attack is made into the left-handed fencer's quarte line, the fencer must keep his fist well to the left to hit the target at an angle with the point.

The left-hander often stands to the right of the fencing line of the right-handed fencer to make the attacks into the sixte more difficult; the right-handed fencer should stand close to the right side of the piste to force his left-handed opponent to stay in the fencing line. After the lunge, the left-hander usually recovers with quarte or counter-quarte, so disengage or counter-disengage ripostes are effective.

Every possible opportunity should be taken to accustom oneself to fencing left-handed partners. From time to time, lessons should be taken with the master simulating the left-handed opponent.

Against each other, left-handed fencers many times become confused because of their constant practice with right-handed opponents. Therefore, they should also have practice sessions in which the master uses his left hand.

Training

PRACTICE

The amount of training required by a fencer depends on the individual. The master regulates the length of each lesson according to the student's endurance and condition. The master must judge how much work the student can digest at one time. The student is usually hesitant to admit he is exhausted, so the master must be alert for signs of strain.

The general rule is to "never fence to the utmost of your energy." A bout with one fencer should not last too long; it is better to fence several bouts, even with the same partner, with interruptions. If possible, a fencer should practice every day, or at least three times a week. If he reaches a point where he feels disgusted with fencing (physical or psychological fatigue from over-training and over-work), he should then abandon fencing for some other sport or entertainment for a few days in order to regain his enthusiasm.

CLASS INSTRUCTIONS

In a class with a large number of fencers, the master is not able to work with each fencer for a long time without neglecting or keeping the rest of the class waiting. His work must be concentrated on the explanation of the exercises, supervision, and control of the classwork.

Class instruction can be very valuable for the practice of footwork needed for fencing. At least 15 to 20 minutes of the practice hour should be spent on footwork since it constitutes 50 per cent of good technique. The master with his assistant or with one of his students demonstrates and explains the exercise in the middle of the salle and than has one pair of students attempt the exercise. After he points out any faults, the class is paired off into two lines, and the students begin to drill.

Examples: When the fencers know the thrust and the positions (parries), they may start to practice the thrust-parry-thrust exercise.

1. Fencers in *A* line make the thrust	Fencers in *B* line take the parry (not before the thrust approaches the target)
2. *B* line makes the return thrust	*A* line recovers with the parry (after the start of the thrust)
3. *A* line makes the return thrust	*B* line returns to on guard, dropping the point to give way to the return thrust

The cadence at first must be very slow, but later it can be speeded up. As soon as the fencers know this routine, they can practice on their own. The master, walking between the lines, watches the parries and, if possible, works with each fencer individually for a few seconds. Consequently, the master can determine who is talented and who deserves more attention.

After the partners have become accustomed to each other's speed, they should change partners to get accustomed to the speed of different opponents.

THE INDIVIDUAL LESSON

Fencers in the class may discover that working with each other is not enough to satisfy their ambitions. Watching the more experienced fencers take lessons usually fascinates beginners, and they quickly realize the importance of individual lessons. In taking their first private lesson, they appreciate that the individual session is worth more because of the increased personal contact with the master and the special attention given them by the master.

The master working with the student directly under his control is better able to analyze the student's individual capability.

The master is an ideal opponent since he can help the student succeed in making attacks and can help correct his bad habits. The student is made aware of his increasing technical perfection and speed, and the master gives the student a chance to catch the opportune moment for action and refine his timing.

The master systematically builds up a program of lessons to assure smooth progress in developing technique. The development of complete harmony between master and student is needed to allow the student to achieve his full potential.

A fencer may learn the principles of fencing from anyone with basic knowledge, but to become a good fencer he must meet and work with a talented teacher. Great masters and great fencers are the product of a fortunate combination of teaching ability and extraordinary student material. Some fencers have a fine technique but are not successful, while others have a less spectacular game but manage to be very efficient. The master has to try to balance these two approaches to produce a complete fencer. Individual lessons should be taken by competitive fencers throughout their fencing life, since there are always movements to be polished and habits to be corrected. The speed acquired in practice must be increased during lessons; timing must become almost an instinct and the movements a habit. In competitive fencing, the fencer is required to use all the physical power and mental ability he possesses and all the dexterity and finesse he has attained during the evolution of his fencing.

Physical Condition

Perseverence, discipline, and will power must be accompanied by good physical condition in order to produce an outstanding fencer. The fencer should have a physical check-up at least every six months, and preferably by the same physician who can oversee his development and general health. Sore muscles are a sign of healthful work, but pulled muscles or sprains can be seriously aggravated or delay recovery. A fencer should never force himself to work with sprained limbs or fingers. With proper equipment, reasonable care, and obedience to the rules, most accidents are avoidable.

Good health is important in modern competitions where the participants must have the ability to withstand day-long tension and strain. Particularly in international competitions in which there may be nearly one hundred competitiors, a fencer may have to participate in about 20 bouts a day. Numerous powerful lunges, rapid advances and retreats, and tense nerves demand physical stamina. Sometimes, a fencer who has a good technical approach may be beaten by a less polished but physically-better prepared opponent. Even between bouts, the fencer must concentrate and plan, and this combined with excessive loss of body heat can result in exhaustion. Therefore, the fencer should strive in all ways to improve his athletic abilities and one of the best methods of doing this is the practice of related sports. Light sprints or high and broad jumps help increase muscular elasticity; swimming tones the muscles and relaxes the body; moderate amounts of skiing (downhill and slalom), waterskiing, tennis, basketball, volleyball, and table tennis condition heart and lung power.

Conditioning the body can be divided into three training stages:

preparatory, formative, and sustaining. These stages should flow into each other gradually without causing strain.

In the initial stages of learning, the fencer should do the preparatory exercises consisting mostly of calesthenics and games. These exercises should be practiced every morning for 15 to 20 minutes to keep the muscles in condition; this is followed by a lukewarm shower and a rub with a rough towel.

In the formative stage, the student should practice fencing three times a week and slowly increase the time he spends working out. After taking a 20 minute lesson, he should fence three or four bouts and then increase his work to six or more bouts a day. Once a week, he should spend some time engaging in one of the suggested sports to improve his overall condition.

In the sustaining period, usually during the competition season, he should spend two or three nights a week fencing. After his lesson, he should fence several bouts in practice and play games. On days he is not fencing, he should take long walks, and he should devote one afternoon a week to other sports.

The program for a fencing evening should be:

1. Warm-up exercises
2. Lesson
3. Bouts with different partners
4. Massage and shower

The master must possess the ability to control and build the training of his student, and time the whole process so that the fencer is at the peak of condition during the most important competitions. If his training was insufficient, the fencer will not be able to perform at his best; if the training was too intense, he will break down at the critical moment. The amount of training is individual and requires professional handling and a great deal of experience on the part of the master. A person may be an excellent teacher, but this does not mean that he is an excellent coach, and vice-versa.

RELAXATION

The fencer must learn how to relax between bouts of a competition or whenever he is tired. The pattern of relaxation described below, which is similar to the yoga relaxation, is recommended.

The fencer lies on his back on a bench or the floor, puts his hands and arms loosely beside his body, and closes his eyes to help concentrate better. Beginning with a slight shaking of the limbs and fingers and continuing by relaxing the muscles of his back, he loosens the tension in his limbs and body, until he rests limply on the floor, exerting no physical tension. By rocking a bit, he places his head in the most comfortable position and relaxes the muscles of his face and chin. Then, the chest and stomach are relaxed and the fencer takes slow, rhythmical breaths. Finally, he attempts to stop thinking, which is certainly the most difficult part of the exercise. With all his muscles relaxed, the fencer tries to ignore exterior noises. At first, he will probably spend all his time thinking about not thinking. Later, sudden short blank periods will come and eventually they will occur more frequently. As he tries to extend these blank moments, he will experience a sinking feeling. Finally, the fencer acquires the ability to doze at will. This pattern may be practiced at home; soft light and quiet music help to increase the relaxation.

Ten minutes of this yoga relaxation, if properly learned and practiced, refreshes the body more than one can easily imagine.

MASSAGE

During the beginning stages of fencing or at the resumption of fencing after a vacation, the fencer will suffer the discomfort of sore and stiff muscles. Lactic acid and other by-products of oxidation from muscular activity have to be eliminated. A massage will speed up this elimination since it stimulates the circulation, increases the suppleness of the muscles, and has a refreshing effect. It is not always feasible to go to a professional massure, so the fencer should learn the system and method of self-massage, primarily of the limbs, fingers, and joints.

A complete massage is divided into the stroking, rubbing, squeezing, kneading, vibrating, and percussion of the limbs or body, in the above order. The stroking and rubbing are made rhythmically with the palms of the hand; the squeezing and kneading with the fingers and hand; vibrating, with the fingers and palm; and percussion, by the edge of the hand. The massage should be directed always inward towards the center of the body. The use of talcum powder or rubbing alcohol will facilitate the procedure. The massage may be obtained with the aid of mechanical devices. Actually, these are probably better than the untrained fingers and hands of most fencers. Although the beneficial effects of massage are mainly of a subjective nature, it plays a role in training and competition.

The types of massage are:

1. Warm-up massage
2. Massage between bouts
3. Massage to alleviate the weariness of the muscles

The aim of the warm-up massage is to increase the working ability of the muscles and to decrease the danger of muscle injuries in cold weather.

The massage between bouts is calculated to temporarily banish muscle fatigue.

The last type of massage is to eliminate the accumulated physiological waste material.

Competition

Exercises strengthen and make the body skillful.

Training prepares the body and spirit for competition.

Competition raises the spirit of the combat. The aim of the competition is to achieve victory in a fair contest.

From the viewpoint of physical education, competition is a necessary evil. It may be considered "evil" because of the demand of the utmost exertion of one's power and the maximum concentration of body and mind. It is necessary because without competition there would be no progress.

Competition is the ultimate goal toward which the accumulated knowledge and power of the fencer are directed. A fencing competition demands the utmost concentration and exertion from the participants.

Before tournaments, and especially before major championships, the fencer should avoid fencing and take two or three days to rest. Rested and charged with energy and enthusiasm, he will be more ready to compete and will perform better. On the morning of the competition, he should take a light, but substantial meal, after his regular exercise. About a half hour before the competition starts, he should warm up his muscles and fence a few practice bouts, until he begins to perspire mildly. After the exercise, he should wear a robe or sweat suit to keep his body and muscles warm and prevent excessive loss of body heat. Between bouts he should cover himself with a robe and, if possible, lie down to relax. Before and between bouts time should be spent watching the other fencers in the pool in order to form an opinion of their momentary condition and good or bad habits. Any knowledge he has gained about his opponents, either from past experience or from current observation, can be put to good use in the bout.

Each participant should observe and understand the method of judging used by the president and members of the jury so he will be able to adjust his fencing to their requirements. The fencer must be aware that members of the jury differ in the ways they see or evaluate actions.

After his pool has finished, the fencer, if promoted, should stay in the area to hear the announcement of the next pool. If he is eliminated, he should offer his help to the organizing committee.

Diet

The energy used in the strenuous physical and mental exercise of fencing has to be stored and available, and must be quickly replaced after it is used. Therefore, the fencer must know general rules of proper diet so that he can have reserves of energy. The sport of fencing does not require a special diet, but it must contain all the nutrients necessary to keep the body in top condition. The caloric requirement depends on age, weight, climate, and physical activity. A grown man of average weight engaged in vigorous activity requires about 3000 calories a day in a temperate climate; a woman requires about 2200. A well-balanced diet of solids and liquids should contain the proper ratio of calories: Carbohydrates, 50 per cent; Proteins, 10 per cent; Fats, 40 per cent; plus the necessary vitamins and minerals.

Carbohydrates provide the fuel for the work of the muscles. They produce quick, readily available, stable energy. They must be taken prior to and during vigorous exercise. Sources of carbohydrates are vegetables, dairy products, fruits, and grains.

Proteins are used for building the bones, tissues, and muscles. Proteins are not readily storeable by the body as are carbohydrates. Sources are meat, milk, fish, and eggs.

Fats give energy. A certain amount of stored fat is necessary for sudden spurts of activity. Food sources are eggs, cream, butter, margarine, olive or vegetable oil, meat, and nuts.

Vitamins help the chemical process of metabolism:

A (Carotene) is found in fish, milk, butter, eggs, oil, animal organs.
B (Thiamine) is found in meat, milk, and vegetables.
C (Ascorbic Acid) is found in citrus fruits and juices.
D (Ergosterol) is found in fish, butter, eggs, and oil. Sunshine is needed to help convert the food into this vitamin.
E (Tocopherols) is found in vegetable oils.

There are other vitamins, but these can also be found in the foods mentioned above.

Minerals such as iron, calcium, and phosphorus are taken from the soil by water and food.

The National Diet Association has made available a table of the amount of calories per unit weight of different kinds of foods. With this information the fencer can choose the kind and quality of foods he needs.

The normal liquid intake (taken partly with food) is about $2\frac{1}{2}$ liters a day, increased when necessary to replace the loss of water through excessive perspiration. The fencer wears a densely woven costume, glove, and mask, only the left hand is free for ventilation. Therefore, the fencer suffers more from heat than the participants in most other sports.

During the course of a strenuous competition, the cost in calories per hour is high. During the competition, there is no time for a full meal (which would be inadvisable anyway), so on the preceding night, the fencer should take a substantial meal two or three hours before bed-time. Two hours before the competition he can eat a light meal composed of easily digestable substances such as oatmeal, sugar, eggs, milk, or butter.

Sugar in the form of lemons or oranges and water with 2 or 3 grams of salt per liter (to replace the loss by sweating) are acceptable during the competition. If there is a lunch break, then juice, fish, eggs, and fruit may be taken.

Fencers should be aware that as far as their general health is concerned, excessive smoking disturbs the blood circulation and immoderate use of alcohol depresses the nervous system and may act as a poison. The proper selection and variety of food and the regularity and moderation in the normal healthy conduct of daily life are the foundation of good body condition.

Manners

Over the years, an extensive code of etiquette defining the acceptable patterns of behavior has developed, giving fencing much of its unique flavor. Throughout the world, the quality of the people attracted to fencing has remained uniformly high; a fencer anywhere may enter a salle d'armes or fencing club with the expectation of meeting people with whom he has a community of interest and education. Higher levels of behavior are required of the competitor in fencing than in most other sports. It follows that there are many rewarding and enjoyable acquaintances to be made in such an intellectually stimulating group. Conversations between the bouts help the fencers recognize and appreciate each other's talents and qualities. Many of these casual conversations lead to lifelong friendships constructed from interest, respect, and affection. For all these reasons, it is most important that the student of fencing develops feeling and appreciation for this formal etiquette.

The manners of the fencer are those of the instinctive gentleman. Behavior learned in the home, the atmosphere of salle d'armes, and the traditional forms of conduct absorbed during the lesson all mould the deportment of the fencer. We list here a set of general rules or suggestions for behavior as an illustration of the expected qualities of the gentleman fencer.

The qualities of modesty, neatness, and polite demeanor are essential characteristics. They recommend their possessor to society much more than a conceited, slovenly, or aggressive self-presentation. This is generally true, both in training at the salle d'armes and bouting in competition.

The fencer must not force his company on the older and better fencers present; on the other hand, when he has occasion to approach his betters and elders, he should do so in confident expectation of a courteous reception. In the same way, he must treat the weaker fencers with the same thoughtful courtesy, giving them help and advice where possible. We should avoid a superior or disdainful manner towards any opponent at any time.

The fencer must be clean and neat, both in costume and deportment. Either in the salle or in competition, the careless fencer in a filthy, ill-smelling uniform creates a general impression of discourtesy and negligence, even before he opens his mouth. No athletic uniform cleans or dries itself satisfactorily while shut in a locker. Fencing is no exception; the costume must be regularly laundered. It is also necessary to keep the surroundings orderly. The fencer must not strew the salle with his equipment or litter any more than he would the homes of his friends.

At the beginning of a bout, the fencer should always introduce himself to his opponent and the members of the jury, if they are unknown to him, and then salute them in greeting. During the bout, he should avoid rough or discourteous play or attacking an opponent who has not put himself on guard. If he disarms his opponent, he should attempt to retrieve the fallen weapon. He must render full and instantaneous apology for any accidental hard blow given. If he, in turn, receives an extremely hard blow, he should not try to take revenge.

The fencer owes courtesy not only to his opponent, but also to the presiding jury. While the jury is deliberating, he should wait patiently for their verdict. Any attempt to influence the jury by intimidation or a display of bad temper at an unexpected decision is strictly forbidden.

At the end of the bout, the fencer again salutes his opponent and the members of the jury with politeness regardless of whether he won or lost.

The cardinal rule is always to behave as the born gentleman must, with toleration and restraint.

Section III
Competitive Fencing

General Background

Fencing, in sport terms, means a friendly contest between two people using blunt swords. Scoring is based on the number of touches made against the opponent during a limited amount of time. The touches must be made on a specific target and certain rules have to be followed. Competitions take place on a strip marked on a floor or on a rubber or metal mat called the *piste*. The bout is judged either by a jury composed of a referee and no more than four nor less than two judges or scored by an electrical signaling apparatus.

As a sport, fencing provides a test of stamina and speed, refines reaction time, improves muscular elasticity and posture, adds grace to the figure, and increases mental and physical coordination and control. It does not require a particular body type since speed and agility are far more important than strength and size. Fencing offers the advantage of being a lifetime sport, and its practice is not limited to certain age groups. Nevertheless, the training of children under 14 years of age presents difficulties from the aspect of maintaining the child's interest during the long training period necessary to produce a good fencer. A younger child's participation in other sports and general physical training will prepare him to be a better fencer when he is old enough to begin his training.

Adam Paul Kovacs—1952 Olympic Champion, 1937 and 1953 World Individual Saber Champion, and Member of the Hungarian Olympic and World Championship Saber Teams 1936–1958.

"To my dear former fencing master, with best regards, Paul Kovacs."

Between the ages of 14 to 16, the young person's attention span and comprehension are sufficient for him to grasp and perfect the complicated movements involved in fencing. When a person matures physically, around age 18, his energy, initiative, and natural impulsiveness can help him attain success in this sport. The peak period of activity for a fencer is between the ages of 20 to 30. During these years, as his training progresses, the student gains finesse, judgment, and control. While muscular elasticity and reaction time do tend to diminish with age, consistent practice and the development of tactical skill can prolong a person's enjoyment of the sport.

The Teaching of Fencing

Fencing is not basically a dangerous sport, but it can be perilous for the inexperienced or the uneducated. Therefore, those who give instructions must be familiar with all the fundamentals and should be permitted to teach only after passing tests proving their skill.

Since fencing cannot be learned from a book, a competent instructor is vital and the student's precision, speed, and timing should always be controlled and supervised by an expert. People who fence solely for recreation or exercise may, after a time, stop taking lessons, but fencers who intend to enter competitions can never forgo their practice sessions. Reaction time slows down when a fencer does not practice consistently; in addition, there is no one whose technique cannot be improved upon.

The most crucial stage in a fencer's life is the period in which he first begins to learn. If, during this time, he is not properly taught, he will develop bad habits which can accompany him throughout his career. It is more difficult to correct the bad habits of an advanced fencer than to teach someone properly from the beginning.

At the start, a novice needs much patience. The basic movements can only be acquired through repetitive, slow, and attentive practice until they become automatic. Usually the student is eager to learn as much and as quickly as possible. The fencing master must convince him that perfection is the ultimate goal. He introduces the student to the secrets of fencing and uses his superior knowledge to give guidance and advice.

Years of constant training, study, and natural ability are needed to produce a capable fencing master. Scientific teaching methods based on current psychological and physiological information have replaced the older methods, which placed the accent on drills. A systematic approach to teaching is imperative. The system used can be derived from the material developed and improved by fencing masters throughout the centuries. The particular method used—the way of adapting movements and exercises to practical use—can be individual and each master can reply on his own ingenuity to arrive at one satisfactory to himself. Some masters emphasize attack, while others concentrate on parries, aesthetics of execution, or efficiency. There are those who prefer teaching beginners and others who concern themselves mainly with advanced students who are planning to enter competitions.

Weapons

In modern fencing the three weapons used are the foil, épée, and saber. Since each weapon will be described in detail in separate chapters of the book, only some general characteristics and scoring will be mentioned here.

Foil: A conventional thrusting weapon used by both men and women. The introduction of an electrical scoring system has eliminated the necessity of judging touches.

Épée: A thrusting weapon used by men (the right of way or priority of actions is eliminated). The touch which lands one-twenty-fifth of a second ahead is scored electrically.

Saber: A cutting and thrusting weapon used by men following conventional rules (and right of way). In use, it can be the most spectacular of all three weapons. Scoring is done by judges.

Styles

The two types of style in foil fencing are the French and the Italian. In saber fencing there are also two, the Italian and the Hungarian. The adaptation of the electrical scoring system in épée fencing has eliminated differences in approach and an international style has evolved.

The characteristics of the two types of foil fencing are related to the nature of the weapon and the temperament of the people who developed it. The Italian foil, with its crossbar, allows a firmer grip, stronger parries, and energetic attacks on the blade. The Italian temperament with its rather explosive nature has led to a style which emphasizes greater agility, vigor, and powerful footwork.

The French foil, with its simple straight handle, permits a looser grip, allowing more finger and wrist work for supple parries, lighter attacks, and greater reliance on deception. The French personality with its compliant nature has contributed to a flexible style with pliant footwork. In practice, both these styles are equally effective.

In saber fencing, the Italian style with its dramatic aspects and circular parries which was very popular in the first third of this century, was replaced by the more rational Hungarian style. The basic Italian technique was developed when the saber was much heavier, and the weapon had to be carried by the forearm for better blade control. The Hungarian approach, using short, simple movements, speeds up actions and makes fencing faster. The lighter saber permits lighter cuts and faster parries. The traditional Italian footwork (similar to the foil footwork) gave way to the athletic footwork with its greater mobility. This form was introduced by the Hungarian fencers and followed by the Poles, Russians, and other nationalities. Motion pictures taken of expert fencers provide an opportunity to analyze the movements of each and adopt the best of each style.

Equipment and Its Proper Use

When selecting equipment, the fencer should be concerned primarily with expediency rather than fashionable appearance. The fencing costume should be neither too tight nor too loose. A tight outfit will impede the free circulation of the blood while a loose costume adds unnecessary surface area, which in turn creates a larger target for the opponent.

Right-handed fencers should never use costumes intended for left-handed fencers, and vice-versa, because such a reversal could easily result in the blade entering through the exposed buttoning area of the jacket. Protective equipment designed for foil and saber fencing should never be used for épée fencing. In addition to the épée jacket, a plastron must be worn underneath in order to give greater protection while practicing or competing with the épée. Worn or torn parts of the costume should be repaired immediately. Clothing worn during fencing should always be completely buttoned or zipped.

The mask should be fitted firmly to the head so it does not press or push on the face or head. A loose mask could easily fall off and the exposed head would naturally be very vulnerable to injury. The mesh of the mask must be checked frequently for flaws or worn wires. Weak and damaged masks must be replaced promptly to prevent possible perforation of the mask by the opponent's blade. Needless to say, the mask must be worn at all times, whether for bouting, practicing, or demonstration purposes. The masks designed for each respective weapon should only be used when fencing with that particular weapon since the corresponding mask is build to protect the fencer from potentially dangerous idiosyncracies of each weapon.

The glove must be properly fitted to the hand. An over-sized glove wrinkles in the hand and causes blisters. A glove which is too tight will constrict the muscles and slow down the circulation, causing fatigue and cramped movements. When saber fencing it is important to use only a saber glove since cuts to the hand can cause permanent injury to the fingers, hand, and arm. It is imperative that the épée be used only with épée equipment. The hand, being a constant target, must be heavily protected from the thrust of the stiff épée blade and using a foil or saber glove would once again expose the fencer to injury. It should be emphasized at this point that in addition to using a saber glove for saber fencing, an elbow protector must also be part of the attire at all times.

In selecting shoes for fencing the most important criterion is that they will not cause the fencer to slip on the floor. Rubber or specially treated leather soles and heels are usually quite adequate. The cut of the shoe can be arbitrary. Some fencers use an extra heel pad in the shoe which receives the impact of the lunging action in order to protect the heel bone from injury. It is advisable to avoid fencing barefooted or with shoes which have untreated leather soles or heels.

With age and usage, blades become worn and chipped due to constant contact. Consequently, a blade should never be adjusted or bent with bare hands. Splinters and rust can cause severe irritation and, at times, serious infection of the hand. If it is desirable or necessary to adjust the bend of the blade, the blade should be placed flat on the floor with one foot firmly pressed against it and then pulled out at an angle which would give the desired bend to the blade. If a fencer is not yet familiar with this procedure, it is best to have an experienced fencer adjust the blade since the blade can easily break or be bent so badly that it cannot be readjusted properly.

Preparatory and Other Exercises

In general, the exercises are divided into five groups: Warming-up exercises and special foot and hand exercises (group work); individual lesson; assault-like exercises with the master; reciprocal exercises with a partner; and free play (assault).

WARMING-UP EXERCISES

These exercises prepare and warm-up the muscles for fencing. Any calisthenics are useful. The fencer should choose exercises that strengthen and loosen up the muscles of the arms and legs, but should avoid those which tend to stiffen his muscles. Some exercises are very essential before every lesson, practice session, or competition. These are:

For the Legs
- (a) Deep knee bends
- (b) Hopping in deep knee bends
- (c) Stretching the legs in deep knee bends (Russian dance)
- (d) Skipping and bouncing on toes
- (e) Lunging from deep knee bend and returning to deep knee bend
- (f) In lunging the stretching and bending of the right knee
- (g) Knee bends in "on guard" position

For the Arms
- (a) Swinging the arms around the shoulders
- (b) Bringing the fists close to the shoulders and describing circles with the elbows

(c) Swinging the arms from front, sidewards and upwards, and back

(d) Bending the arms in front of the chest with tearing-like movements

(e) Stretching the arms in front and grasping the fingers

SPECIAL FOOT AND HAND EXERCISES

The special foot and hand exercises condition the muscles and joints in positions and movements which are not natural but are expedient for fencing.

The special foot movements for fencing, the positions of the hands, and the transitions from one to the other have to be practiced first separately then in connection with each other to achieve harmony between them. These exercises are usually practiced in groups.

INDIVIDUAL LESSONS

The individual lesson must be practical and theoretical. Every lesson should consist of attacking and defending exercises supervised by the master. These exercises and others will be extensively discussed in the appropriate sections of the book.

ASSAULT-LIKE EXERCISES WITH THE MASTER

Assault or combat-like exercises give the fencer a chance to put his knowledge (obtained in previous lessons) into practice in the different situations presented by the master. The student has to find the proper, most effective attack or defense.

RECIPROCAL EXERCISES WITH A PARTNER

In reciprocal exercises (between two fencers) the actions are specified and limited to certain movements for each fencer.

FREE PLAY (ASSAULT)

In free-fencing, the fencers use all their knowledge and imagination to hit the opponent while not being hit themselves. Fencing with different opponents prepares a fencer for competitions.

Chapter 1

The Foil

The foil is generally considered the basic weapon; all fencers, young and old, should learn to handle it competently before turning to the épée or the saber.

The foil is a thrusting weapon. The blade is quadrangular and tapered to the end, which is blunt or has a *point d'arret*. The guard consists of the cup (*coquille*) and the handle. The handle may be French—straight and simple, Italian—with crossbar and *ricasso*, or Belgian—pistol shaped. Inside the small cup is a fitted leather pad to make it more comfortable for the top of the thumb and the first two joints of the index finger (Fig. 3-1).

The Grip

The handle of the French foil should be held close to the guard with the thumb flat, opposite to the second portion of the forefinger so that it almost touches the pad. The handle rests along the axis of the length of the palm, between the cushion of the thumb and the outside. The other fingers hold the handle in a relaxed manner. The thumb and forefinger lead the point; the other fingers only help to hold the foil properly.

The Italian foil must be held with the thumb over the crossbar. The index finger is under the crossbar and the middle finger is hooked inside it.

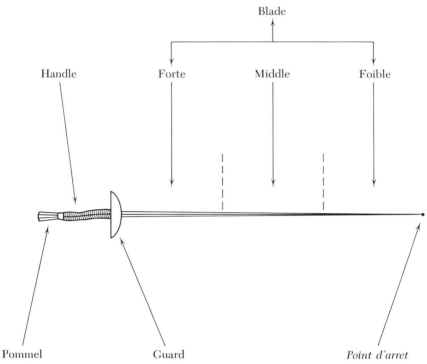

Blade

Handle   Forte   Middle   Foible

Pommel   Guard   *Point d'arret*

Fig. 3-1   *Parts of the foil.*

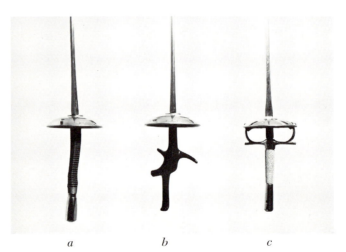

a   *b*   *c*

Fig. 3-2   *The foil:* a) *French* b) *Pistol* c) *Italian.*

The Belgian foil is held with the thumb and forefinger so that the top horn of the handle protrudes up between them. There are two horns on the bottom of the handle. The first comes between the middle and ring fingers and the second between the ring and little fingers (Figs. 3-2, 3-3, 3-4).

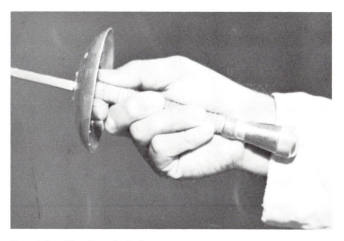

Fig. 3-3   *The French foil grip.*

Fig. 3-4   *The Italian foil grip.*

Positions of the Body

THE FIRST POSITION

This is similar to the one of *attention* used by the military, and it is assumed when the fencers are facing each other, each with mask and foil in his hands. The mask is held at the left side of the chest and the foil with the blade pointing obliquely down, the guard touching the thigh. (In the balance of the book right and left are used to describe actions as performed by a right-handed fencer. Left-handed fencers will reverse the instructions.)

THE INITIAL OR BASIC POSITION

From the front position the fencer takes the inital or basic position. He turns his body approximately 90 degrees to the left, places his feet at right angles and brings his weapon with a straight arm to shoulder height. The right foot is pointed straight at the opponent with the blade directed toward his chest. The fencer's left shoulder is turned back and his head turned toward the opponent. In this position, the mask is donned with the left hand; the chin is put into the mask first, and then the back hook of the mask is slid to the nape of the neck. After this, the left arm is stretched behind, so that both arms are parallel to the floor.

THE ON GUARD POSITION

From the basic position, the fencer moves into the on guard position. This should be the position most comfortable for the body, one in which the fencer can most easily approach the opponent or retreat from the opponent to execute an effective lung. The more the body is turned to the side, the smaller is the target the adversary can attack. To take the on guard position, the fencer steps directly forward with his right foot about 18 inches in the direction of his opponent. Both knees are bent, spread apart so that the left knee is above the left toe and the right knee is over the right heel. Simultaneously, the left arm is bent with a slight curve over the left shoulder, the hand a little higher than the head. The right arm is relaxed, blade in line with the forearm, with the point directed to the opponent's eyes. The fencer leans slightly forward

FIG. 3-5 *On guard posed by P. Dumenieux, former Canadian Ladies' Foil Champion.*

from the hips. The weight of the body is equally distributed, with the center of gravity between the feet (Fig. 3-5).

Foot Movements

STEP FORWARD

The step forward starts with the right foot and is completed by bringing the left foot up again into the on guard position. The feet should be lifted, not slid along the floor. When executed repeatedly, the continuous movement is known as the *advance*.

STEP BACK

The step back is executed like the step forward, but in reverse order. When done repeatedly, the continuous movement is called the *retreat*.

JUMP FORWARD

The jump forward starts with the forward forceful movement of the right lower leg, followed by a short jump on the left foot.

The soles of both feet should hit the floor at the same time with a decisive pincer-like snap.

To begin the jump back, the fencer swings his right foot behind his left leg. At the same time, he jumps back with his left foot and throws his body backward. Both feet should land at the same time to regain the balanced on guard position.

THE LUNGE

The lunge is the most important foot movement since it enables a fencer to reach his opponent with the point of his weapon from the on guard position. Initially, the right leg is energetically thrown forward so that it reaches out as far as possible. At the same time, the left knee is snapped into a locked position; the left foot is kept flat on the floor.

Upon completion of the lunge, the right leg below the knee should be vertical to the floor, the right thigh almost parallel to the floor, and the body leaning slightly forward. It is of utmost importance to start the lunge by lifting the toes of the right foot prior to moving the knee or heel. In the first stages, the forward step and the lunge should appear indistinguishable to the opponent. The recovery is completed by pulling the body with a semi-circular motion of the left knee and at the same time pushing back with the right foot until the on guard position is attained (Figs. 3-6, 3-7).

Fig. 3-6   *Lunge posed by P. Dumenieux.*

Fig. 3-7 *Thrust with lunge posed by P. Dumenieux.*

Step-lunge (Pattinando).° This movement is a combination of a quick step and a lunge. The step-lunge is different from the advance and lunge. After the lower part of the right leg is extended, the toes of the right foot are kept off the floor until the left leg is brought up to the on guard position. Both feet are then snapped flatly on the floor; the next move is a lunge. When this entire movement is executed correctly only two phases should be heard; the sound of both feet simultaneously hitting the floor on the forward step, and the sound of the right heel touching the floor during the completion of the lunge.

Jump-lunge (Balestra). As the name implies, this action is a combination of a jump followed immediately by a lunge. During the final phase of the jump forward, the right leg is thrown forward into the lunge position.

Repeated-lunge (Raddoppio). This movement is made up of an

° The terms in parentheses (French, Italian, or both) are included because of their general international acceptance. In some cases where there is no accepted English name, the original French or Italian is used in the text.

almost continuous repetition of lunges. After the first lunge the left leg is brought forward to the on guard position while the body remains at lunge level from the floor. The second lunge is initiated immediately after the completion of the first by an energetic forward thrust of the left leg which drives the body forward.

The lunge must be practiced to gain precision. From the on guard position the right arm is extended, followed by the simultaneous extension of the right leg. The left arm is thrown to a horizontal position, and the left knee is snapped into place. In the lunge position, all the limbs except the right leg are extended and stretched. On the recovery to the on guard position, all the limbs are bent and relaxed. It should be noted that the left arm can be used to add momentum to the lunge by being moved rapidly backwards; in the on guard position this arm gives balance and poise.

In order to prevent the student from dragging or sliding his feet along the floor while stepping, lunging, and recovering, the master can place his blade in front or behind one of the student's feet in such a way that the student will be forced to lift his feet properly.

THE FRENCH FLÈCHE

The flèche in foil fencing is accomplished by throwing the torso forward as the left foot crosses in front of the right foot. The movement is completed by resuming a balanced on guard position. The *Passe on avant* of the eighteenth century is the forerunner of the flèche as we know it today. The use of the flèche has become increasingly popular since the beginning of the present century. Its effectiveness is sustained only if it is used sparingly. The movement is best left to advanced fencers since the failure of a flèche attack renders the fencer vulnerable through a momentary loss of balance. Furthermore, a penalty may result from an incorrectly executed flèche, e.g. by causing body contact (*corps à corps*). Regular and systematic practice of the flèche is very important in order to learn the movement correctly. At first, while the foot movement is being mastered, arm movements should be restricted by placing the hands on the hips. Later, the arms can be used freely, and, finally, the foil should be placed in the hand and the complete attack practiced.

The Hungarian flèche, previously used exclusively in saber fencing, has now been adopted by foil fencers. (See section on the saber for discussion on the Hungarian flèche and footwork used in saber fencing.)

This is a movement which is initiated like a regular step. In the midst of the forward step, the action is broken by a sudden stop of the right foot followed by a retreat or a lunge depending on the reaction of the opponent. This movement is used to frighten the opponent, to interfere with his timing, or to force him into a rash action.

FIG. 3-8   *Silhouettes of the foil target.*

The Target

In foil fencing, the target is limited to the torso area. The exact target area, as defined in the 1959 edition of the F.I.E.* rule book, is as follows:

The target in foil, for ladies as well as for men, excludes the limbs and the head. It is confined to the trunk, the upper limit being the collar up to 6 cm. (2½ in.) above the prominences of the collar bones; at the sides to the seams of the sleeves, which should cross the head of the hu-

---

* Rule book of the Federation International d'Escrime (F.I.E.). This book regulates the order, place, time, number of hits and other rules of the bouts, judging procedures, equipment, and general information.

merus; and the lower limit following a horizontal line across the back joining the tops of the hip bones (ilium) thence following in straight lines to the junction of the lines of the groin. The bib of the mask is not included in the target. (Fig. 3-8)

If the anterior part of the target is divided equally into four quadrants by a horizontal line bisected by a vertical line, each of the resulting quadrants is covered by two parry positions (Fig. 3-9).

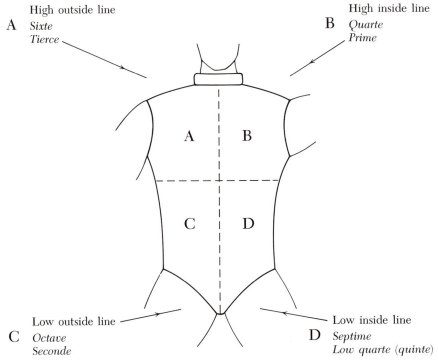

A   High outside line
A   *Sixte*
     Tierce

B   High inside line
B   *Quarte*
     Prime

C   Low outside line
C   *Octave*
     Seconde

D   Low inside line
D   *Septime*
     Low quarte (quinte)

FIG. 3-9   *Division of the target area.*

The Salute

Before and after each lesson or bout the fencer must salute his fencing master or opponent. It must be remembered that the salute is both begun and terminated in the initial position.

There are two types of salute—the simple salute and the combined salute. The simple salute is directed only towards the master or opponent and is completed as follows:

1. The blade is brought to a vertical position with the arm bent and the hand at chin level.
2. The arm is then extended towards the master or opponent until the blade is parallel to the floor in the initial position.
3. The mask is held with the left hand against the left side of the chest.

The combined salute is directed towards the opponent or master, the judges, and the spectators.

1. The opponent is first saluted in the above described manner.
2. The same salute is given towards the judges and audience from the fencer's left side.
3. The weapon and arm, in a horizontal position, are next moved to the right side of the fencer at chest level with the hand turned downward.
4. The initial position is then resumed.

The Positions of the Weapon

Before describing the various positions, it is necessary to point out the distinction between *pronation* and *supination* of the hand. Pronation is a covering motion, the process of turning the hand with the palm down. Supination is the exact opposite, the palm is turned up.

The positions are traditionally called by the old French words for the ordinal numbers from first to eighth. These are prime, seconde, tierce, quarte, quinte, sixte, septime, and octave. This system is recognized universally in the fencing world.

Fencing masters generally stress only four of the eight positions: quarte, sixte, septime, and octave. These four primary positions are favored because the thumb is almost in the same position in all, necessitating only a slight movement of the hand when a thrust is executed from any of the four positions (Figs. 3-10 to 3-13). Also the return-thrust from the secondary positions (prime, seconde, tierce, and quinte) is uncertain and difficult; therefore, their use is rapidly

Fig. 3-10   *Quarte.*

Fig. 3-11   *Sixte.*

Fig. 3-12   *Septime.*
Posed by Maitre Alpar.

Fig. 3-13   *Octave.*

Photos by W. Snedish.

declining in spite of the beginner's desire to use them for their extra power. Secondary positions are now usually taught after the primary positions have been mastered (Figs. 3-14 to 3-18).

The sixte position should be learned first because it is the easiest and represents the least change from the initial position. The hand is supinated about 45 degrees from the initial position with the arm relaxed and shifted slightly towards the right side. The point of the blade should be approximately at shoulder level pointing towards the opponent's left eye. This position covers the right upper quadrant.

The quarte position should be learned next. The guard is moved diagonally across the body to the left of the fencer, and the hand is pronated 45 degrees from the initial position. This movement from sixte should bring the elbow within 4 inches of the body, with the point of the blade directed towards the opponents right eye. The quarte position covers the left upper quadrant of the target. This position should be held a little lower and closer to the body than the sixte position.

From the sixte position, with the fist on the right side of the body in the same supinated position, a counter-clockwise, semi-circular movement of the point to the level of the opponents left knee will produce the octave position. The arm should be slightly bent with the guard at hip level. The octave position covers the right lower quadrant.

After the octave, the septime position is learned. This position is produced by moving the guard diagonally across to the left side of the body at the same time raising the fist to approximately chest level. The arm is slightly bent with the point directed towards the opponents right knee with the hand maintaining a 45 degree pronation from the initial position. The septime covers the left lower quadrant.

In order to avoid rough touches, the blade should be slightly bent downwards. Rules of fencing state that the bend may not exceed 4 cm. ($1\frac{9}{16}$ in.) from a straight line. This bend in the blade automatically establishes a closer distance to the opponent when positions on the right are supinated and those of the left are pronated.

After becoming thoroughly familiar with the primary positions, the fencer finds the secondary positions relatively easy to learn. If

FIG. 3-14   *Prime.*

FIG. 3-15   *Seconde.*

FIG. 3-16   *Tierce.*

Posed by P. Dumenieux.

FIG. 3-17   *Italian Quinte (High septime).*

Photos by W. Snedish.

Fig. 3-18 *French Quinte (Low quarte). Posing: Maitre Alpar.*

the hand is pronated completely in the septime position and the point directed towards the floor, the prime position is assumed.

If the hand is completely pronated in the octave position, the seconde position is attained. Similarly, if the hand is completely pronated in the sixte position, the tierce position is attained.

According to French interpretation, the quinte position is considered to be a very low quarte position. The Italians, however, regard quinte to be a very high septime position. The latter is positioned so that the blade is at head level with the guard slightly to the right of the fencer. This position is especially effective in preventing cutover attacks from hitting the target area (Fig. 3-19).

These eight positions are classified according to their use and relationship to the opponent's blade. If the positions are held without contacting the opponent's blade they are called *basic positions* or *invitations*. When in contact with the opponent's blade they are called *engagements*. When used for the purpose of deflecting the opponent's thrusts, thereby covering the target, they are called *parries*.

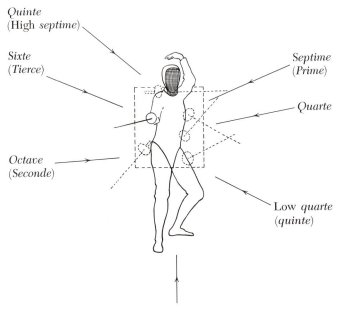

Quinte
(High *septime*)

Sixte
(*Tierce*)

Septime
(*Prime*)

Quarte

Octave
(*Seconde*)

Low *quarte*
(*quinte*)

Fig. 3-19   *The defensive box in foil fencing.*

Fundamental Movements and Definitions

THE PASSAGES

The passage is the manner in which the blade is moved from one position to another. These are direct, semi-circle, three-quarter circle, circle.

The direct passages are quarte to sixte and reverse, and octave to septime and reverse.

Semi-circular passages are sixte to octave and reverse, quarte to octave and reverse, and sixte to septime and reverse.

Three-quarter circle passages are quarte to septime and reverse, and quarte to quinte and reverse (Italian).

Circular passages are full circles made with the point of the blade, which place the blade in the same position as it was held originally or the way that the point moves when changing engagement.

Fencing distance is determined by the closeness of the fencers. *Close distance* or *close quarters* is the distance maintained when the opponent can be reached by an extension of the arm without any foot movement. The *middle distance* requires a single foot movement, either a step or a lunge, and the extension of the arm in order to reach the opponent. *Far distance* means two or more foot movements plus the length of the extended arm are necessary to reach the opponent.

The term *lines* can be used in fencing in two respects.

The imaginary line passing through the feet of the two opponents in the on guard position is the *fencing line*. When the point of the blade is directed with an extended arm to the opponent's target, the *blade is in line*. The blade in line may be high or low.

In foil fencing the hit is a definite touch with the point of the blade on the opponent's target. To practice the correct touch, the pupil brings the point of the blade onto the master's target with a straight arm, and then with slight pressure of the thumb and forefinger bends the blade a little upwards. The fist is held a little higher than the shoulder.

The *absence of blades* occurs when the fencers' blades are not in contact with each other.

When the blades are in contact, crossing on either side or being held so that the foible of one blade contacts the forte of the other, the blades are in *engagement*. This means that if two right handed fencers cross blades in high line with the left sides of the blades, they are engaged in quarte. Similarly, the engagement in right high line is the sixte; in low left, septime; in low right, octave. If the fencer pushes the opponent's blade with the engagement so far to the side that the opponent will not be able to hit with a straight thrust, the fencer is said to be *covered*. The engagement is done in order to test the opponent's grip on the weapon. It is useful in training the fingertips to feel the moment when the opponent breaks the engagement.

Simple Actions

THE DIRECT THRUST (COUP DROIT)

The direct thrust is a hit which arrives without any hesitation, in a straight line, by one complete movement to the opponent's target. The point should hit the target before the heel of the lunging foot touches the floor.

The direct thrust should be learned from the middle distance in two stages: first, the arm is extended in line; second, the hit is made with a lunge. This sequence later should be speeded up so that the extension and the lunge seem to occur simultaneously. The lunge should appear to follow the point rather than bringing it forward.

After the student has practiced the straight thrust from the original on guard position of the hand, he should exercise the thrust from different positions and from varying distances. When completing the thrust, the fencer's fist should cover the line in which the opponent's blade lies.

To practice the direct thrust and the recovery after a lunge, the master should direct his blade to different sections of the student's target, thus requiring the student to return to the on guard position while engaging the blade with the appropriate engagement.

THE DISENGAGE ATTACK (DEGAGEMENT; CAVAZIONE)

The disengage is an indirect, simple attack of the opponent's engagement to the opposite side of the blade. The blade is liberated from the engagement, and the point passes the opponent's guard or blade in a semi-circular, spiral movement. The disengagement from the quarte or sixte engagement passes beneath the opponent's guard, and from the septime or octave, above the opponent's guard.

Finger play is the delicate work of the fingers in relaxing pressure on the handle during the manipulation of the point and in pressing firmly again after the movement is completed. This action is a characteristic of the French school in which the last three fingers direct the circular movement while the thumb and forefinger lead the point.

In the Italian style, the firmer grip does not allow this finger work so the circular actions are controlled by the wrist.

Defense

The defense against an attack may be passive or active. Passive defense is the fencer's movement of withdrawal or displacement of his body at the moment when the opponent's point is approaching the target. Active defense is executed with the weapon. The simplest form of the active defense is the direct parry.

THE DIRECT PARRIES

The direct parry is a defensive position. It is assumed by moving the blade across the body from one side to the other to engage the opponent's blade and deflect the point at the moment when it is approaching the target. The parry should be taken with the guard or the forte of the foil, either with a pressing or beating movement (*picco-parries*). The parry can be taken at a point farther or closer to the defended target, depending on the distance of the opponent. The parries must be made with short, definite, limited movements without any hesitation, and the speed with which they are taken should be appropriate to the opponent's attack. The parry should be made with the fist, and not by swinging the point across the target.

When the student has acquired the ability to make the movements of the parry correctly, he should practice taking the parry only at the last possible moment before he is hit.

The names of the parries are similar to the names of the engagements given above, prime through octave.

After the student is familiar with the thrust from different positions and the thrust-recovery to different positions, he should be able to practice an exercise of thrust with lunge, parry with recovery, second thrust with lunge (thrust-parry-thrust). In the beginning, this drill should be practiced in a slow rhythm enabling the master to control the proper taking of the parries and to develop the mobility and suppleness of the student's recovery.

When the students have mastered these movements, they can practice so that one uses a thrust-parry-thrust sequence while the other uses a parry-thrust-parry. Usually, beginners are restricted to lunges in the quarte line and parries of quarte. When the students are able to control the movements of thrust and recovery, the master should show them that the recovery need not be complete. By taking his front foot back only half way, the fencer is able to speed up his return thrust.

When the pupils are proficient at this three movement sequence, the group drill can be extended to include five movements. This exercise serves to introduce to the student a basic concept of foil fencing, the idea of cadence or of right of way. If the first thrust does not hit or is parried before it arrives, the right of way goes to the second fencer who now may make a counter-attack with a return thrust. If this return is parried by the first fencer, he has regained the right of counter-attack. This sequence of attack, parry, and counter-attack proceeds until one fencer is hit.

This exercise also gives the student an opportunity to learn to adjust his speed to that of his partner. The beginner usually executes all his movements with much the same speed and is often puzzled at how to hit the opponent since all his thrusts are parried. After explaining that there are other attacks to be learned later, the master may demonstrate the effect of different rhythms by speeding up his return thrust and making a hit before the student is able to parry.

At a later stage, this sequence of associated movements should be practiced with all possible combinations of thrusts and parries.

This exercise of thrust-parry-thrust may now be practiced in a combat-like manner. The master allows himself to be hit from time to time by any thrust to see whether the student is always trying to hit with first intention, which is a direct, simple attempt to hit not taking into account the opponent's possible reaction or response. The master can also change his parries from simple parries to counter-parries to teach the student a variety of forms.

THE DIRECT RIPOSTE

The direct thrust executed immediately after a successful parry in the same line, with or without a lunge, is called the *direct riposte*.

The beginner, after a successful parry, is usually so amazed at his success at defending himself that he often forgets the riposte. The master must make the pupil practice the riposte after a parry until it becomes a reflex action of the hand itself. To speed up the riposte, the master has the student take the parry slowly and concentrate on making a quick return thrust. It is quite important to practice a retreat with the parry followed by an immediate lunge with the riposte. Timing the parry to occur with the retreat of the back foot and the thrust to come with the lunge helps the student to improve the coordination of his hand movements with his feet. The retreat also gives a little more time for the parry to be taken.

THE RIPOSTE ALONG THE BLADE (COULÉ) (FILO)

The riposte which hits the opponent in the same line as the parry without breaking the contact of the blades is called *filo* riposte. The most useful filo ripostes are those from sixte (tierce) or octave (seconde) parries when the opponent has failed to cover the line completely with his thrusts.

THE CONTRA-RIPOSTE

The immediate riposte after a successful parry of the opponent's riposte is called the *contra-riposte*. When practicing with the student, the master may change his second parry from a high line parry to a low line parry or the reverse in order to change the contra-riposte. For a second intention attack—a premeditated offensive action which attempts to elude the opponent's reaction or parry his counter-actions—the fencer stays in the lunge after the attack, parries, and makes the contra-riposte from the lunge position.

THE CIRCULAR (COUNTER) PARRIES

If a fencer on guard in the high line takes a parry to cover himself against an attack directed to the low line or vice-versa, he must take a *semi-circular parry* in the manner described in the section on passages (p. 86). These are parries passing from sixte to septime, from octave to quarte, from sixte to octave, and their reverse.

When the fencer from one position or from his own engagement, parries an attack (directed into the open line) with a circular motion he takes a *circular parry* (*counter-parry*). The circular parry is a full circular motion passing from one position back to the same position. The circular parries against the high line attacks pass under the opponent's blade; the quarte is made with a counter-clockwise movement; the sixte with a clockwise movement. The counter-parries against the low line attacks in septime and octave pass over the opponent's blade in clockwise and counter-clockwise directions, respectively.

COMBINED EXERCISES

At each level of the fencer's development he should practice compound exercises consisting of movements of attack and defense, with a variety of hand and foot work designed to polish his discipline, coordination, speed, and timing. We speak of such groups of exercises as *combined exercises*. These exercises should become increasingly complex as the student increases his knowledge of tactical maneuvers.

An example of such a combined exercise (using actions we have already discussed) might be the sequence: straight thrust and recovery with quarte, followed by a circular quarte parry with retreat and direct riposte. After the initial thrust and recovery, there is a pause. The second half of the exercise is then executed without a pause. As the student's ability increases, the two halves should be performed with greater speed, and the interval of the pause should be varied, with one or more forward or backward steps included.

THE CHANGING PARRIES

Against an opponent's attack along the blade, the fencer may attempt a parry with opposition—that is, he may use the simple parry. Alternatively, he may parry by changing the parry to the opposite line from the attack. If, for example, the opponent's quarte parry, direct riposte is parried with sixte instead of quarte by passing the blade below the opponent's guard, the fencer has taken the changing parry of sixte. If the riposte was a filo reposte from the sixte parry, the changing parry would be quarte. In the low lines, the septime (octave) parry riposte would be met with the changing parry of octave (septime).

Those *changing parries* are very much like the circular parries except that the point describes an arc of only three quarters of a circle. These parries are very disturbing and confusing to the opponent. The fencer should observe the way the point moves in these changing parries and try to practice the same movement by himself, as often as possible, without an opposing blade. This movement makes the wrist supple, and when mastered, gives the fencer the ability to break the line unexpectedly.

CHANGE OF ENGAGEMENT

Starting from his own or his opponent's engagement, the fencer changes the engagement by disengaging his blade and engaging on the opposite side of the original blade contact. The purpose of this movement is to confuse or disturb the opponent. It may be practiced by two students with engaged blades, who alternately change the engagement and then stop briefly. The movement should also be drilled with advances and retreats.

THE DISENGAGE RIPOSTE

The fencer may use the indirect riposte with disengage against an opponent who always parries the direct riposte with a direct parry or who after a thrust covers himself with a simple position. In the disengage riposte, the point describes a larger circle than in the disengage attack. This happens because the fencer's foil is in a parry position with his point farther from his opponent's guard. In the case of the disengage riposte from the quarte parry, it is especially important not to make a lunge before the point has passed the opponent's guard; starting the lunge too soon will only result in having the blade blocked by the opponent's forearm.

Unless the fencer is sure of his opponent's reactions, the disengage riposte from quarte or septime parries made at the first opportunity may fail to hit. The opponent may not react and cover himself with the expected parry, but may leave his blade in line, thus blocking the riposte.

After the disengage attack and riposte have been learned, the thrust-parry-thrust exercise may be modified to become a disengage-thrust-parry-disengage-riposte sequence. The second student executes a circular-parry-direct riposte-direct parry.

Example of Combined Exercise: At this point an appropriate combined exercise drill might be: disengage attack against quarte engagement, a recovery with quarte position, circular quarte parry with retreat, disengage-riposte.

FENCING TIME

Fencing time is the length of time needed to execute a simple attack with lunge, a parry followed by a direct riposte, or an appreciable interval of time between two hits. The speed of execution is assumed to be that of an average fencer.

Making an unexpected attack or the removal of the blade as the opponent is about to engage it are examples of actions executed *in time.* This is discussed in more detail on p. 109.

Timing exercises should be begun during the very early stages of fencing. Keeping the proper distance from the master who moves backward and forward is the first exercise which refines the student's reactions. Another early timing exercise consists of having the student make a thrust with a lunge at the moment when the master changes positions or takes his blade away from engagement. Later, two students may drill timing exercises together. With blade engaged, the first student initiates a change of distance by advancing and retreating, while the second tries to keep his distance without losing blade contact. Then, the first student opens the line of engagement and the second tries to attack with a thrust at the same time. If the master allows both students to regulate the distance and open the line at will, they soon learn that they must be very careful in moving to avoid having a collision or losing blade contact. They will also find that they are unable to take advantage of every opportunity given by the opponent.

THE EVASIVE THRUST (DEROBEMENT, CAVAZIONE IN TEMPO)

The evasive thrust is a simple attack in time against the opponent's attempt at engagement. The movement is similar to the disengage attack, but the point must be removed before the opponent touches the blade.

The evasive thrust must be practiced against the simple, semicircular, and circular engagements. To teach finger work and evasions, the master instructs the student to put his blade in line and the master slowly but evenly crosses the line with various engaging movements, trying to catch the student's blade. The student evades the engagement by swinging his point to the opposite side of the master's blade. At first only hand movement is practiced, but later the action is combined with footwork.

COUNTER-EVASIVE THRUST

If the blades have been in engagement and the opponent is changing the engagement, the *counter-evasive thrust* is made in the direction opposite to that from which the engagement was broken. The difference between the counter-evasive and evasive thrusts is illusory; we are misled by the engagement of blades. The motion of the counter-evasive thrust from quarte engagement to sixte is the same as the evasive thrust against the simple or counter-sixte engagement.

To make the student use his sense of touch (rather than sight), the master may make him close his eyes after an engagement. The student then makes the thrust against the change when he feels the engagement being broken. When the student is able to feel this kind of evasive thrust with his fingers, he can proceed to practice the attack with footwork.

Example of Combined Exercises: The master engages the blade in quarte, then changes to sixte. The student makes the counterevasive thrust and recovers with quarte. After a pause, the pupil retreats with circular quarte, (parrying the master's thrust) and finishes with disengage riposte.

THE CUT-OVER (COUPÉ) (TAGLIATA)

We have delayed the discussion of this simple, indirect attack until now because it is a fairly wide movement and we feel it best to restrain the naturally large movements of the beginner.

The cut-over is a kind of simple disengage which, instead of passing the opponent's blade near the guard, passes around the point of the opponent's blade. This attack is used only against engagements in the high lines. In executing the cutover, the fencer's lunge must not start before the blade has already passed the point of the opponent's blade or else the attack is likely to land flat or pass the opponent's target. If the distance is short, the cut-over may be executed with a bent elbow. At longer distances, wrist and finger action is usually sufficient.

After any kind of quarte or sixte parry, the cut-over executed as a riposte may land on the upper part of the body. After a quarte parry, the cut-over riposte may also land on the flank. During the riposte after the quarte (sixte) parry if the wrist is brought towards the left (right) shoulder, it will help the fencer to pass the opponent's point, especially if he is opposing. The evasive cut-over may be made against simple, semi-circular, circular, or changing quarte or sixte engagements. In parrying the cut-over, the fencer may use the simple or circular quarte or sixte parries to catch the attack in time, but is better to use the high septime parry (or, according to the Italian school, the quinta).

ATTACKS INTRODUCED WITH ENGAGEMENT (PRAISE DE FER)

Against an opponent who stands with his blade in line, the fencer may not attack without first removing the threatening point from line. The attack used could be the *engagement thrust,* the *bind;* or introduced with the *transfer,* and the *envelopement.* These are discussed below.

The Engagement Direct and Indirect Thrust. After engaging the foible of the opponent's blade with the forte of his own, the fencer may execute a direct thrust. If the opponent reacts with counter-pressure against the original engagement, the fencer may attack instead with a disengage-like, semi-circular, indirect thrust. From a distance, the fencer begins the action with a touch on the opponent's blade, followed by a step with the covering engagement, and a lunge with thrust.

The Bind, Flanconnade (Croisé, Fianconata). The flanconnade begins with engagement in quarte. Without breaking the contact of the blades, the fencer leads the point above the opponent's guard to the outside of his blade. The movement ends in a thrust that hits on the flank. The engagement should flow smoothly into the thrust; the opposing blade should not be forced down into the low line. The flanconnade may be used as a riposte after the quarte parry. It is especially effective when the parry is taken with a retreat and the thrust with a lunge.

Another form of this attack is initiated from septime engagement. The extension brings the point smoothly under the guard of the opponent and around into his sixte line. The attack finishes with a thrust along the blade toward the sixte to the upper part of the opponent's target.

Transfer (Transporto di ferro). The transfer of the blade is an action which carries the opponent's blade from high to low line (or the reverse), starting from an engagement and without a break in blade contact. Examples of such an action would be the transfer from quarte to octave, from sixte to septime, or the opposite.

The transfer may be practiced from the far distance with a step-lunge. The engagement is taken as the front foot moves; the bind as the left foot moves and the thrust with the lunge.

The Envelopement. In the envelopement the foible of the opponent's blade is engaged, then carried in a circular movement around and back to the same line without a break in blade contact.

PARRYING THE ATTACKS WITH ENGAGEMENT

The attacks begun with engagement can be parried with direct parries or with changing parries. The bind from quarte to octave can be parried with yielding quarte, the bind from septime to sixte can be parried with yielding prime. This yielding parry allows the blade to be carried along without resistance by the opponent's engagement to the line he desires, and then is taken at the last moment by placing the fist in low quarte or prime.

ATTACKS ON THE BLADE

The *glide* is defined as a smooth, even movement along the blade with no pressure; the *slide* is a similar movement with some force, and the *pressure slide* is a slide with increased force. We can then see the distinction between the *gliding disengage*, the *sliding thrust* or *disengage,* and the *pressure slide-thrust* or *feint* (*filo* or *filo-feint*). These movements along the blade are discussed in many books under the collective name of *coulé,* even though each is distinguished from the others by the position and type of opposition offered by the opponent, the degree of pressure, and the intention of the attack. Here, each is presented separately.

The Gliding Disengage. The gliding disengage attack can be very effective against an opponent who habitually covers the side of the engagement. The glide starts with a constant slip of the foible along the opponent's blade towards his guard. Simultaneously, the foil arm is extended, the body leans to bring the point forward, and a lunge is started. At the last possible instant before the lunge is finished, the point is led around the opponent's guard in a flowing movement to make a hit. The motion must flow smoothly and evenly with the blades in constant contact until the point is disengaged to touch the target.

The idea of this attack is to keep the opponent in doubt as to the exact moment of the disengage and to keep him frozen in position as long as possible. When executed correctly, the movement is extremely hard to parry, especially for an opponent who likes to parry at the last moment. The best and most useful of these gliding disengages starts from sixte. From a greater distance, the glide has to be taken with the advance and the disengage with the lunge.

This delicate and difficult attack cannot be perfected until the student is able to completely relax; a certain amount of muscular tension is inevitable in the beginner. When explaining the movement, the master instructs the student to try only the gliding motion from point to guard, making sure that although the blade contact is not lost, no pressure is exerted during the forward movement. As a reciprocal exercise, one student tries to hit with the gliding disengage, while the other tries to parry at the last moment. This gliding disengage also serves as a transition from a simple attack to an attack on the blade.

The Sliding Thrust and Disengage. The sliding thrust and disengage looks to the spectator very similar to the gliding disengage, but actually differs in two ways. First, unlike the glide, the attacker exerts a slight pressure against his opponent's blade; second, there is a moments pause at the end of the slide while the fencer evaluates his opponent's reaction. If the opponent shows no reaction, the attack is finished with a straight thrust along the blade. If the opponent reacts with opposition, the attacker passes the guard with a disengage. This attack is useful against an opponent who is not well protected on the side of the engagement in his on guard position.

Pressure Slide-Thrust (Coulé, Filo). The opponent may hold his blade firmly or with a relaxed grip. The firmly held blade has to be taken out of line with *pressure* and, because of the opponent's resistance, the thrust must be made by maintaining contact with the opponent's blade. Once contact is lost, the opponent is able to bring his blade back into line. This attack is also called the *filo thrust* or *forced thrust attack along the blade* and is most effective in the sixte and octave engagements when directed toward the right upper and lower quadrants of the opponent's target.

Violent Pressure (Froissement, Copertino). This attack is an exaggerated pressure slid movement. The opponent's blade is moved forcibly aside, out of line, by extending the arm in a rather stiff manner with the hand held in extreme supination in sixte and extreme pronation in quarte.

THE BEAT (BATTEMENT, BATTUTA)

The beat is primarily used against an opponent who holds his blade in line in a relaxed position. The aim of the beat is to slacken the grip, thereby knocking the blade aside or drawing it into opposition. The beat is executed with the middle of the blade against the foible or middle of the opponent's blade. The various beats are named according to the direction in which the executing fencer's blade is moved—quarte, sixte, etc.

The beat must be short, sharp, and limited. It must be short in order to prevent the opponent from moving his blade and avoiding the beat; sharp in order to move the blade out of line while hitting only at one point; and limited so that the position of the blade will be controlled after the meeting of the blades.

The beat can be direct, semi-circular, circular, or a change-beat, according to the relationship of the blades:

1. From a position against a blade in line.
2. From a position against a blade in position.
3. From a line on the blade in position

4. From a line on the blade in line.

5. From position of engagement on the same side as the engaged blade.

6. From position of engagement to the opposite side of the engaged blade (change-beat).

7. From the opponent's engagement to the same side of the engaging blades.

8. From the opponent's engagement to the opposite side of the engaging blade (change-beat).

From the middle distance the beat should be made simultaneously with a stamp of the right foot followed by a thrust with a lunge. From the far distance the beat should be made simultaneously with a forward movement of the right foot followed by a stretching movement of the left knee, a thrust, and a lunge.

In order to perfect the beat, which can only be accomplished when a definite *blade feeling* is established, the fencer should practice the following:

1. The student beats the blade and thrust.

2. The master beats the blade, gives the line, and the student counter-beats in the line and thrusts.

3. The student beats, the master counter-beats in the given line, and the student then counter-beats in the line given by the master, following with a thrust and lunge.

The following exercise can be used in determining the limitations of the beat:

1. Fencer A holds his blade in line. Fencer B makes a beat without a lunge.

2. Fencer A tries to avoid the beat by moving his blade in a circular manner. Fencer B continues with the beat attempt until contact of the blades has been established.

If B makes the slightest move with his sword point prior to the actual beat, the evasion by A will be easy since B has telegraphed his intention. If, on the other hand, the beat by B is executed exclusively in a forward direction, any evasive efforts by A will be almost impossible.

Other exercises can be useful for establishing both the timing and precision of the beat movement.

1. Two fencers exchange beats with intermittent disengages.
2. One fencer periodically brings his blade into line and the other tries to beat the blade.

All the parries can be executed with a beat. These are called the *picco-parries* or *beat-parries* and the riposte from the beat-parry comprises the fastest counter-attack in fencing. The beat-parry riposte should be executed so that it will intercept the attacking blade in one motion.

COMBINED EXERCISES

The student makes a beat-thrust attack against the master's blade and resumes an on guard position with his blade in line. The master makes a beat-thrust attack on the student's line which is followed by a changing parry with a retreat, completed with a riposte.

In teaching these movements, the master sometimes reacts and sometimes remains passive in order to force the student to judge for himself when to end the attack. This type of attack serves as an introduction to the feints.

PARRYING AN ATTACK ON THE BLADE

Attacks on the blade can be parried with opposition or with changing parries. The pressure slide-thrust from sixte may be parried with yielding prime; from octave, with yielding quarte.

Compound Attacks

THE FEINT (FINTA)

The feint is a deceiving or false thrust which invites and lures the opponent to make the appropriate parry. As the opponent takes the parry, the fencer's blade passes the opponent's parrying blade and the thrust is completed in the opened line. The feint is composed of a *false thrust* and a real *evasive thrust*. The false thrust must appear to be the real thrust in order to convince the opponent to take the parry (*trompement*). The false thrust from the middle distance is made in two movements: the first is an extension of the arm with a slight forward movement of the upper body; the second is the evasive thrust with a lunge. The feint should be made with the point close to the opponent's guard, and the pass should be made close to the opponent's bell. It is of utmost importance that the blade does not touch the opponent's blade or guard in the midst of the evasive movement since this would cause the right of way to be lost.

The feints are classified as follows:

1. Initial presentation and introduction of the feint
2. The type and quality of the taken parry
3. The number of parries to be evaded

The introduction of the feint can be:

    (a) direct thrust
    (b) disengagement
    (c) evasive thrust
    (d) cut-over
    (e) engagement
    (f) pressure
    (g) violent pressure
    (h) beat

The quality of the taken parry can be:

    (a) simple
    (b) circular (counter or changing parries)

The number of evading parries can be:

    (a) single
    (b) dual
    (c) plural

In order to properly understand the verbal description of a feint all three separate movements comprising the feint must be given, e.g. *direct thrust - simple-single feint* means that the direct thrust passes a simple parry once prior to reaching the target; *disengage-simple-dual feint* means that after the disengage-thrust the point passes two simple parries prior to reaching the target.

The *simple-single* feint is generally called the *one-two*, and the *simple-dual feint*, the *one-two-three*. The one-two from the far distance is divided into two movements. The arm is extended on the first step and passes the opponent's blade as the lunge is completed. The one-two-three from the far distance is executed in such a way that each hand movement is synchronized with each foot movement; the first feint with the right foot; the second feint with the left foot; and the real thrust with the lunge. The cadence of the one-two-three should be adjusted to the opponent's reactions and may be one of the following:

1. The length of each feint is the same
2. The first feint is long and the second and third are short
3. The first is short, the second long, and the third short

Highly trained fencers may modify the one-two when in the opponent's quarte engagement by initiating the feint simultaneously with the lunge; however, the thrust must be completed prior to the termination of the lunge at all times. The effectiveness of this particular action depends on the fencer's facility in passing the blade when the opponent takes the sixte parry.

If the feint is a direct thrust or a simple disengage, with the final thrust passing a circular parry, it is referred to as a *direct-circular* and *disengage-circular feint*, respectively. These types of feinting actions are generally categorized as *doubles*. If the point of the feinting blade passes two or three circular parries the feint is called *double* or *triple circulation*.

The variations and combinations of feints which can be used are numerous, and they can be changed at will to adjust attacks to the different styles used by opponents. Dual feints, for example, a combination of two feinting actions, can be varied in both sequence and manner of execution depending on the opponent's parrying positions. The simple-single, circular-circular, simple-circular, and circular-simple feints can be used. Special mention must be made of the *pressure slide-feint* since it is similar to the gliding disengage and coulé, and is one of the most effective attacks on the opponent's blade. In executing the pressure slide-feint, the opponent's blade is held with the forte until the middle of his blade has been reached. This action forces opposition which, in turn, makes it possible to complete the action by a passing thrust.

In order to understand the relationship between the gliding disengage, sliding disengage, and the pressure slide-feint, a brief summary follows. The gliding disengage is a constant movement of the point along the opponent's blade without pressure followed by a disengage. The sliding disengage is executed with the point passing along the opponent's blade with slight pressure until it reaches the opponent's bell or guard. The fencer must determine how the opponent will react; at the instant the reaction occures, the disengage is carried through. In order to time the attack with the opponent's reaction, a slight break in the forward motion should occur between the slide and the disengage. The pressure slide-feint is a stronger and more forcible attack; no hesitation should occur from the time of initiation to termination. The opponent's reaction should always be predetermined and the disengage should follow as soon as the opponent gives the desired opposition against the blade.

The *cut-over* (*coupé*) can be used interchangeably with a series of feints, e.g. one, cut-over; cut-over, two, etc. The one-two-three feints, however, are rarely combined with a cut-over action.

Feints against the Sweeping Parries. The *sweeping parries* are special parries taken from the high line to the low line and vice-versa. The action is completed with a counter-circular movement which sweeps the front of the target and breaks the opponent's line of attack. These parries are from quarte to septime and from septime to quarte. The movement is similar to the changing parries except the terminating position is changed from either high to low line or from low to high line.

The advantage of these sweeping parries is that simple-single feint attacks need not be parried by two individual cover movements, but can be checked by a single sweeping parry. The simple-single disengage from engagement in quarte can be parried with the sweeping septime and the same attack from an engagement in septime can be parried with a sweeping quarte. The circular quarte-septime and the circular septime-quarte can pick up almost any kind of attack.

The feint attacks used against these types of parries are the *circular-counter-circular* feints. In the opponent's quarte or septime engagement the circular feint is executed in the opposite direction of the regular double after completion of the disengage. The circular-counter-circular-dual feint is made against the counter-quarte-septime and counter-septime-quarte parries. After the disengage, the first circular movement enables the fencer to avoid the opponent's primary parry and the second circular movement should be in the opposite direction to avoid the secondary part of the opponent's dual parry. This attack should only be executed with a step and a lunge. If a slight hesitation is used between the step and the lunge each part must be synchronized with the step and lunge, respectively.

1. The student executes a disengage one-two and recovers in position (short pause). The student then parries with retreat; the one-two attack is executed by the master. Each parry position should be completed by moving one foot backward each time. The student then completes the exercise with a direct or disengage riposte.

2. The student makes a double of the master's engagement, and recovers (short pause). He then retreats with a counter and direct parry, followed by a direct or disengage riposte.

3. A series of beats is executed by both student and master. At the right moment the student makes a beat-one-two attack, recovers in line (short pause). Parries the master's beat attack with a changing parry and terminates with a riposte along the master's blade.

These exercises increase in complexity within a set pattern of similar movements. The purpose is to teach the student proper co-ordination of hand and foot work in conjunction with the different phases of the exercises. The following are examples:

Direct thrust with lunge (recovery),
One-two with step-lunge (recovery),
One-two-three with jump-lunge.

Thrust along the blade with lunge (recovery),
Coulé with lunge (recovery),
Pressure slide-feint with step-lunge.

Disengage with lunge (recovery),

Circular disengage (recovery),
Circular-dual feint with step-lunge.

Beat, thrust with lunge (recovery),
Beat, disengage thrust with lunge (recovery),
Beat, disengage feint, thrust with step-lunge.

Direct thrust with lunge (recovery),
Thrust feint with cut-over and step-lunge (recovery),
Thrust feint, cut-over feint, cut-over with step-lunge.

Disengage with lunge (no recovery) (master parries but there is no riposte),
Repeated thrust with repeated lunge. . . . . . . (master parries but there is no riposte),
Reprise feint with step-lunge.

MIXED PROGRESSIVE EXERCISES

Disengage with lunge (recovery),
Double with lunge (recovery),
Beat, one-two with step-lunge.

Composite Parries

Composite parries are a series of successive parries which keep the numerous feints of an attack in check. The final thrust of the opponent can thereby be parried effectively. The one-two attack can be parried with either two simple parries or a simple and a circular parry. The parries which keep the opponent's feints in check are only half parries in contrast to the final parry which should be complete and sufficient to cover the target. The double can be parried with a circular-simple or a circular-circular composite parry. In defending a plural feint attack, each feint must be checked with the appropriate parry and the final parry (complete) can be either simple or circular.

The attacks on the blade are parried in the same manner as other attacks. The circular disengage feint should, however, be parried with a changing parry during the first stage of the attack. The final parry of the composite cut-over feint should be parried with a high septime if the final feinting movement is a cut-over.

Compound Ripostes

The riposte, essentially an attack, can also be executed with the same feints as an original attack after a successful parry. The lunge must be slightly delayed in order to give the hand sufficient time to complete the feinting movements. The lunge should be completed simultaneously with the final feinting action. Thus, if an attack is made in the quarte line and is successfully parried, a disengage-one-two riposte would be made with a feint in sixte and the thrust with the lunge in quarte. The riposte is terminated, in this case, in the same line as the original parry. If quarte and septime are used, the feint is made outside the opponent's blade with the thrusts landing on the inside; in sixte the feint is underneath (or inside) and the thrust over the opponent's blade. In octave, the feint is over and the thrust underneath the opponent's blade and the circular riposte describes a circle and a half around the opponent's blade.

COMBINED AND PROGRESSIVE PARRY RIPOSTE EXERCISES

When the fencer has advanced enough and is thoroughly familiar with the above mentioned parries and ripostes, he will be able to practice various, more demanding parries and ripostes with his master. Some of these exercises are listed below, and they can pose a difficult task for even an advanced fencer. The actions of the master are described in the parentheses.

1. Half and full parry riposte.

The master makes a feint, the student takes a half parry, e.g. half quarte. If the master continues with a direct thrust, the student takes a full parry. If the master completes the feint and thrust, the student takes the complete parry in the opposite line of the initial feint. After completing the final parry, the student ripostes either directly or with a disengage.

2. Counter-sixte, feint riposte (disengage, octave-semi-circle quarte, direct riposte),

Quarte parry, disengage riposte (responding quarte).

The responding parries are parries the master or the opponent uses to react to the feint. They are not the real, final parry.

1. Quarte parry, direct riposte (disengage, quarte parry, direct riposte),

   Quarte parry, disengage riposte (quarte, counter-quarte, direct riposte),

   Quarte parry, disengaged-feint, riposte (responding quarte-sixte).

At the disengage-feint riposte (after quarte parry) the feint is in the opponent's sixte line and the final thrust in the quarte line.

2. Quarte parry, direct riposte (disengage, quarte parry, direct riposte),

   Quarte parry, flanconnade riposte (ceding quarte parry, direct riposte),

   Quarte parry, disengage riposte (quarte, counter-quarte parry, direct riposte),

   Quarte parry, feint riposte (quarte, sixte-quarte parry, direct riposte),

   Quarte parry, cut-over riposte (responding quarte).

3. Counter-quarte parry, disengage riposte (disengage, quarte, counter-quarte parry, disengage riposte),

   Quarte, counter-quarte parry, disengage riposte (quarte, counter-quarte parry, disengage riposte),

   Quarte, counter-quarte parry, disengage riposte (responding quarte).

The above exercises should be reversed for the sake of variety and to give the student practice in executing the numerous parries and ripostes. The exercises can also be varied to eliminate any set reactions on the part of the student.

Renewed Attacks

After a successful parry a fencer has earned the right to riposte. If this riposte is delayed or omitted, he may be hit by a renewal of the original attack since he has lost the right of way. There are three kinds of renewed attacks: The *remise* (*rimessa*), the *redouble-*

ment (*rimessa di filata*), and the *reprise d'attaque* (*doppia botta di rimessa*).

The remise is a second thrust after the original attack in the same line, executed from the lunge position without withdrawal of the arm. The remise may be made with a stamp of the front foot (*apell*). This movement helps maintain the force of the original attack. It should not be confused with the repeated jabbing motions made by withdrawing the arm that frequently occur when the fencers have missed each other several times (*répartée*).

The redoublement is a repeated action (thrust, disengage, or feint) with prolonged or renewed lunges made against the opponent who retreats with the parry.

The reprise d'attaque is a new attack made against the opponent who cannot be reached with repeated lunges. This action is usually made with a step-lunge.

Actions in Time

Actions in time are made when the opponent is unprepared or has let his attention flag. Such an action may catch the opponent when he is preparing to attack or even when he is in the midst of executing his attack. Timing or *tempo* is the choice of the proper moment to attack or counter-attack. A well-trained body and a developed capacity for sudden decision give the fencer the consistent ability to make such actions in time.

It is not necessary to execute an action in time with a quick or violent motion. A movement that starts from rest without obvious preparation and proceeds smoothly without hesitation may be so unexpected that it succeeds in hitting the opponent before he is alerted. The attack, even though executed quickly, may look slow and easy because of the lack of preparatory motion. Such a movement is often more effective than a powerful movement made with obvious preparation or with vacillation during execution.

We have previously discussed the improvement of timing through the use of evasive thrusts and feint attacks. Now, we will consider counter-attacks—attacks which are actions in time or attacks made into attacks. The counter-attacks are classified in two groups: the *stop-hits* and the *time-hits*.

THE STOP-THRUST (COUP D'ARRET, COLPO D'ARRESTO)

The stop-thrust is a counter-attack that stops the attacker from proceeding. The stop-hit must land before the final movement of the attack. It should not be attempted in the face of the opponent's direct thrust. In case of a double touch (*ambo*), the counter-attacking fencer does not have the right of way and so is declared touched. Even if the attack develops slowly, only a very fast fencer can make a stop-hit arrive ahead of the straight attack.

THE TIME-THRUST (COUP DE TEMPS)

The time-thrust is a stop-hit that blocks the course of the attack and covers the fencer who executes it. The time-thrust thus serves simultaneously as a parry and a counter-attack. This action may be executed in first measure into one-two (simple feint) attacks, in the first or second measure into the one-two-three attack (dual feints), or in the last measure against the direct thrust or simple or composed feint attacks.°

The time-thrust executed against the indirect riposte as a remise (with apell) is called the *appuntata*. This is discussed on page 114. The master, in teaching the time-thrust against the single feint attack, must understand the theory behind the time-thrusts against each of these attacks. Thus, against a simple-single feint attack (one-two), against which the reaction to the feint would be quarte or octave position, the fencer substitutes the time-hit to the upper target. Against such an attack in which the reaction would be the sixte or septime position, the hit is to the lower part of the target.

Against the circular-single feint attacks (double) in place of the circular or changing quarte or octave reactions, the time-thrust is now made to the lower target. Against an attack where the reaction is a circular or changing sixte the time-thrust is made to the *outside* part of the lower target. The circular or changing septime reaction is replaced by the time-hit to the upper target.

If a time-thrust is to be made in the second measure against

° The measure is the length of time of a movement. The direct thrust has only one measure (last). The one-two has first and last measure. The one-two-three has first, second, and last measure.

the dual feint, the first (reacting) parry is taken and then the time-hit is made instead of the second parry.

The time-thrust in the last measure applies to an action against the final movement of the attack. There are three such last measure time-thrusts specified in the Italian school—the *inquartata*, the *imbroccata*, and the *passata sotto*.

The Inquartata. The inquartata is a last measure time-thrust made by moving the body sideways against an attack meant to land on the upper left section of the target. Placing the point in the upper line towards the opponent's target, the fencer steps to the outside with his back foot, simultaneously turns his body to the left, and pushes his fist to the left to block the opponent's blade to the side and evade his thrust (Fig. 3-20).

Fig. 3-20 *Inquartata.*

The Imbroccata. The imbroccata is a last measure time-thrust against the opponent's thrust with pressure in octave. The fencer opposes the pressure with his fist and forces his point a little upwards to the right lower section of the opponent's target. This is a difficult action and is rarely done.

The Passata Sotto. The third last measure time-thrust is the passata sotto, used against attacks in the high line. The thrust is made with hand in pronation while the left leg is stretched backwards, the right knee is bent even more, and fingers of the left hand touch the floor beside the right foot. The fencer attempts to avoid the thrust of the opponent by displacing his body beneath the attack, while impaling the attacker on the out-thrust blade (Fig. 3-21).

The time or stop-thrusts are difficult actions to master. They require accurate judgement of the right moment, and definite, quick execution. The slightest delay or indecision betrays the action to the attacker.

Fig. 3-21 *Passata sotto. Posing: Maitre Alpar and Imre Hennyey former Intercollegiate World Champion.*

ATTACKS WITH SECOND INTENTION (SECONDA INTENZIONE)

Against an opponent who customarily ends his riposte in the same line or against an opponent who favors the stop-thrust or time-thrust, the fencer may use an attack with second intention.

A second intention parry is taken by making an original attack designed to draw an expected parry and riposte or a counter-attack. When the desired motion comes from the opponent, it is taken over with the parry and the riposte that was really meant to hit. The second intention parry and riposte against the expected riposte is called contra-riposte and is made from the lunge or while the fencer is moving forward after parrying the opponent's riposte.

A second intention attack against an evasive thrust, time-or stop-thrust is the second intention parry and riposte described above. The attack is a false move made up of only a step or short lunge to lure the opponent into the counter-attack.

FEINT IN TIME (FINTA IN TEMPO)

If the fencer recognizes the opponent's second intention attack against his own evasive stop-or time-thrust, he may only indicate the first movement and then continue by evading the second intention parry. The feint is made with apell, the thrust is continued with the lunge.

COUNTER–TIME (CONTRO TEMPO)

The counter-time is a time-thrust made into the feint in time. To practice this action, the student stamps his foot to indicate a false attack. The master stamps his foot to indicate the feint. Then the student executes the time-hit with lunge while the master tries to finish the feint attack with a short lunge. Both complete the action with the lunge.

In summation, we list the sequence of actions leading to the counter-time of the Italian school.

1. Attack (*attacco*)
2. Evasive thrust or stop-hit (*cavazione in tempo, colpo d'arresto*)
3. Second intention (*intenzione seconda*)
4. Feint in time (*finta in tempo*)
5. Counter-time (*contro tempo*)

In contrast, the French school and the International Fencing Federation rules define counter-time as "every action made by the attacker on a stop-hit made by his opponent." [*]

---

[*] International Fencing Federation Rule Book, Paris, 1959, p. 164.

Thus this sequence is:

1. Attack (*attaque*)
2. Time-thrust, stop-thrust (*coupé de temps, coup d'arret*)
3. Counter-time (*contre-temps*)

Examples of combined exercises:

A. 1. Student: Quarte beat, thrust
   2. Master: Evasive thrust
   3. Student: Second intention parry (sixte)
   4. Master: Feint in time (outside-inside)
   5. Student: Counter-time (indicating the beat; time-hit to the low right line of the master's target)

B. 1. Student: Direct thrust
   2. Master: Counter-sixte parry (from sixte position), disengage riposte
   3. Student: Second intention octave parry
   4. Master: After the counter-sixte parry, feint riposte (low-high)
   5. Student: Remise to the upper right section of the master's target, with the fist to the right and high, (*appuntata*)

APPUNTATA

Appuntata is a time-thrust similar to the counter-time into the opponent's feint riposte (a remise in time). The action is directed to the part of the opponent's target which had just been successfully defended by a parry. This action is usually accompanied with a stamp of the foot in the lunge. The appuntata must block the conclusion of the riposte.

Examples:

1. If a direct thrust was parried by the opponent with a quarte, an immediate remise blocks the disengage riposte and scores at the same time.

2. If a thrust was parried by the opponent with an octave, an immediate remise blocks the feint riposte and scores at the same time.

The False Attacks (Fausse Attaques, Attacco Simulato)

False attacks are imitation attacks designed to test the opponent's reactions, intentions, or to mislead him. Correctly made the false attack lures the defender into a premature parry or stop-thrust, allowing the attacker to evade the one or to take over the other. One could say, all feint attacks start with a false movement. Also, the first movement of an attack in second intention is false in that it is not really designed to hit and so is a little exaggerated to draw the opponent's reaction. These false motions are an important element in the preparation of any composed attack.

Disarmament (Desarmo, Sforzo)

The disarmament is a bind or strong beat with a spiral twist done on the opponent's blade. It is used to loosen the opponent's grip (making him unable to parry), or to wrench the weapon entirely from his grasp. The FIE rules require that the point must land without a break or hesitation in the disarming movement.

From quarte position, the blade is given a spiral twist with the hand in pronation. This binds the opponent's blade from the foible down to the forte and forces it into seconde. From sixte with supinated hand the blade is bound into septime with a quick and vigorous transfer of the blade. These actions are of very limited utility and are rarely used.

COMBAT-LIKE EXERCISES

In combat-like exercises, the student has to find out for himself the right attack or defense from the various opportunities the master offers. This is the first step in preparing the student for free play.

Examples:

1. In the thrust-parry-thrust exercise the master from time to time allows himself to be hit with the first thrust in order to force the student to attack always with first intention.

2. The master gives different invitations or brings his blade into line. The student tries to execute feints or makes beat attacks on the blade in line.

3. The master changes positions constantly, quarte-sixte or octave-septime; the student makes feints into the opening line. Next, the master changes the distance forcing the student to discover for himself whether the lunge is sufficient or whether a step-lunge is needed.

RECIPROCAL EXERCISES

Reciprocal exercises are practiced by two fencers working together. They limit themselves to certain types of attacks and defenses. One fencer initiates the attack, the other defends himself with parries and ripostes. The defender should stand against the wall, forcing himself to rely on the parry of the weapon (not distance) for his defense. These movements should also be practiced from the far distance.

Examples:

1. *A* invites in sixte; *B* attacks with a direct thrust; *A* tries quarte parry. If *A* parries too soon, *B* hits in sixte evading the parry. If *A* quesses that *B* wants to finish the attack in sixte line, he remains in sixte and makes a parry riposte.

2. *A* gives high or low line; *B* makes a beat-thrust attack; *A* parries the attack or, if the beat was wide or slow, makes an evasive thrust. If *B* anticipates the evasive thrust, he parries and ripostes.

Free Play

When the master feels his students are ready for combat, he should arrange them in pairs. At first the range of attack and defense should be limited. From time to time the master should stop the action and give constructive criticism and advice. He should make the student repeat any unsuccessful action and indicate to him the reasons why it failed. Later, a wider range of action is permitted until the students are fencing entirely on their own initiative. In addition to the mechanical principles they now know, some finer tactics should be explained to them since in competion the fencer encounters opponent's who have a wide variety of styles, both orthodox and unconventional. The student should take every opportunity to fence with the various types of opponents.

Following are some basic fencing rules:

A good hit must land clearly and distinctly on the opponent's valid target.

Every hit which arrives a good fencing tempo ahead of another must be considered as valid.

If both fencers hit each other at the same time, from the same distance (with footwork of uniform measure) because the conception and execution of each attack was simultaneous, both hits are counted as good (*tempo comune*), and neither hit is scored (except in épée, where both hits are counted).

If, as one of the fencers attacks, the opponent counter-attacks and does not anticipate the attack by a fencing tempo, the hit is scored against the counter-attacker who provoked the double touch (*ambo*).

An attack executed correctly and without hesitation must be parried. If the defender does successfully parry, he has earned the right of way. The right of way alternates in this fashion until one fencer is hit.

The riposte should follow the parry immediately. If the defender delays or hesitates, the attacker may seize the initiative.

The evasive thrust or cut executed against attacks on the blade has the right of way.

If the fencer touches his opponent's blade during the feint, and continues on to make a hit, the blade contact may be considered a parry by which the defender has earned the right to riposte.

The time-thrust must block the opponent's attack.

The stop-thrust must arrive ahead of the attack by an ending tempo.

Electrical Fencing

There is little doubt that the introduction of the electrical scoring system revolutionized épée fencing a generation ago, and that a similar revolution is going on now with foil fencing. Scoring has become easier, and has eliminated any uncertainty which may be connected with decisions made by referees.

In addition, this scoring system has brought the game closer to the principles of dueling and simplified the method of fencing. Although foil fencing has lost a good deal of its old spectacular beauty, the enforcement of the rules and the correct signaling time hopefully will help retain some of it.

The increased weight of the foible of the blade (because of the point and tape needed for electrical scoring) has given rise to a tendency to hold the foil incorrectly (more like the saber). The fencer embraces the handle more securely with middle, ring, and little fingers. This change in the grip causes very wide movements of the blade, eliminating the possibility for fine control of the point.

To curb this tendency, the fencer has to exercise his fingers to gain strength in them so that he will be able to hold the foil properly. To secure the foil to his hand, he should use a wrist strap.

The change in the balance of the blade means movements are wider and parries have to be more expansive so the target will be cleared and there will not be a possibility for an insufficient parry.

The so called picco-parries (tik-tak parries) must now be taken well ahead of the body and the riposte must be made with great speed so that it will arrive before the continuation of the attack reaches the target. Many hits previously considered flat are now recognized by the machine, and this has increased the fencer's confidence in his attacks.

The remise, stop-hits, and second intention are now more frequently used; the fencer has had to learn not to stop after a supposed touch, but rather to continue until he becomes aware of the light and the buzzer. Simplicity, speed, timing, and aggressiveness are the primary factors through which success is gained.

To accustom the student to the weapon he will use in competitions, lessons must be taken with a foil having the same balance and weight as the electrical foil. Some lessons should also be taken with the electrical weapon itself to increase the student's confidence in replacement of the point, in remises to the attack, and to the remises of the riposte.

Finally, we must emphasize that the principles of fencing have remained the same, and the fencer still has to practice composed movements (attacks and parries), as before with the standard foil to acquire flexibility and the ability to diversify his fencing.

Chapter 2
The Épée

The épée, a thrusting weapon, is a heavier edition of the foil with its technique based on that of the foil. The difference in use lies in the extension of the target area and the rules and regulations of the bout. The target is the entire body including fencing uniform, gloves, shoes, and mask (Fig. 3-22).

The blade is triangular, stiff, tapered towards the point d'arret, and mounted to the guard with the widest side on top.

The guard is larger than the foil-guard, with a depth of $1\frac{1}{8}$ to $2\frac{3}{16}$ inches (30 to 55 mm.) and $1\frac{3}{8}$ inch (35 mm.) in diameter. The

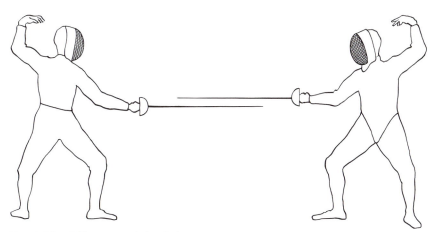

Fig. 3-22   *Silhouettes of the épée target.*

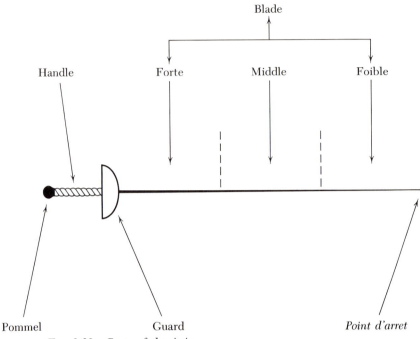

FIG. 3-23   *Parts of the épée.*

blade may be mounted to the guard eccentrically, but this eccentricity cannot be more than $1\frac{3}{8}$ inch (35 mm.). The handle can be either French, Italian, or pistol-shaped (Fig. 3-23).

The On Guard Position

Because of the exposed right knee, the knees in the on guard position are less bent than in foil fencing. The right (sword) arm is held in an easy, flexed position, the forearm parallel to the ground, the hand in slight supination, and the elbow held in. The blade and the forearm are kept in one line. The on guard position can be taken by placing the right foot forward, or putting the left foot backward.

The Footwork

Since épée fencing has been simplified by the introduction of the electrical scoring system, footwork has become more natural also. The advance may be started with either foot. If it is started with the right foot it is done the same way as in foil fencing; if started with the left foot, the movement is done by bringing the foot forward, close to the right heel, and then moving forward into the on guard position.

The retreat with the left foot is the same as in foil fencing. Initiated with the right foot, it starts by moving the right foot back close to the left, and then moving the left back into the on guard position.

The lunge is a complete extension or slightly less, depending on the distance. The half lunge can be lengthened by a stamp of the foot or with the repeated lunge. The *retraction* is a withdrawal of the right foot from the on guard position, moving it close to the left with extension of the knees. This is usually made with a stop-thrust to the opponent's wrist or arm.

The *flèche*, either the French or the Hungarian, is often used, but must always come as a surprise.

The Hit

The épée rules, unlike those of foil or saber, award the touch to the fencer whose hit arrives a fraction of a second $(1.\frac{1}{25})$ ahead. The thrusts may be directed to any part of the body. *Angle* (diagonal) thrusts to the wrist against the opponent's straight arm are executed with the forearm held straight along the blade, and the arm bent at the elbow. Since the arm presents a small target area, accurate thrusts requiring careful and constant practice are needed and the fencer must be able to project the feeling in his finger-tips to the point of the weapon. The point should be kept close to the rim of the opponent's guard at all times, so that the slightest opening can be caught.

The Parries and Ripostes

The parry must either protect the arm or cover the body depending on the type of attack. Parries against attacks to the wrist or forearm are oppositions to thrusts, rather than the formal parries of the foil. The parries protecting the body are quarte, sixte, octave, or seconde and, more rarely, the septime. (Actually, the septime is dangerous in that it is taken far forward and leaves the arm exposed.)

The parries may be simple or counter; the latter done many times with *envelopment* to keep the opponent's blade well under control. In defense against attacks, displacement or withdrawal of the body is often used, especially when the attack is directed to the head. Also, retraction is the best way to protect the front foot against a thrust.

The ripostes are usually simple and are most effectively made along the blade with glide or bind.

Accuracy, precise timing, and speed dominate the game.

Other Actions

Because the action in épée fencing is quite similar to the foil fencing, it will not be discussed again. However, some characteristic differences will be pointed out.

The épée game is dominated by second intention. The fencer using the épée must be very cautious, with the attention concentrated on the arm.

FIG. 3-24   *Flèche to the body.*

FIG. 3-25   *Flèche to the knee.*   *Photos by W. Snedish*

FIG. 3-26   *Arrêt on the arm with retraction. Posing: Alpar and Hennyey.*

Any forward movement of the arm made to bring the point in touch with the opponent's target is considered an attack. Attacks on the body should be executed at the most opportune time or on the blade (Figs. 3-24 to 3-26).

The beat has to be strong enough to divert the blade and open the target. Stop-or time-hits are basic in épée fencing and are directed into any kind of attack, even into the opponent's stop- and time-hits. The beat may be made with second intention in order to provoke the opponent's disengage or evasive thrust into which a stop-hit can be made.

The remise and redoublement are frequently used, especially against a retreating opponent or one who does not riposte. They are usually executed with the apell, the stretch of the lunge, or the repeated lunge (Fig. 3-27).

To practice the timing and point control, a fencer can hang a

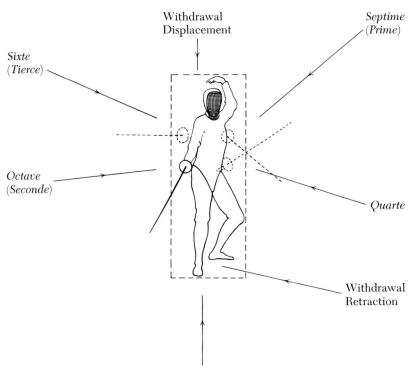

Withdrawal
Displacement

Septime
(Prime)

Sixte
(Tierce)

Octave
(Seconde)

Quarte

Withdrawal
Retraction

Fig. 3-27   *The defensive box at épée.*

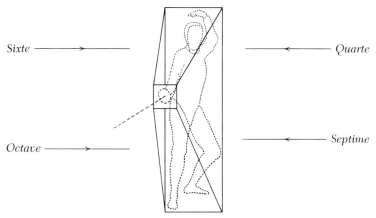

Sixte ———————→ ———

Quarte ←——————— ———

Octave ———————→ ———

Septime ←——————— ———

Fɪɢ. 3-28   *The projection of homologous exercises.*

small ball on a string from the ceiling, set it in motion, and then try to catch it with a thrust at the nearest and at the furthest point on its course.

HOMOLOGOUS EXERCISES

These exercises are helpful for the épée and saber fencer only. They emphasize the fact that these are two separate target distances in épée and saber fencing: the arm distance and the body distance. The exercises are arranged into groups which combine both target distance, e.g. a thrust (cut) to the arm followed by a thrust (cut) to the body (Fig. 3-28). They are an aid in learning the respective differences between the amount and speed of the action that must be directed toward the nearest and farthest target.

In each group of exercises the master allows himself to be hit on each segment of the target. The student carries out an action, and then, without stopping, continues to the next part of the exercise. In the examples given here the exercises are given from the point of view of the student, and, consequently, the master must adjust himself to the student's needs by giving the necessary reactions and assistance.

Examples:

1. Thrusts to the wrist, arm, and body (one after the other).
2. Thrusts to the foot, knee, and body (one after the other).

3. Stop-hits to the wrist, arm, and body (one after the other).

4. Parry ripostes to the wrist, arm, and body (one after the other).

5. Remises; both hits on the arm; first on the arm; second on the body; both hits on the body.

6. Repeated thrusts in close quarters (note that the *corps à corps* is allowed in épée fencing).

COMBINED EXERCISES

A.   1. Thrust to the forearm, retire to on guard.

2. Stop-hit to the wrist with retraction, against the master's attack to the foot.

3. On guard with the back foot, counter-sixte parry, riposte against the master's attack to the body.

B.   1. Beat and thrust to the forearm.

2. Changing parry with recovery against the master's filo riposte.

3. Envelopment and bind riposte.

C.   1. Disengage with lunge (the master parries with counter-parry but does not riposte).

2. Remise with the stretch of the lunge (master retreats).

3. Recovery to on guard by pulling up the left foot, flèche attack to the body.

Chapter 3

The Saber

The saber (Fig. 3-29), a cutting and thrusting weapon, consists of a blade and handle with guard; it is used with conventional rules and rights of way. The weight of the weapon must be less than $1\frac{1}{10}$ pounds (500 grams). The blade is rectangular in the section near the guard and is gradually tapered to a blunted point that is used for thrusts. A groove runs along each side from the forte, past the middle, and stops at the foible. This lightens the blade and makes the section triangular. The foible, about 8 inches long, is flat. The front and back edges (used for cuts) are rectangular. The middle of the blade is used for beats while parries are made with the forte. The guard is made up of the basket, handle, and pommel. At the present time, the saber is the only weapon used in tournaments without an electrical scoring apparatus.

The Grip

The saber should be held with the upper part of the thumb and forefinger below the small metal band so that the thumb rests on the flat part of the handle. The handle lies on the cushion of the palm under the little finger. The other two fingers are bent over the handle lightly (Fig. 3-30).

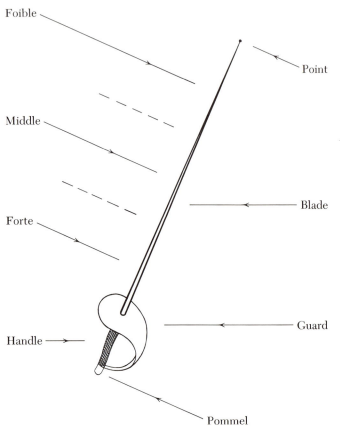

Foible

Middle

Forte

Handle →

Point

Blade

Guard

Pommel

FIG. 3-29   *Parts of the saber.*

FIG. 3-30   *The Saber grip.*

Position of the Body

The front and initial (basic) positions are the same as those in foil fencing except that the saber is held with the hand in pronation and the blade at an angle of approximately 45 degrees.

In the on guard position, which must be flexible, the right foot moves forward about 12 inches in the direction of the opponent, landing in the same position as in foil fencing. The left hand is placed on the left hip and the sword arm is slightly bent downwards with the elbow held 4 to 5 inches from the hip. The point of the blade should be about the height of the right eye and the guard should be turned about 45 degrees to the right. The upper part of the body, above the hip, leans slightly forward (Figs. 3-31 to 3-33).

In advanced fencing, the weight of the body is slightly shifted from the front or back foot, depending on whether the fencer wants to attack or defend himself. Many fencers, for an easier start, turn the left foot at a slight angle forward with the weight of the body resting on the ball of the foot. This position facilitates the execution of the flèche.

FIG. 3-31   *Tierce on guard.*

F̲ɪ̲ɢ̲. 3-32   *Seconde on guard.*

F̲ɪ̲ɢ̲. 3-33   *Lunge with head-cut. Posing: Maitre Alpar.*

Foot Movements

The foot movements used by the saber fencer are identical with those used in foil play with the addition of the double-step, jump-step, apell, stamp, slide, check, and the flèche.

The double-step is made up of two steps executed without any break. On the first step both soles hit the floor at the same time. The right foot then rolls on the heel immediately into the second step, while the left foot, after a slight pause, smoothly follows the forward moving body and is placed easily on the floor.

The jump-step is a combination of a jump and a step. After the completion of the jump the step is started immediately. The left foot follows the forward motion in the same manner as in the double-step.

In the slide, a step is started with the right foot. Just before the step is finished, the weight of the body is thrown forward with a quick motion so that both feet slide simultaneously on the floor for a distance of one or two feet. This movement is designed to give the opponent the impression that an attack is being developed. As he reacts or tries a stop-hit, the attack is continued towards the open target or a parry riposte may be used to complete the action.

The check is a movement which starts out as a slide, but instead the body is suddenly halted by the right foot. This maneuver is intended to frighten the opponent or provoke his counter-attack.

The slide and check are second intention movements designed to breakup the rhythm and sequence of the expected timing.

One of the most important foot movements in modern saber fencing is the flèche attack. Modern saber fencing with its emphasis on speed, subtle timing, and carefully kept distances has required the adoption and development of the flèche. The simple step-lunge is often not enough to reach the opponent and the jump-step-lunge action is far too slow as compared to the perfectly executed modern flèche.

Before describing the execution of the different types of flèche, we have to distinguish between the modern and the classical forms of this kind of attack. The classic flèche attack was a movement similar to running; when the back leg was crossed in front of the forward leg, it was the crossing foot which gave the body the final push to reach the opponent. The crossing movement took a fairly long time, and if the opponent was able to react quickly, he could detect the beginning of the flèche and so defend himself by drawing away or by jumping back.

If the modern flèche is started from a stationary position, it is technically almost identical to the start of a sprint; if it starts while the fencer is in motion, the movement is similar to a successively accelerating flying-start. An important difference must, however, be noted: when a right-handed sprinter takes his starting position, his left leg is in front. When a right-handed fencer is in the on guard position, his right leg is in front. Therefore, he has to learn the opposite start to that which he would use in a sprint. For this reason it is necessary to strengthen and train the right leg. To learn the motion-technique of the flèche from the stationary position, the fencer should practice at first without his saber. The fencer can perfect the execution of the flèche to the point where it seems to be an almost slow, short movement, needing the minimum of strength (Figs. 3-34, 3-35).

When the flèche is started from a stationary position, the body must be at such an angle in relation to the feet that the line of thrust from the legs corresponds as closely as possible to the direction in which the body must go. Otherwise, the flèche will become a jump directed upwards rather than a movement towards the opponent. Thus, the fencer has to bring his body into the correct angle before he leaves the floor with his feet. In order not to betray the actual

FIG. 3-34   *How to teach the flèche. Posing: M. Demeter, I. Hennyey, Maitre Alpar.*

Fig. 3-35   *Head-cut with flèche.*

moment of the start of the flèche, the fencer should shift the weight
of his body slightly and imperceptibly back and forth several times.
The powerful take-off of the modern flèche is made from the sole
of the right foot and is instantly followed by a definite snap of the
right knee. The left leg plays its part in thrusting the body forward,
but the abrupt start depends primarily on the action of the right
leg. The body is in an extended position, following as closely as
possible the line between the starting point and the target. The left
leg, crossing in front of the right, stops the body's natural tendency
to fall, and restores the balance so that the flèche ends in a slowing
run. Thus, the order of movement is as follows: first, the weight
shifts onto the right foot as the left leg is straightened, and the center of gravity is slightly lowered; second, the forceful extension of
the right knee throws the body forward at an oblique angle, so that
every part of the body and weapon is directed toward the opponent;
and finally, as the left leg crosses in front of the right, the fencer
regains his balance and passes his opponent.

The flèche from a flying start can be executed in various ways:

1. the rolling flèche; 2. the step- or jump-flèche; 3. the stamp and flèche; 4. the slide or check and flèche; 5. the retreat and flèche; and 6. the lunge and flèche.

1. *Rolling Flèche.* In this basic movement, the fencer starts by advancing his right leg, but does not bring his left foot forward. Instead, he straightens his left leg, forcefully puts his right foot down, and, with a rolling movement on the sole of the right foot, thrusts his body toward the opponent. The right knee, acting like a spring, propels the body out and forward.

2. *Step- or Jump-Flèche.* Here the fencer makes a step or jump before starting the rolling flèche.

3. *Stamp and Flèche.* This is begun by having the weight of the body on the left leg, while the right foot is stamped vigorously several times. Then, with a sudden motion, the fencer shifts his weight to his right foot and completes the flèche as described above. Here the use of the left leg is more important than in the other type of flèche.

4. *The Slide or Check and Flèche.* After completing a slide or check, the fencer throws his upper body forward with a quick motion and continues the flèche as before.

5. *Retreat and Flèche.* To surprise and mislead his opponent, the fencer can take a short step back without moving the upper part of his body, grasp the floor with his feet (the right knee bending more than the left to get the necessary angle) and complete the flèche.

6. *The Lunge and Flèche.* The lunge and flèche requires strenuous work since the right leg must push the body forward and up into the flèche after the weight of the body has been transferred to it by the lunge. This attack may be used against a retreating opponent who cannot be reached with a repeated lunge.

FENCING TIME

Fencing time or measure means the length of time needed to execute a simple cut, thrust, or parry riposte when the riposte immediately follows the parry. In other words, the interval of time between two consecutive cuts or thrusts made at the speed with which the average fencer moves.

The execution of an unexpected attack or the removal of the blade as the opponent tries to catch it are examples of actions in time.

Following are some attacks which depend on time:

1. *The Evasive Cut or Thrust.* This is an indirect attack, in time, made against an opponent's engagement or beat. The point is deflected around the opponent's guard before the opponent touches the blade. The evasive cut (thrust) can be used against any engagement or beat.

2. *The Evasive Cut-Over.* This also is a simple indirect attack against the opponent's attempt at engagement or beat. Here the blade is deflected around the point rather than the guard, before the opponent is able to touch the blade. The evasive cut-over can be used only against tierce or quarte engagements or beats.

3. *Counter-Evasive Cut or Thrust.* When the blades are engaged and the opponent attempts a changing of engagement or wants to make a change-beat, the evasive movement has to be made in the direction in which the contact of the blade was broken. Here, too, the techniques mentioned with regard to foil fencing are valid for the saber.

The Moulinets

The moulinets are circular movements made toward and away from the body by the forearm. The spectacular Italian style of saber fencing used in the first quarter of the Twentieth century was based on moulinets and short swings of the arm, but it became apparent that this technique exposed the arm to stop-hits and remises. Since our aim is to reduce the scope of movements rather than enlarge them, we recommend that moulinets be dispensed with except for theatrical fencing or for warm-up exercises for the arm and wrist. Even then, they should be used only after the fencer has mastered the simple passages so that his technique in handling the blade will not be spoiled.

The Target

The target in saber fencing consists of the whole upper part of the body, including the head and arms, "above a horizontal line drawn between the top of the folds formed by the thighs and the trunk of the fencer when in the on guard position." [*] The cuts and thrusts may be delivered to the front or, if the fencer turns away, to the back (Fig. 3-36).

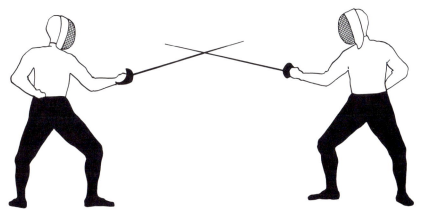

FIG. 3-36 *Silhouettes of the saber target (white area).*

The Salute

The simple salute is taken from the initial position. The fencer: 1. brings the guard with bent arm close to his chin, turning the guard to the left while the blade is held vertically; 2. stretches his arm toward the opponent with the guard in the same position; 3. returns to the initial position. In the composed salute, the fencer: 1. salutes his opponent as above; 2. salutes the president of the jury; 3. keeping his arm straight, he turns his hand into supination, moves the saber across to the right side in front of his body, and follows the point by turning his head.

---

[*] F.I.E. Rules, 1959, p. 410.

The Positions of the Saber

The positions of the saber, like those of the foil, are named traditionally with the ordinal numbers from one to five: Prime (Prima), Seconde (Seconda), Tierce (Terza), Quarte (Quarta), and Quinte (Quinta).

The positions are called *invitations* if the intention of the fencer is to provoke his opponent to attack his open target. They are the same as the above position except for the tierce and seconde. In the tierce on guard position, the point is directed to the opponent's eye; in the seconde, it is directed to the opponent's thigh. In the invitation; the point is moved out to open the target. The positions are called parries if the fencer's intention is to stop the opponent's attack by holding the saber against his cuts or thrusts.

Prime covers the left side of the body from hip to shoulder. In taking this position from the initial position, the point is lowered to the height of the knee, the guard is turned and moved to the left side in front of, and level with, the left shoulder, and is held with slightly bent arm.

Seconde covers the right flank from the hip to the shoulder. In taking this position the point is lowered from the initial position to the height of the thigh, the guard is turned a little upward and moved to the right side with slightly bent arm, the upper rim of the guard is held at the height of the right shoulder.

Tierce covers the right flank and right cheek. To assume this position the elbow is pulled back two to four inches towards the hip, the wrist and guard are turned outwards, the point of the saber is held obliquely upward. The parry can be made closer, lower, or higher depending on the opponent's attack.

Quarte covers the left side of the body and cheek. It is taken from the initial position by lifting the point as the elbow is pulled back to the hip, turning the wrist and guard to the left, and holding the point of the saber obliquely up.

Quinte covers the head. It is taken by turning the guard and the edge of the blade upward, simultaneously lifting the fist and blade with the arm slightly bent. The guard is held in front of the right shoulder, a little above the head (Figs. 3-37 to 3-41).

When the opponent attacks, the parries should always be made so that the forte is held across the direction from which the cuts come to form a right angle with the attacking blade.

As auxiliary positions, we mention the saber sixte and septime. These parries, unrelated to the foil positions of the same name, are used only by masters in giving lessons to students who riposte with great speed, or for meeting a beat-attack on the false edge of the blade. The sixte, used to cover the head, is done by holding the fist to the left of the head, palm turned toward the head with the blade held obliquely across the top of the head with edge upwards. This action is used against an attack on the false edge in the quinte position. In the septime position the hand is held in the same position as in sixte except that the fist is moved to the right side of the head and the blade down beside the right shoulder with the edge to the right. The septime is used against the very fast quarte parry-cheek-riposte or against an attack on the false edge on the tierce position.

THE PASSAGES

Passage means the path described by the blade as it moves from one position to another. The passages are simple, semi-circular, and circular (counter).

Fig. 3-37   *Prime.*   Fig. 3-38   *Seconde.*

FIG. 3-39   *Tierce.*

FIG. 3-40   *Quarte.*

FIG. 3-41   *Quinte.*

Posing: Maitre Alpar.

The simple passages are from:
> seconde to prime, and the reverse
> seconde to quinte, and the reverse
> tierce to quarte, and the reverse
> seconde to tierce, and the reverse
> tierce to quinte, and the reverse
> quarte to quinte, and the reverse

The semi-circular passages are from:
> seconde to quarte, and the reverse
> tierce to prime, and the reverse
> tierce to quinte, and the reverse
> quinte to prime, and the reverse

The circular passages are full circles (described with the point) from one position back to the same position. Against the high line, the point passes below and against the low line above the opponent's blade. The use of the counter-tierce and the counter-seconde are practiced as preparation for an attack.

The definitions of *distances*, *lines* and the *relationship of the blades* are the same as in foil fencing.

THE HIT

In saber fencing the hit is a touch on the opponent's target with the point or with either the front or back edge of the weapon. A touch with the point is called a thrust, while a touch with either edge of the foible is called a cut. The cuts are made with a striking rather than with a pushing or drawing movement, except in the case of the chest or inside arm cuts, in which case the point crosses the target and the hand returns the guard with a continuous movement into the tierce position.

Simple Actions

DIRECT CUTS AND THRUSTS

In the on guard position the fencer may be in tierce or seconde depending on his distance from his adversary or his intentions. (The preventive arm-cut or thrust is easier from the seconde position.)

Direct cuts or thrusts are simple attacks and must be delivered without hesitation in a straight line by one continuous movement to any part of the opponent's target. The point or cutting edge should hit the opponent's target before the heel of the lunging foot touches the floor. After the completion of the cut or thrust, the guard must be in position to cover the proper line.

The cuts and thrusts should be practiced first from the middle distance and then, with different foot movements, from the far distance. The thrust, as in foil fencing, must be practiced in two parts: first, with the extension of the arm; second, with the lunge. The thrust must hit the target at an angle to fix the point, usually with the guard well to the right.

The cut should take into account the direction of the blade, the stretch of the arm, and should be made with the help of the thumb, forefinger, and a slight wrist action (with or without a lunge).

The pressure of the thumb and forefinger should be relaxed at the moment the cut is made so that the blade easily rebounds from the target.

When these movements are practiced in detail, they should be performed:

1. In progression
2. With progressive speed
3. Energetically
4. In time

To perfect the execution of the cut, the fencer may use the following exercise: The master, without sword, extends his arm forward. The student from tierce position tries to hit the master's hand with the foible of his saber as described above, while the master attempts to avoid the cut by withdrawing his hand. If the cut is well executed without preliminary swinging of the blade it should arrive before the master is able to withdraw his hand. In the reverse exercise, the master can prove that even from an extreme tierce position the cut will be successful if properly executed.

Cuts can be delivered to the head, flank, chest, either cheek, upper and lower arm, and the inside and outside of the arm. The upper and lower arm cuts must be executed with the blade and guard at an angle so that the rim of the guard will not be hit. The lower arm cut can be executed with the false edge of the blade.

Thrusts can be delivered to the body, head, and arm. After the cuts have been practiced separately, they should be practiced in a continuous manner to relax the arm, to gain better control, and to perfect handling of the blade. Starting with a first cut, and without changing the position of the fist or withdrawing the extended arm, the fencer should make other cuts without a pause.

Examples:

Head-flank-chest-cuts, tierce position. The master, from seconde moves up to quinte after the student's cut to the head, allowing the other cuts to land. The final movement of the student is a quick return to a tierce on guard.

Chest-flank-right cheek-cuts, tierce position. The master, from quinte position, moves to seconde after the student's chest and flank-cuts, allowing him to land a cheek-cut. After the chest-cut, the immediate flank-cut helps to reduce the swing of the chest-cut. The same cuts should also be practiced on the arm.

HOMOLOGOUS EXERCISES (See also p. 125) (Fig. 3-42)

Examples:

Cut on the upper arm, continue to cheek or head
Cut on inside arm, continue to chest
Thrust on the arm, continue or follow by thrust to body

MIXED EXERCISES

Examples:

1. Upper arm, flank. The master, after the student's cut to the upper arm moves from seconde to quinte, opening for a flank cut.

2. Upper arm, thrust. The master, after the student's upper arm cut, moves from seconde to tierce while the student, passing the tierce, continues with a thrust.

3. Inside arm, cheek. The master, after the student's inside arm-cut, moves from the tierce position over to quarte. The student passes his blade below the master's guard and continues immediately with a cut to the cheek.

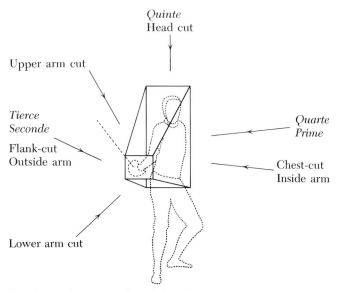

Quinte
Head cut

Upper arm cut

Tierce
Seconde

Flank-cut
Outside arm

Lower arm cut

Quarte
Prime

Chest-cut
Inside arm

FIG. 3-42   *The projection of homologous exercises.*

COMBINED EXERCISES

Examples:

Upper-outside-inside-arm-cut followed by head-flank-chest-cut, tierce. The first three cuts to the arm are made without a lunge, the cuts on the body with a lunge, followed by recovery to tierce.

The same combined cuts can be made with a continuous retreat in order to develop independence of handwork and footwork.

FINGERING

Fingering is the delicate play of the fingers in pressing and releasing the handle or rolling the guard to the required position. The rolling of the fingers is always simultaneously followed by a slight movement of the wrist so that the thumb will remain on the back of the handle.

THE DIRECT PARRIES

The direct parry is the transfer of the blade to one of the defensive positions in the simplest possible way to impede the opponent's cut or deflect his thrust. The parry can be taken further away from or closer to the body depending on the distance of the opponent. The names of the parries are the same as the positions: prime, seconde, tierce, quarte, and quinte.

In saber fencing, we made a distinction between two defensive systems: the prime-seconde-quinte or the more favored tierce-quarte-quinte (Figs. 3-43, 3-44).

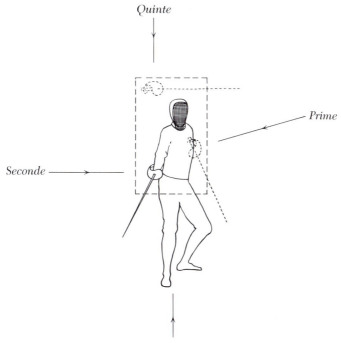

FIG. 3-43 *The* prime-seconde-quinte *defensive box in saber fencing.*

In the prime-seconde-quinte system, the point is closer to the opponent and the parries are further away. The tierce-quarte-quinte is easier to execute and the parries are made closer to the body. A good fencer will use a combination of these systems, according to the momentary need.

Since the hand and arm are part of the target, attacks directed at them must also be parries; however, the motions of such parries are reduced versions of the regular parries.

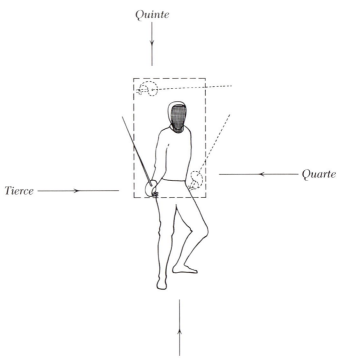

Quinte

Tierce

Quarte

Fig. 3-44   *The* tierce-quarte-quinte *defensive box in saber fencing.*

Parries must be short, definite, limited movements without any hesitation and their speed should match the speed of the opponent's attack. When the parries have been mastered they should be done only at the last moment, just before the cut or thrust arrives at the target.

BASIC ROUTINE EXERCISES

After learning the direct cut and parry, the student will be able to practice the parry-cut (thrust) and later the cut-parry-cut (thrust-parry-thrust) exercises as basic exercises in fencing.

The cut (thrust) is executed with a lunge; the parry with a recovery; and the final cut (thrust) with another lunge. In the beginning, this exercise should be practiced with a fairly slow rhythm so that the master can control the taking of parries, the mobility and suppleness of the recovery, and the second lunge.

After the student has practiced these three movements with the master, he may be pitted against another fencer to carry out his part of the reciprocal exercises. In a fencing group formed by two opposing lines, each line can do the same routine, first as directed by the master's call and then later on their own.

Example:

1. *A* line makes a head-cut which, just before its arrival, will be parried with quinte by the *B* line;

2. *B* line makes a return head-cut which will be parried just before its arrival with recovery and quinte by the *A* line;

3. *B* line recovers with the quinte into an on guard position and the *A* line finishes the exercise with a flank-cut.

The cut-parry-cut exercise can be practiced like an assault with the aid of the master if he lets himself be hit from time to time by the first cut (thrust) in order to make sure that the student always cuts with the intention of hitting or his return cut is alternately directed to different parts of the target. This will teach alertness and readiness for any kind of parry.

THE DIRECT RIPOSTE

The immediate counter-attack with cut (thrust) executed with or without a lunge after a successful parry to the nearest open part of the target is called the *simple direct riposte.*

The direct ripostes are:
        after prime—flank or head
        after seconde—right cheek
        after tierce—head or chest
        after quarte—right cheek
        after quinte—flank

One might ask why the riposte to the head after the prime parry and to the chest after the tierce parry are called direct ripostes, when the flank and the chest, respectively, are the nearest parts of the target. It must be noted that in the first case if the opponent's chest-cut is directed high, the flank will be open, but if the attacker's fist is low, the guard will cover the flank and the blade will cover the cheek. In this case, the head will be the nearest and easiest open target. In the second case, after the tierce parry, if the opponent's flank-cut is directed low, the head will be open to attack. However, if the attacker's fist is high and the cut directed to the cheek, the guard will cover the head. The chest, therefore, will be the nearest open target.

THE INDIRECT RIPOSTE

The type of riposte that is made when the blade passes the nearest open part of the target or land on an initially covered but later exposed part of the target is called the indirect riposte. Many fencers react instinctively with a parry, even before the riposte is started. Against such a fencer, the indirect riposte is effective.

THE FLYING PARRY RIPOSTE

A well-trained fencer, knowing the exact speed of the opponent's attack, may make the parry riposte in a continuous movement, catching the opponent's blade during the course of the action. This sweeping motion, in which the parry and riposte blend together, is termed the flying parry riposte.

RIPOSTES ALONG THE BLADE

After the opponent's attack has been parried in tierce or seconde, the thrust riposte may be made along the blade without losing the blade contact (coulè, *filo* riposte).

At first, all the parry ripostes are practiced without using foot movements and then with a forward or backward movement of the feet. The parry should be taken with the step and the riposte made with or without the lunge.

THE COUNTER (CONTRA)-RIPOSTE

The riposte executed after the successful parry of the opponent's riposte is called the counter-riposte.

HOMOLOGOUS EXERCISES

After the parry ripostes to the arm and the body have been practiced separately, they should, for comparison, be practiced in combination.

Examples:

1. Quinte parry—lower arm riposte
   Quinte parry—flank riposte (the master makes two head-cuts in a row giving a chance for both ripostes).
2. Quarte parry—upper arm riposte
   Quarte parry—cheek riposte (the master makes two chest cuts in a row, giving a chance for both ripostes).
a. Parry the cut to upper arm with half quinte, riposte to the lower arm
   Parry the head with full quinte, riposte to the flank (the master cuts the upper arm first, then the head).
b. Parry the cut at the inside arm with half quarte, riposte to the upper arm
   Parry the chest-cut with full quarte, riposte to the cheek (the master cuts the inside arm first, then the chest).

OTHER COMBINED EXERCISES

1. A sequence of the different parries followed by different ripostes.

2. A sequence of the different parries followed by the same riposte.

3. A sequence of the different ripostes from the same parry.

Examples:

1. Seconde parry—cheek riposte
   Quinte parry—flank riposte
   Prime parry—head riposte
2. Tierce parry—head riposte
   Quinte parry—head riposte
   Quarte parry—head riposte
3. Quinte parry—flank riposte
   Quinte parry—head riposte
   Quinte parry—chest riposte

The master does not parry at first, but later parries the first two ripostes. He sometimes lets one or all of the ripostes land to see if the student always ripostes with the intention of hitting.

After the same exercises have been practiced on the arm as

well, the sequence exercises should be practiced in homologous combination as follows:

Tierce parry—upper arm riposte
Tierce parry—head riposte
Quinte parry—lower arm riposte
Quinte parry—flank riposte
Quarte parry—inside arm riposte
Quarte parry—cheek riposte

THE INDIRECT PARRIES

Semi-circle Parries. The opponent's chest-cut (thrust) can be parried with the semi-circle prime (besides the simple quarte) from the defender's tierce; the head-cut with the semi-circle quinte (besides the simple quinte) from the tierce position; opponent's chest-cut (thrust) can be parries with the semi-circle quarte (besides the simple prime) from the defender's seconde. In these parries the point describes a semi-circle from high to the low and from low to the high positions.

Circle Parries. The opponent's direct thrust or attacks ending with the thrust can be parried with circular parries (besides the semi-circle parries). In saber fencing three circular or circle parries are used: *circle tierce, circle seconde,* and, rarely, the *circle quarte.* The circle tierce and quarte pass below the opposing blade; the circle seconde passes above the opponent's blade.

The direct and circle secondes are the most effective parries against the opponent's thrust attacks. The other circle parries have limited practical use. Circle parries are sometimes called *counter-parries,* but I prefer to use the term given here.

Changing Parries. The changing parries are practically never used in saber fencing since they could be dangerous when used against thrusts along the blade because they could carry the point of the opponent's saber onto the target.

THE ENGAGEMENTS

The engagement means crossing either side of the opponent's blade with the edge of the weapon, and bringing the blades into contact. The engagement can be made in the high or low line and against the tierce or seconde positions. The engagements are named for the positions taken: prime, seconde, tierce, quarte, and quinte, but the prime and quinte engagements are almost never used.

The place of the engagement could be:

1. In engagement against the opponent's line
2. In opponent's engagement against our own line
3. Both in the engagement of the blades.

THE INDIRECT ATTACKS

The Disengage-thrust or Cut. From the opponent's engagement of the blade, the indirect attack is the disengage thrust or cut, executed in the same way as in foil play. The point passes under the guard from the engagements of tierce, quarte, and quinte and over the guard in the case of the prime or seconde. The disengage can be parried with simple, semi-circle, or circle parries.

The Cut-over. The disengage executed by passing our blade over the point of the opponent's blade is called the *cut-over* attack. These casting cuts or thrusts can be used only from the tierce or quarte engagements.

ATTACKS INTRODUCED WITH ENGAGEMENTS

The Gliding Disengage. The Gliding disengage, after the engagement of the blades, is a constant slide with the foible of the saber along the opponent's blade without any pressure so that the point, in an uninterrupted flowing action, passes under the opponent's guard at the last moment. This attack can be made into the opponent's high line or tierce, but is more effective in his low line or seconde position.

From a far distance, the gliding action is made during an advance and the disengage made with a lunge. To practice the gliding movement the master lets his student try the slide, from the point, along the blade, to the guard, several times before making the cut. This movement is a very cautious one ending with a quick cut on the arm or cheek, or with a thrust.

Bind (Transporto di ferro). This is a movement which takes the opponent's blade from the high line to the low or the reverse, without losing contact with his blade. The bind could be taken from quarte to seconde and the reverse; from tierce to prime or quinte and the reverse.

The Envelopment. Theoretically, the envelopments are similar to those used in foil fencing except that in saber fencing they are very dangerous and almost never used in practice since the circular movement brings the opponent's blade back to the target.

FORCE ATTACKS ON THE BLADE

Pressure. Pressure is used against an opponent's blade held stiffly in line. With the forte of the blade, the foible of the adversary's blade is taken out of the way. The type of pressure is named after the position in which the blade is touched: prime, seconde, tierce, quarte or quinte.

The pressure can be introduced with simple, semi-circle, circle, and changing engagements. In practice only the seconde, tierce, and quarte are used.

The *changing engagement* is an engagement from one side of the blade to the other. The first is the *false engagement* (only a touch); the change is the one made with real pressure. The change can be made from tierce to quarte and from quarte to tierce and quinte by passing the blade below that of the opponent; from seconde to prime and the reverse by passing it over the adversary's blade.

The Pressure Slide-Thrusts (Filo). The pressure slide-thrust is an attack on the opponent's blade, keeping it under pressure all the way until the thrust is executed. There are only two attacks of this kind: the tierce and the seconde pressure slide-thrusts. The seconde pressure slide-thrusts will be effective when the opponent's guard is a little higher, and the tierce if the opponent's guard is a little lower than the correct position hence not entirely covering the target.

Execution from a far distance: 1. The engagement with advance of the right foot; 2. The pressure with advance of the left foot; and 3. The slide-thrust with the lunge.

The pressure slide-thrust can be parried with simple, changing, and ceding parries.

The simple parries are practically the only effective opposition to the slide. The changing parries are less effective, again, because of the danger of carrying the opponent's blade into the target. The prime ceding parry should be used against the pressure slide-thrust in tierce and the quarte against the seconde.

The engagement and the pressure attacks are only rarely used in saber fencing since there is some danger of exposing the hand and the distance is usually too great to permit successful execution of these attacks. The pressure slide-thrusts can be used successfully as ripostes after the tierce or seconde parries.

Violent Pressure (*Froissement, Deviamento*). Violent pressure is used against a stiffly held blade when the point of the opponent's blade is brought forcefully down with an almost horizontal tierce or quarte. The best riposte after the tierce parry is the slide-thrust, and after the quarte, the cheek-cut.

THE BEAT (BATTEMENT, BATTUTA)

Against the adversary's blade held with a relaxed grip, the beat attack is used to knock the blade aside or loosen the opponent's grip thus making it more difficult for him to parry. The beat must be short, sharp, strong, and confined. It must be short so that the adversary will be unable to avoid it in time; sharp so the blades will meet in one point; strong so that it will startle the opponent and take the blade out of line; and confined or limited so that the beating blade will not go too far out of line after the beat is executed. The fencer must hit the foible or middle of his opponent's blade with the middle of his blade. The beat can be executed with the front or with the false edge of the blade on the front or the false edge of the opponent's blade. The attacks on the front edge of the seconde and tierce positions (and on the foible) must be strong enough to slacken the opponent's grip; otherwise the action may often be judged to be the opponent's parry riposte.

The beat can be simple, the semi-circle, the circle, or the change beat, according to the correlation of the blades:

1. From the invitation onto the other blade in invitation, the direct or counter-beat.

2. From the invitation onto the other blade in line and reversed, the direct or counter-beat.

3. From line onto the other blade in line, the direct or counter-beat.

4. From the fencer's own engagement onto the engaged blade, on the same side or on the opposite side.

5. On opponent's engagement onto the engaging blade on the same side or on the opposite of the opponent's blade.

Execute the beat first from the middle distance, perhaps with a stamp of the right foot followed by the cut (thrust) with a lunge.

Execute the beat from a far distance with the beginning of the forward movement (step, jump, or flèche) followed by a cut on the lunge or during the course of a flèche.

The most frequently used attacks are against the high line or tierce position with the quarte beat; against the low line or seconde position with the seconde beat attack.

HOMOLOGOUS EXERCISES

1. Against the low line or seconde position: seconde-beat upper arm cut; seconde-beat external cheek cut.

2. Against high line or tierce position: quarte-beat upper arm cut; quarte-beat head cut.

3. Against high line from seconde position: tierce-beat outer arm cut; tierce-beat thrust.

MIXED EXERCISES

1. Seconde-beat—upper arm cut, quarte-beat—head cut, quarte parry cheek—riposte (at the first attack the master is in seconde then moves up to the high line and finally makes a chest-cut).

2. Quarte-beat—upper arm cut, quarte-beat—head cut, quinte parry head riposte, (the master makes a head-cut after the beats).

The seconde-beat cheek cut can be parried only with tierce.

The quarte-beat head cut can be parried with semi-circle quinte (or sixte).

The quarte-beat cheek cut can be parried with circle-tierce (or septime).

The other beat-attacks are not used in competitive fencing and if employed in practice, they are only used for an exercise of controlling the blade.

Compound Actions

The feint is a false attack designed to lure the opponent into a parry position. The attacker must be careful not to let his blade come into contact with the opponent's blade since this would give the opponent the right to riposte. With the feint the following factors must be taken into consideration: 1. the method used to make the feint; 2. the type of parry the opponent makes; and 3. the number of parries to be evaded.

The ways of executing the feint include direct, disengage, evasive cut or thrust, evasive cut-over, pressure-slide, and the feint introduced by the beat.

The parry given in response can be either simple or circular. One or two feints may be made depending on the number of parries to be evaded. In saber fencing, feints are commonly named according to the part of the body at which they are, or appear to be, aimed.

Examples:

1. Direct head feint-flank cut (a direct one-two attack)
2. Direct head feint-flank feint-head cut (one-two-three attack)
3. Quarte-beat, head feint-chest cut (beat one-two attack)
4. Seconde beat upper arm feint-thrust feint-cheek cut (beat one-two-three attack)

The Single Feint. A single feint attack consists of a false cut or thrust and a real cut or thrust. From the middle distance the first movement is the feint made with the stretch of the arm followed by the cut or thrust done with a lunge. From the far distance, (except for attacks introduced with engagement or pressure) attacks can be made with the step-lunge, the jump-lunge, or with the flèche.

The engagement-pressure-feint can only be safely made with the lunge or step-lunge. With the step-lunge, the engagement is made before the step, the pressure and feint with the step, and the cut or thrust with the lunge. Other single feints can be made with the step or jump and the cut can be made with the lunge. The feint can be made at the beginning of the flèche and the cut at the end of the flèche. When the beat single feint is done with a step-lunge, the beat comes as the right foot touches the floor, the feint when the left foot is put down, and the cut with the lunge. With the jump-lunge, the beat and feint are done with the jump and the cut with the lunge. When the flèche is used, the beat and feint come at the beginning.

COMBINED EXERCISES

1. Head-feint, flank-feint with step forward, continued with prolonged flank-feint, head-cut with flèche.

During this exercise, the master, after taking the first parry (with retreat), stops for a moment in order to give the student a chance to prolong his flank-feint and real cut.

2. Cheek-feint, thrust-feint with a step forward continued with a prolonged thrust-feint, cheek-cut with flèche. This is executed in the same manner as used before except the master starts from the seconde position.

These attacks should not be confused with the one-two-three attacks.

COMBINED MIXED EXERCISES

1. Upper, under-arm-feint continued with head-feint, chest-cut.
2. Upper, under-arm-feint continued with beat-head feint, flank-cut.

HOMOLOGOUS EXERCISES

1. Upper, under-arm-feint continued with head-feint, flank-cut. The first feint is done without a lunge, the second with a lunge.
2. Thrust, outside-arm-feint continued with thrust-feint, cheek-cut.
The first with a short lunge, the second with a step-lunge.
3. Beat, upper, inside-arm-feint continued with beat, head-feint, flank-cut.
The first is done with a short lunge (delayed recovery forward to on guard position), the second with flèche.

4. Head, flank-feint done with step forward continued with head-feint, flank-cut with flèche.

5. Slide-thrust-cheek feint continued by thrust-feint, cheek-cut with flèche.

During the first part of these exercises the fencer should make an exploratory feint before the real feinting attack.

The following are some attacks which have been found to be extremely effective in competitive fencing.

1. Head-feint, thrust. Many fencers when defending themselves against the head-feint with quinte immediately take the tierce, covering the cheek, flank, and arm. After the head feint the attacker passes the defender's guard with a three-quarter counter-clockwise circle to complete the thrust. The wrist is used flexibly to execute the upcoming thrust.

2. Chest-feint, outside-cheek cut. After the chest-feint, the attacker passes the opponent's quarte parry below the guard, and with a turn of his wrist, finishes the cut on the cheek.

3. Feint outside the opponent's tierce, cut-over head-cut. If the opponent assumes an insufficient tierce on guard position, the attacker makes a feint (similar to a head-cut) outside the opponent's blade and passes the point of his blade with a cut-over to finish the cut on the head.

4. Under-arm-feint, head-cut. After the attacker initiates a false-cut to the underarm with the back edge of his saber, he passes the opponent's tierce outside and finishes the attack with a cut-over to the head. This is done to make the opponent react by lowering or withdrawing his fist.

Attacks with circular movements (double). The straight thrust or disengage thrust can be parried with counter-tierce or counter-seconde. If these parries are passed with a circular movement, the fencer executes a double (direct-circular or disengage circular attack). In saber fencing, this action is only used against tierce or seconde position or engagement when the reacting parry is a circular tierce (semi-circular quinte) or circular seconde (semi-circular quarte).

Composite Parries

The composite parries are two or more parries used to cover the target against the opponent's feints. The single feint should be parried with two consecutive parries (the first a half parry; the second a full parry) according to the nature of the attack (simple, circular, or attacks on the blade). The simple-single feints can be parried with two simple, or with one simple and one semi-circular parry. The double can be parried with one circular and one simple (semi-circular) or two circular parries. The attacks on the blade vary depending on whether the attacked blade is in line, in invitation, or in engagement; therefore, the parries used are opposition, changing, semi-circular, or circular in combination with simple, semi-circular, or circular parries.

Examples:
The head-feint, flank-cut can be parried with quinte-seconde or with quinte-tierce parries.

The head-feint, chest-cut can be parried with quinte-prime, but the quinte-quarte parries are better in this situation.

The flank-feint, chest-cut can be parried with seconde-prime or with tierce-quarte parries.

The thrust-feint, circular thrust of tierce with circular tierce-quarte (seconde, semi-circular prime, semi-circular quinte) or two circular tierce parries.

The disengage-feint, circular-thrust of seconde engagement with circular seconde-tierce (prime, quinte, semi-circular-quarte) or with two circular seconde parries.

The quarte-beat, head-feint, flank-cut against tierce or high-line with semi-circular quinte-seconde (tierce) parries.

The seconde-beat, cheek-feint, thrust against seconde or low-line with tierce-quarte (seconde, semi-circular prime, semi-circular quinte) or two circular tierce parries.

HOMOLOGOUS EXERCISES

The master makes feints on the arm, and then on the body to give the student a chance to compare the parries and ripostes.

Examples:

The upper-arm-feint, under-arm-cut is parried with small quinte-seconde parries, riposte to the arm, and continued with head-feint, flank-cut parries with full quinte-seconde riposte to the cheek.

Inside-arm-feint, outside-arm-cut is parried with small quarte-tierce parries, riposte to the arm; this is continued by thrust-feint, cheek-cut parried with full quarte-tierce parries, and riposte to the chest.

SPECIAL EXERCISES

At this stage of the parry riposte exercises two new exercises should be practiced. The first helps to parry the feint, the second to use the *last minute* parry.

1. The master executes different feinting-cuts in a constant movement to different parts of the target; the student follows these movements with the corresponding half-parries. When the master makes a real cut the student makes a real parry and a riposte.

2. The master tries to get the student to move from his position by making threatening cutting motions and stamping his foot. The student should refrain from reacting to anything but a real cut.

Compound Ripostes

The feint ripostes are used against an opponent who is able to parry a rapid direct simple riposte. Some of the feint ripostes are executed in such a manner that the feint is held for a period of time, while others simply pass certain parts of the target.

Examples:

1. Quarte parry—head-feint, flank riposte; the feint to the head is decisively made.

2. Quinte parry—head-feint, flank riposte; the feint to the head is made with the arm only slightly stretched in order to avoid touching the opponent's quinte parry while riposting.

3. Seconde parry-cheek-feint, chest riposte; this is a riposte in which the feint passes the opponent's cheek and head.

The feint ripostes must be completed very quickly and with no hesitation. The speed and timing must be such that the opponent is unable to make a cut against the arm during the feinting movement.

COMBINED EXERCISES

1. Quinte parry, direct arm riposte; quinte parry, head-feint, flank riposte.

2. Quarte-tierce parry, direct arm riposte; quarte-tierce parry, head-feint, chest riposte.

3. Small quinte-seconde parry, direct arm riposte; quinte-seconde parry, external cheek-feint, thrust riposte.

Dual Feints

Each single feint attack or riposte can be further developed into a dual feinting movement. These dual feinting actions can be used against an opponent who either reacts to the feinting movement or one who makes complete parries. Since numerous combinations of actions on the arm and body are possible, the master usually regulates specific exercises of three movements or less.

The timing pattern of the dual feint can be one of the following:

1. All three movements done with the same timing. This can be used effectively against a nervous opponent who reacts to each feinting motion.

2. A long first movement followed by two short ones. Useful against calm opponents who hesitate to parry and do not follow each feint immediately.

3. A short first movement, a long second, and a short third. This is recommended for use against opponents who react to the first feinting action but who stop or hesitate at the second feint.

The movements of the hand are syncronized with those of the feet. From the far distance the sequence is as follows:

1. Step-lunge with first feint executed with forward movement of the right foot, the second feint is done with the left foot and the cut or thrust done with the final lunge.

2. A step forward with the first feint, followed by a quick feint-cut or feint-thrust with the lunge.

3. The first feint is executed before the step forward, the second feint with the first step, and the cut or thrust with the lunge.

If the dual feint is used with either a jump-lunge or a flèche, the first feint is executed before the jump or initial flèche movement respectively, the second feint with the jump or initial flèche, and the cut or thrust with the lunge or at the end of the flèche.

PROGRESSIVE EXERCISES

This is a group of exercises which are built up from the simple attack to the dual attack in a progressive manner.

1. Simple head-cut without lunge, head-feint, flank-cut with lunge, (recovery); head-feint, flank-feint, head-cut with a step-lunge.
2. Seconde beat, arm-cut without lunge, head-feint thrust with a lunge, (recovery); head-feint, thrust feint, external cheek-cut with step-lunge.
3. Upper-arm, under-arm-feint with lunge, (recovery); head, flank-feint, head-cut with a flèche.

The parry of the dual feints must consist of three complete movements with the final parry being followed with a quick simple or dual riposte. In actual competition the dual feints are rarely used because the arm is exposed for a relatively long period of time and is very vulnerable to a stop-cut.

Renewed Attacks

Should the opponent fail or hesitate to make a riposte immediately after a successful parry, the attack can be renewed to great advantage. There are three types of renewed attacks: The *remise* (*rimessa*), *redoublement* (*rimessa with raddoppio*), *reprise d'attaque* (*ripressa d'attacco*).

The remise is used against an opponent who does not riposte or delays his riposte. It consists of a repeated cut or thrust immediately following the original attack; usually, it is executed without withdrawing the arm and while the lunge is being made.

The redoublement is made against an opponent who retreats with the parry and does not follow-up with a riposte. It consists of a repeated simple or composed action usually executed with a renewed lunge.

The reprise d'attaque is used against opponents who retreat in order to protect themselves. This action is initiated in the on guard position after the first attack. It is usually executed with two or more foot movements.

The remise is used primarily as a second intention attack. The initial feinting cut is made in order to draw the opponent into the parry position, this is followed immediately with a cut to the arm before the opponent makes a riposte. The premeditated action of executing a cut to the arm prior to receiving the riposte is called a *second intention remise*. The parry position must be such that the opponent's forte is struck close to the guard. The cut to the arm is then repeated with a quick snap of the thumb and forefinger just below the guard. The body is withdrawn at the same time to avoid the riposte. This attack is most effective against prime, seconde, and quinte positions.

The following exercises build a good sense of timing for the cut, remise, and parry.

1. Quarte parry head riposte, remise to the arm; quinte parry head riposte, remise to the arm; tierce parry head riposte, remise to the arm. (The master makes cuts to the chest, head, and flank and follows with a quinte parry position each time.)

2. Quinte parry chest riposte, remise to the arm; quinte parry head riposte, remise to the arm; quinte parry flank riposte, remise to the arm. (The master cuts to the head three times and follows with the chest, head, and flank positions, respectively.)

At a later stage of training, when the above movements become precise and smooth, the exercises should be practiced with constant advances and retreats. These remise exercises are excellent for developing the thumb and forefinger and for the acquisition of speed, suppleness, and timing needed in executing perfect cuts.

Actions in Time (Tempo)

Actions executed as surprise attacks, counter-attacks, or stop-hits are known as time-hits. The previous discussion on timing in foil fencing is entirely applicable to saber fencing as well. The exercises used in saber fencing further improve and refine the sense of timing.

During the early phases of teaching the student to make the proper direct cuts, the master should extend his arm and have the student try to cut the arm before it is withdrawn. A similar exercise can be used for refining the student's sense of timing. The master, without a saber in his hand, extends his arm and quickly withdraws it. The student has to try to hit the arm from the tierce position. The cut must be timed so that it will land at the moment when the arm is fully extended. When a high degree of proficiency has been reached, the exercise can be made more complicated by the master if he creates distracting actions while extending and retracting his arm.

TIMING EXERCISES

1. In middle distance the master moves from one position to another and the pupil cuts or thrusts as soon as the master initiates his movement.

2. A more advanced exercise consists of having the master move constantly in quinte-seconde (quarte-tierce) while the student cuts or thrusts at the target area of his choice.

3. The above exercise can be changed so that the master's movements are made from seconde-quinte to tierce-quarte and reversed.

From the far distance an attack must be initiated at the exact moment when the desired target area is in the process of being covered. This will ensure the success of the attack since the target will be open after the advance because of the constant motion of the master's blade. This is an exercise which demands much attention and precise timing.

4. The master moves back and forth with quarte-tierce and the student keeps the appropriate distance. From time to time, the master gives either high or low line and the student executes the proper beat and cut exercise.

5. Change in both position and distance adds to the complexity of the exercise.

The possible actions in time are:

1. Preventive arm-cut
2. Evasive cut or thrust (*cavazione in tempo*)
3. Time-cut or thrust (*colpo d'arresto*)
4. Second intention parry riposte against any of the above mentioned actions (*seconda intenzione*)
5. Feint in time (*finta in tempo*) (an action into the second intention which avoids the second intention parry)
6. Counter-time (*contro tempo*), stop or time-hit into the feint in time

THE PREVENTIVE ARM-CUT

This is a stop-hit on the arm, executed either during the development or in the midst of the opponent's attack that must land prior to the final phase of the attack. These cuts are successful against slow fencers or against opponents who make their attacks with wide movements and by the lifting of their arm (Fig. 3-45).

Fig. 3-45   *Preventive arm-cut.*

In the first phase the body leans forward as the arm is extended to make the cut to the opponent's arm. The second phase consists of an immediate retreat after the cut. This is done with a backward jump and an adequate parry position is assumed in case the cut is short or is parried by the opponent.

The preventive stop-cut or thrust is a stop-hit on the body used against very slow opponents or opponents who move forward with careless invitations.

Both the preventive cuts and thrusts must hit the opponent ahead of the attack in order to take the right of way.

THE EVASIVE CUTS OR THRUSTS

These are time actions used against opponents who try to beat or take the blade with wide strong or slow movements. As the name implies, the opponent's blade is evaded prior to blade contact which, in turn, should halt the opponent's planned attack.

THE TIME-THRUST OR CUT

This is a movement made with a short, quick, and energetic lunge. The blade is placed directly in the path of the attacking blade and covers the line being attacked. This action synchronizes the parry and thrust or cut into one action and causes the attack to be blocked and makes a simultaneous hit. This action can be executed:

1. Into a single attack
2. Into the first or second time measure of the dual attack
3. Into the first to last measure of the compound attack

The last measure of the time-hit, a contracted movement of the parry riposte, serves to both parry the opponent's attack and score a simultaneous hit. Attacks, simple or compound, which are designed to hit the flank can be easily blocked with a time-thrust if the guard is held high and well over to the right.

A time-thrust or time-cut can be made into attacks ending with a head-cut by the use of the *inquartata* action, which is an evasive movement used in the last measure of the attack. A thrust made with the fist forced well to the left or an inside cheek-cut with a pronated hand position can be used while the body, with the help of a side step with the left foot, is turned towards the left thereby completing the evasive movement of the body.

Against thrust attacks ending in the high line, the *passata sotto* may be used effectively with a time-thrust. This is a hit executed with the aid of body evasion by stretching the left leg backwards, which in turn lowers the body. The right knee continues beyond the normal angle of the lunge and the left hand supports the lowered body position by touching the floor with the finger tips close to the right foot.

Last measure time-hits are very difficult to master and are only executed with success if almost perfect timing, speed, and accuracy has been attained.

Appuntata: The appuntata, a time-thrust or arm-cut executed into an opponent's feint riposte, is a remise in time. The action is directed to the part of the opponent's body which has just been successfully defended by a parry. This action is usually accompanied with a stamp of the foot.

Examples:

1. If a head-cut was parried by the opponent and the flank-feint head riposte is detected, an immediate thrust is executed which blocks the riposte and scores at the same time.

2. If a head-cut was parried by the opponent and a head-feint, flank riposte is detected, an immediate arm-cut with a quick retreat prevents the riposte from allowing time and distance for a hit.

SECOND INTENTION PARRY RIPOSTE

This action is used against opponents who riposte automatically to the same part of the target or who favor the time- and stop-hits. The second intention parry riposte against the opponent who habitually ripostes is called the counter (contra)-riposte and is executed after a successful parry of the opponent's riposte.

The second intention parry riposte can be used very effectively against opponents who use the preventative arm-cut. In order to bait the opponent into making the arm-cut the fencer should put his arm forward. The resultant cut to the arm should be parried immediately and followed by a lunge or flèche depending on the opponent's distance.

Against opponents who favor the stop- or time-cut (thrust) to the body, the second intention parry riposte should be initiated with an invitation. The target area should be opened and followed by a step forward with the parry. In this way, the distance is closed for the final riposte.

FEINT IN TIME (FINTA IN TEMPO)

If an opponent attempts to make a second intention parry against a stop or time-hit, a feint should be executed and an evasion of the opponent's second intention parry effected. This is actually a second intention action into a second intention. The feint is executed with a stamp of the right foot and the cut or thrust done with the lunge.

COUNTER-TIME (CONTRO TEMPO)

A time-thrust or preventive cut into the opponent's feint is called the counter-time. The most refined and difficult actions in the actions in time are the time-thrust with a lunge and the preventive arm-cut with a backward jump.

THE DISARMAMENT (DESARMO, SFORZO)

The disarmament is a forceful, grazing beat or transfer of the opponent's blade toward seconde or tierce made to loosen the opponent's grip on the handle. From tierce position against an opponent in seconde, the fencer's action on the blade is made downward on the side of the saber blade. Against an opponent in tierce position, the fencer makes the disarmament with a clockwise circular forward and downward movement. The rules require the hit (cut or thrust) to arrive without a break from the disarming movement. This action is rarely used in modern fencing.

COMBAT-LIKE EXERCISES

1. The simplest form of this exercise is the cut-parry-cut exercise. The master from time to time allows himself to be hit with the first cut so that the student always attacks in first intention.

2. The master engages the student's blade, and then cuts to different parts of the student's target (these cuts should be parried by the student). Alternatively, the master brings his blade into line, and the student makes a pressure-slide thrust. This exercise may also be executed with a beat attack as the final movement.

3. The master gives different invitations or brings his blade into

line. The student tries to execute feints on the invitations or makes beat-feint attacks on the blade in line.

4. The master moves with quinte-seconde into which the student attempts a straight attack. The master either allows himself to be hit, or makes a parry-riposte. This in turn should be parried by the student.

5. The student attacks with direct head-cut from the far distance. The master either lets himself be hit, makes a stop-cut at the beginning of the attack (which the student must parry), or moves forward lifting his arm. At the latter action, the student makes a preventive cut to the arm and jumps back.

6. The master either gives line or advances with quarte-tierce, pauses, and makes a head-cut. The student makes either a beat arm-cut on the master's line or attempts a preventive cut to the arm into the master's head-cut.

7. The master either gives a line and parries the beat attack by the student or takes an evasive thrust against the beat. The student makes a counter-riposte after parrying the master's riposte or tries a preventive cut on the master's arm with a jump back.

8. The student makes a beat, returns to tierce, and beats again (provoking an evasive thrust). If the master attempts the evasive thrust, the student picks it up with a parry-riposte. If there is no thrust, the student continues with a simple feint.

RECIPROCAL EXERCISES

(all from the far distance)

1. A invites in seconde, B stands in tierce on guard.
   B attacks with a direct head-cut, A tries a quinte parry riposte.
   If A parries too soon, B finishes his attack to the flank.
   If A guesses that B wants to finish the attack on the flank, he remains in seconde and makes a parry riposte.
2. A gives high or low line, B makes a beat cut attack.
   A parries the attack or, if the beat was wide, makes an evasive thrust.
   If B anticipates the evasive thrust, he takes a parry and ripostes.

3. *A* makes a direct head-cut or feint, *B* tries either to parry or to make a time-hit on the feint.
4. The fencers cross their blades in seconde.
   A slides on the blade, releases it, and attempts an arm cut. *B* tries to parry the cut or makes a counter arm-cut on the slide, which should be parried by *A*.

Fig. 4-1   *Marcel Marceau—Inscribed: To Julius Alpar my fencing master with deep admiration and friendship, always, Marcel Marceau.*

Section IV

Theatrical Fencing

Introduction

For the student of the theater, a great deal of knowledge of historical fencing is required before he can fence in an authentic manner on the stage. Theatrical styles of fencing differ from combat or competitive fencing in several respects because the aim of the bout is different. In competitive or combat the bout is personal, with one participant trying to defeat the other. The theatrical bout is an attempt to establish the illusion of such a bout in the minds of an audience. Thus, the actors dress in costume, use weapons appropriate to the period of the play, and the movements of attacks and defense are wider and slower to allow the audience to grasp the course of action.

The fight must be conducted without danger, but has to give the impression of reality. The fencers on stage are partners rather than opponents and safety must never be forgotten. Any action depicting wounding or killing must be executed with the utmost precaution since the actors almost never wear masks or protective armor.

Fencing on the stage, therefore, is a set of routine exercises that have been practiced step by step by the actors from a plan. The actors must be drilled very carefully so that they maintain the proper distance from each other. Until they are able to control their movements, they should use masks and study with a fencing master.

Fig. 4-2 *Robert Goulet, stage and television star—Inscribed: Dear Mr. Alpar, I am soon obtaining a sword cane and I assure you that much posturing will be inflicted upon the unwary passersby. But each time, it shall be done in the memory of you. All the best, Bob Goulet.*

Ancient Combat

Greek and Roman swords have already been described. Since both these weapons were simple, short, and clumsy, they could not be used very efficiently for parrying. The Greek swords, which were made of bronze, were not effective thrusting weapons because this relatively soft metal bent easily. The Roman iron swords were sufficiently strong for both cutting and thrusting. In later times, the introduction of longer swords meant that weapons could be used for limited defense. The shield provided defense against attack while additional protection was provided by a helmet and leather or metal leg and arm plates. The sword was held by the handle with the fingers forming a fist so that the thumb touched the top of the first joint of the forefinger.

To salute (or rather to challenge) the opponent, the swordsman beat on the middle of his shield with the pommel of the sword or with the flat part of the blade. Sometimes, especially after a victory, both arms, with weapon, were raised over the head one or more times.

In the on guard position, the left foot was put about twelve inches forward and the weight of the body was carried equally on both slightly bent legs. The shield, held with bent arm, was kept close to the left side of the chest and the sword was held with the point forward and below the edge of the shield.

Cuts could be delivered to the head or shoulders or to the right or left side of the opponent's body. When the cut was directed to the opponent's right side, the soldier stepped forward with his right foot. The thrust could be made to the right or left side or beneath the shield.

In defense a soldier could hold the shield over his head, in front, or to the left or right of his body. When the right side was threatened, the right foot was crossed behind the left and the body turned behind the shield. Defensive body movements included volting (jumping to avoid very low cuts), ducking, or bending forward below the high parallel cuts. The swords sometimes exchanged beats during preparation or execution of an attack.

In the duel, the fighters turned or danced around each other waiting for the best moment to attack. One fighter could pass the other, jump forward or backward, and keep the opponent in uncertainty about the actual moment of attack. If the opponents struck their weapons against each other (clashed), the shields were used to push each other away. If they fought at close quarters, one fighter might try to trip the other by crossing his leg behind his opponent's leg.

To adapt these movements for the stage, we may use the following exercises to imitate the Roman style of combat.

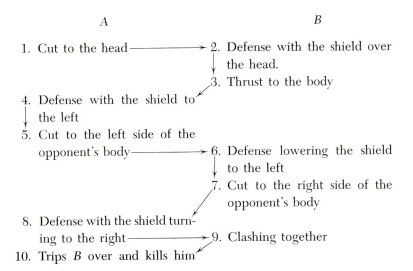

A

1. Cut to the head ──────────→ 2. Defense with the shield over the head.

3. Thrust to the body

4. Defense with the shield to the left

5. Cut to the left side of the opponent's body ──────→ 6. Defense lowering the shield to the left

7. Cut to the right side of the opponent's body

8. Defense with the shield turning to the right ──────→ 9. Clashing together

10. Trips *B* over and kills him

B

NET AND TRIDENT

The gladiator called the *retarius* held a net with one hand and tried to throw it over his opponent. Meanwhile, he kept his opponent away with a trident which he held in his other hand. The opposing gladiator attempted to avoid the netting by jumping away, stepping on the net, cutting it with his sword, or by trying to break the trident with his own sword. In most other ways, the body movements were similar to those described above (Fig. 4-3).

FIG. 4-3 *Practice with net and trident—sword and shield. Posing: D. Vilner and H. Olguin, University of California.*

Middle Ages

The sword used in the Middle Ages was longer and heavier than the Roman gladius. Consequently, the cuts were made with a wider swing and the thrusts from a greater distance. The longer sword allowed some parry-like defense. During this time, the Roman style of fighting prevailed (Fig. 4-4).

FIG. 4-4 *Sword and shield. Posing: H. Zenk and D. Mundie, University of California.*

Fig. 4-5. *Two-hand sword (grip).*

TWO-HAND SWORD

The two-hand sword was a heavy weapon used by foot soldiers either against mounted enemies or in fighting with each other. The heavy blows were capable of damaging armor, knocking the opponent unconscious, killing the horse, or even felling the horseman and the horse with one stroke. There were usually only one or two men in a group with this heavy weapon since it was so expensive and re-quired extraordinary power and strength to wield. The weapon was held with both hands. The right hand grasped the long handle near the crossbar, the left was placed behind the right at the end of the handle (Figs. 4-5, 4-6).

In the at ease position, the soldier held the sword, point down, in front of him with both his hands resting on the crossbar. In another relaxed position, the arm was stretched to the side while the hand grasped the handle with the sword point resting on the ground near his foot. During marches, the sword was carried over one shoulder, the handle held at the end with the point angling obliquely up.

For the salute the sword, pointed upward, was brought with both hands to the front of the chest. The salute was executed by first lifting the crossbar of the sword to the height of the mouth. The sword was then carried over to the left shoulder. Finally, the point was lowered to about 4 inches (10 cm.) from the ground while the right foot was moved a short step back. These actions were performed in reverse order to complete the salute.

The ready position was the same as that used with sword and shield but the left knee was bent a little more.

Fig. 4-6   *Two-hand sword. Posing: D. Mundie and H. Zenk, University of California.*

The blades could be engaged in high position (with points up) or in low position (with points on the ground). The cuts could be delivered vertically down, obliquely down, parallel from right to left, or reversed. The engaged blade could pass over or under the opponent's blade.

When a thrust was made from a shorter distance, the left hand passed over the crossbar and grasped the blade behind the leather covered false guard in front of the hilt. The low cuts delivered to either side of the body could be parried with the sword held downward to block the cuts; cuts delivered high were parried by holding the sword vertically to the left or right of the body. The vertical cut could be stopped either with crossbar or with a parallel parry above the head. The aim was to beat the opponent's blade aside, and any body movements needed to accomplish this were used.

Mail gloves were worn to allow the swordsman to grasp his opponent's weapon and twist it out of his hand.

The following is a simple exercise for a theatrical fight with the two-hand sword.

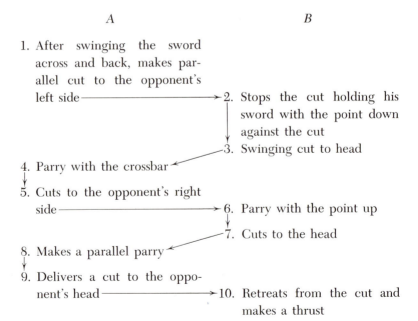

A   *B*

1. After swinging the sword across and back, makes parallel cut to the opponent's left side ──────────────→ 2. Stops the cut holding his sword with the point down against the cut

3. Swinging cut to head

4. Parry with the crossbar

5. Cuts to the opponent's right side ──────────────→ 6. Parry with the point up

7. Cuts to the head

8. Makes a parallel parry

9. Delivers a cut to the opponent's head ──────────────→ 10. Retreats from the cut and makes a thrust

FIG. 4-7   *Halberd. Posing: D. Vilner and C. Cronyn, University of California.*

The spear and the halberd were weapons used by foot soldiers against each other or against horsemen. The halberd, a form of spear with an axe near the point for chopping, was the common weapon of palace guards (Figs. 4-7, 4-8).

When the soldier was at attention, he held his weapon near to his right foot with the right hand on the handle at about shoulder level. The salute was made by stretching the right arm to the right while keeping the end of the weapon fixed and turning the head in the direction the salute was to be given. Standing at ease, the soldier held the weapon with both hands, arms straight in front of his body and parallel with the ground. During marches, the weapon was carried on the right shoulder, point obliquely up.

The on guard position was assumed with the left foot slightly advanced and both knees slightly bent. The weapon was pointed to the left and the handle was grasped by both hands in front of the body.

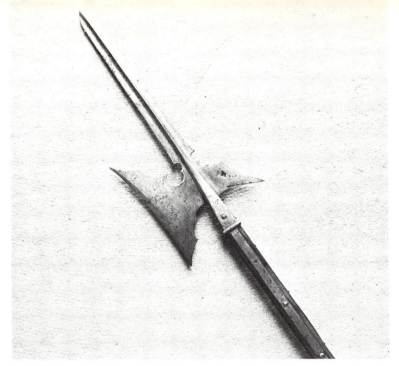

Fig. 4-8   *Sixteenth century halberd.*

Courtesy of De Young Museum, San Francisco, California.

Fig. 4-9   *Halberd. Posing: D. Mundie and H. Zenk, University of California.*

Cuts with the halberd were directed mostly to the opponent's head; the point was employed for thrusting. If the weapons were engaged, the disengage thrust or cut could be used. A head-cut was parried with the handle lifted parallel above the head. Thrusts could be knocked away or parried with circular movements (Fig. 4-9).

The dagger was used either alone or as a secondary weapon in rapier play. When used alone, the dagger was held in the fist of either hand with the point down or up, possibly being changed from one hand to the other during a fight. From the on guard position (rather a wide side-stance) the opponents circled each other with weapons extended. Stabs could be delivered from above (dagger held with point down), from below (dagger held with point up), or from the left or right. The free hand was used for parrying; if a cape or cloak was worn it could be wrapped around the free arm for extra protection. Evading blows by suddenly bending the body or jumping was a very important part of the defense.

The dagger was also used as the final weapon at the end of fights, when other weapons were used, to kill the wounded opponent.

Marozzo, an Italian master of the sixteenth century, taught 13 ways to disarm an opponent. The following are some examples of his method.

1. Grab the opponent's right wrist with your left hand from below, step with the right leg behind the opponent's right leg, and by pushing his right shoulder with your right hand, throw him.

2. Grab with the left hand the opponent's right wrist from below and with the right hand pull the opponent's front leg up, throwing him backwards.

3. With the right hand, grab the opponent's right wrist from above. With the left arm crossing below his right arm, grab his left shoulder and force his dagger-arm downwards, while placing your left leg behind his right leg.

4. Grab with the right hand the opponent's right wrist from above, push his right elbow with your left hand from below with a circular upward motion, and twist his arm around to his back.

Early Modern Period

The rapier was used either alone or in combination with other offensive or defensive weapons. If the rapier was employed alone, the left hand was used defensively. This hand, protected by a mail glove, could grab the opponent's blade, push it away, and grasp the opponent's wrist, pulling him close, so that he was unable to use his weapon.

To hold the rapier, the fencer placed his index finger in the *pas d'ane* (ring in the front of the crossbar) and the middle finger on the *quillon* (crossbar). In earlier times when the pas d'ane consisted of two rings, the index and middle finger were put through the rings (Fig. 4-10).

During the sixteenth century, Agrippa described four offensive-defensive on guard positions used with the rapier.

The *prima* position was assumed with the hand in pronation over the left side about the height of the left shoulder (the point a little downwards, directed to the opponent's chest).

Fɪɢ. 4-10   *Seventeenth century Spanish rapier. Proper grip shown.*

Courtesy of De Young Museum, San Francisco, California.

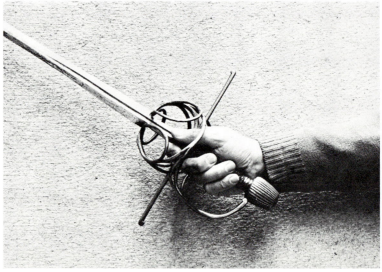

In the *seconda*, the hand was in pronation over the right side about the height of the shoulder (the point directed to the opponent's chest).

In the *terza* position, the hand was again in pronation, the fist on the right side about the height of the hip (point directed to the opponent's eye).

The *quarta* position was assumed by placing the hand in half supination (thumb on the top of the grip), the fist on the left side about at the height of the hip (point directed to the opponent's head).

In the sixteenth century, the rapier was primarily used as a cutting weapon to attack the head, flank, chest, and legs. Both edges were employed with straight or circular motion or with a flick of the point. Thrusts were delivered to the face, chest, or the lower part of the body. The parries consisted of what we today would call time-hits executed from one of the above described guards in an attempt to hit and cover at the same time.

For the on guard position, either the left or right foot could be in front. Attacks were delivered while passing, jumping, or circling around. The defense was carried out by ducking to avoid high cuts or by volting to avoid attacks directed to the legs. In the preparatory phase, the opponents tapped each other's blade or exchanged beats. The disarm was executed with a violent, twisting slide or beat toward the quarta (forward and downward) or toward the terza (sideward and downward).

RAPIER AND BUCKLER

The use of the rapier and buckler was the result of an application of sword-and-shield fight ideas. The buckler, a small round shield commonly constructed with a spike in the center, was held with the arm almost straight in front of the body and the fencer in the left side on guard position. The action was similar to that of the sword and shield, but much faster.

RAPIER AND DAGGER

When the rapier and dagger were used together, the dagger was held in the left hand and was used defensively or for stabbing in close quarters; the point was directed either up or down. The crossbars were curved and were supposed to hold the opponent's blade until the other arm delivered the cut or thrust with the rapier (the offensive weapon) (Figs. 4-11, 4-12, 4-13).

In the stoccata guard position, the rapier-hand was kept near to the hip and the dagger's point close to the rapier's point. In the high guard position, the rapier was held in the high seconda and the dagger near to the left hip. The right foot was in front in the on guard position, and the weight of the body was on the left leg to keep the head safely out of the way. The cuts and thrusts were delivered with the rapier, and the parries were taken by the combined use of the dagger and rapier to the left, right, or above the head.

In the second half of the sixteenth century, thrusts became more popular and the lunge came into vogue. All the other movements mentioned above in connection with the single rapier continued to be employed.

RAPIER AND CLOAK

Before the fight, the cloak was removed from the shoulders and wrapped around the left forearm with the end of the garment

Fig. 4-11 *Rapier and dagger.*

Fig. 4-12 *Rapier and dagger.*

Fig. 4-13 *Rapier and dagger.*
          Posing: J. Spencer and M. Small, University of California.

being held by the hand. The cloak was used to ward off attacks or to stop the attacker's blade. It might also be thrown over the opponent's head or blade to impede his attack. The wrapped arm was good protection against cuts, but when the triangular blade allowed better thrusting attack, the cloak proved to be inadequate; so the dagger was used for better defense.

TWO RAPIERS

A further development in rapier play, in the last part of the sixteenth and the beginning of the seventeenth centuries, was the use of two rapiers. The regular rapier was held in the right hand, while the left hand held a shorter rapier. Considerable skill was needed to carry out attacks and parries at the same time.

In the on guard position, the fencer alternated his right and left foot forward as the fight required. The stance was changed with high speed as the combat developed. The lunge was executed with either foot, depending on the on guard position. In order to repeat the lunge, the back foot was moved up to the front one.

In the attack position, the body leaned a little forward and in the defensive position, a little backward.

The parries, cuts, or thrusts could be executed with both weapons at the same time or alternated at the fencer's will.

Practicing the various movements requires dexterity and patience, and usually only expert fencers are able to perform with two weapons.

TRANSITION RAPIER

Towards the end of the sixteenth century, the rapier became lighter and shorter, allowing faster and more controlled movements. At the beginning of the seventeenth century, eight parries in four lines were in use and different attacks were invented.

The eight parries were prime, seconde, tierce, quarte, quinte, sixte, septime, and octave (See the section on Modern Fencing). Even the counter-parries were known by this period. The so-called *universal parry* was a parry from tierce through quarte to seconde in one movement and was regarded by some as infallible against any attack. The left hand was also used for defense, although some masters were already opposed to this practice.

The thrust gained more attention, and the disengage, beat, and feint were used.

The salute was elaborated and consisted of four movements:

1. The on guard position was assumed.

2. The fencer stood upright, removed his hat, and raised his sword arm to about the height of his head.

3. The on guard position was again taken with hat in hand.

4. The fencer resumed the upright position, raised his sword arm, and put his hat on.

Modern Period

SMALL SWORD

From the second quarter of the seventeenth century, the small sword, used exclusively for thrusting, permitted all the movements we know today. Fencing became very precise. About the middle of this century, the mask began to be commonplace in practice, and the on guard position evolved to its present appearance.

The small sword was the weapon of the eighteenth century. In the nineteenth century this sword lost it's importance since it was no longer part of the dress of the time, but it continued to be used in duels and in sports.

A theatrical student using the small sword on the stage must know at least the basic fundamentals of modern fencing.

SABER

Fencing with military sabers was somewhat cumbersome and slow; cuts were delivered with swings (moulinets) and parries made with circular motions. The on guard position was similar to that of rapier fencing, but the left arm was kept behind the back. On foot, the fights were conducted in circles. The positions and attacks of saber fighting (except for cavalry fights) have to be practiced on the basis of our modern saber fencing. On horseback, the same parries and attacks were used, but the heavier weapon and the problem of controlling the horse made fencing slower and more difficult. The horseman fighting against foot-soldier used swinging cuts made from both sides of the horse and tried to disarm him in order to run him down with the horse.

The bayonet, attached to the gun barrel, was used for thrusts or cuts with direct or circular motion. Parries were also made with direct or circular motions to knock the opponent's weapon away. In close quarters the butt-end of the gun was used for beating or tossing.

A fight which involves the gun and bayonet is not a part of fencing and those seeking instructions should consult military books dealing with this form of defense.

By the nineteenth century, weapons were divided into those used for fighting (dueling) and those used for exercise.

The weapons used for sport became lighter and the point and edge were blunted. The weapons were still ornately decorated; the handle of the small sword was often covered with velvet and gold, and the guard of the saber was frequently artistically perforated.

Exhibitions and bouts were conducted with great ceremony, and the on guard position and salutes were taken with prescribed movements and attitudes. The on guard position was elaborated to incorporate spectacular swings.

1. From the initial position, the weapon was lifted with straight arm obliquely up above the shoulder.

2. From this position, the weapon was brought down to point obliquely down.

3. The weapon was then brought back, crossing in front of the body and held with both hands (arms straight). The left hand held the foible of the weapon.

4. Both arms and the weapons were raised over the head.

5. The on guard position was finally resumed.

At exhibitions the so-called *grand salute* was done. This consisted of a series of movements performed without masks. The fencers faced one another in the initial position with arms held straight. They saluted facing each other, and then to the left and to the right. Both took the on guard position for five counts. Coming back to the upright position they separated and one made a lunge while the other executed a prime parry. Again both took the on guard position for five counts and then engaged in various movements showing the basic methods of attack and defense. At the end, stamping twice with their right foot, both returned to the initial position. They saluted both to the right and to the left, took the on guard position once again for five counts, then stamping with the right foot they returned to the upright position, saluted each other and shook hands.

Exercises Useful for Stage Movements

These exercises are designed to develop the coordination, balance, suppleness, and body control necessary for both fencing and general stage movements. Training consists of a number of selected exercises from different fields of sports. On stage, it will probably be necessary to only do simple attacks and parries, but the rhythm and speed learned in routine fencing exercises help give the impression of a real fight.

BASIC WARMING-UP EXERCISES

1. Deep knee bends, stretching one leg after the other forward and sideways
2. Bouncing in a deep knee bend
3. Russian dance—simultaneous quick changes from one outstretched leg to the other in deep knee bends
4. Skipping
5. Bouncing on the toes
6. Rotating the head in both directions
7. Rotating the arms in clockwise and counter-clockwise directions from the shoulders, both simultaneously and alternately
8. Rotating the arms with the arms bent (fists held closed and placed tight at the shoulder)
9. Pulling bent arms apart after having the fists clenched tightly in front of the body
10. Walking across the stage with slow and then fast steps
11. Running across the stage with small and then larger steps
12. Leaping across the stage (frog leaps, arabesque)
13. Jumping up to and down from a platform (lower, higher)
14. Vaulting over a side-horse or table

If the actor has to fall or stumble either forward or backward, rolling may be used to accomplish a spectacular recovery. The roll must first be practiced without a weapon. Later, when the actor can perform the roll with facility, he may use a weapon.

When doing the *forward roll* the actor steps into the roll with one foot a short distance forward. He then bends his front knee and puts both hands with arms bent to the floor close to his front foot. He touches the floor with the nape of his neck first and then rolls over onto his back. He must pull his knees up to his chest to execute a smooth roll and enable himself to jump quickly into the upright position, which finishes the roll. After mastering the roll with the use of both hands, the actor should try it with one hand and then with no hands. Those who are not able to do the roll over their head may try it sideways over one shoulder.

A *backward roll* takes more skill and practice. The actor has to lift one leg while bending the knee of the other leg until his back is almost down to his heel. As he begins to roll backwards, he places his chin against his chest, bringing his head slightly forward; then, reaching backwards over his shoulders, he pushes the floor with his hands, puts his knees close to chest, and rolls over into an upright position. This roll can also be done with the neck bent to the side.

When rolling with the weapon in hand, the weapon should be held to one side.

All exercises should be practiced on a mat before they are done on a bare stage.

The actor should learn to fall foreward, backward, and to the side. In falling sideways, he touches the floor with the knee corresponding to the direction in which he is falling. When the fall is almost complete, he extends his hand and arm to the same side breaking the impact.

The *dead-man forward* fall looks extremely difficult. Keeping both feet together, the actor leans forward until he reaches about a 45 degree angle. He then slightly bends his knees and when they touch the floor, he falls forward. In the last moment of the fall he brings both hands up to about the height of his chest to diminish the impact with the spring of his slightly bent arms. After perfecting this fall, the actor must try a similar exercise—falling with straight knees and breaking the fall with his arms.

The *dead-man backward* fall seems even more startling than the forward fall. The actor starts falling backwards keeping his body straight. Just before hitting the floor, he relaxes his body so the seat hits the floor first. The hands, as before, hit the floor to break the impact. It is important to keep the head forward so it does not hit the floor. If the actor is unable to accomplish this fall, he should turn to one side at the last moment of the fall and finish on his side.

MISCELLANEOUS EXERCISES

The following should be mastered:

1. Balancing on a beam
2. Climbing a ladder
3. Swinging on a rope
4. Holding, lifting, and carrying a body (A body can be carried by one person in his arms, on his back, or by dragging. Four or six persons can carry a body in their arms, on their shoulders, or over their heads.)
5. Basic Judo movements (Neck throw—grabbing the opponent's neck with the arm and throwing him to the ground with a circular motion. Hip throw—lifting the opponent across the hip and throwing him in the same manner as above. Trip throw—tripping the opponent by crossing one leg behind the opponent's leg or legs and pushing him backwards causing him to stumble. Overhead throw— grabbing the opponent's upper arms and put one foot up to his abdomen, roll back and throw him overhead.)
6. Basic boxing movements

FENCING EXERCISES IN A GROUP

(a) On guard, advancing, retreating, lunging, passing, volting, jumping forward and backward, jumping up (pulling the knees high), quick turns with the front and back foot (a pivot), and dancing around in an on guard position.

(b) Cuts, thrusts, parries, return-cuts (thrusts) after parries, different attacks, and beats of the blades.

Frequently, especially in films, actors are compelled to fence on stairs. For a forward movement, the fencer moves up the first step with the front foot; the other foot then follows taking in the same distance. Moving backward is more difficult because the fencer cannot look to see where he is going. The back foot must search for the next step while the front foot keeps his body in the on guard position.

The most difficult thing, while moving up or down stairs, is to make certain the opponent is fully occupied. Steps should be taken one at a time without crossing the feet. If the fencer should happen to cross his feet, chances are he would miss a step and lose his balance. When he reaches the foot of the stairs, he may jump the few remaining steps to the level, turn around, and continue to fence in reverse order. If there is a railing on the side of the stairs, the left hand can be used to hold the railing thus helping to maintain a more secure balance.

FENCING AGAINST TWO OR MORE OPPONENTS

If a single fencer is attacked by two or more opponents, the play should be organized so that the single fencer alternates a few strokes with each opponent, leaving none of them unoccupied for any length of time. For example, a single fencer might disarm one of his opponents, fight and wound the second opponent while the first is looking for his weapon, and then continue to fight with the first.

When fighting against two or more opponents, the single fencer should back into a wall or corner or jump behind a table or bench (perhaps turn a table over or throw chairs in the opponents' path) to avoid being surrounded. The attacked fencer can draw one of the attackers into his trap and begin to fight with him. It is extremely easier to fight one than ten! To enliven a scene, a fencer can swing from a chandelier, knock down opponents while swinging on a rope, or jump from a balcony into the enemies' midst. The possibilities for this type of action are so varied that the fencers and director of the show can work out numerous variations without ever having to repeat an action.

After mastering the falling exercises, an actor will find that fainting will be easy by comparison. Fainting can be done anywhere or from any object. One can faint by falling into or out of a chair, to the floor, against a wall, down stairs, or into someone's arms.

Fainting into a chair does not need any special explanation. The actor has only to make sure that his limbs and head hang loose and relaxed. Sometimes he may roll down (after hitting the chair) and fall to the floor with a twisting movement.

Fainting to the floor is a vertical collapse. The actor bends both knees, touches the floor sideways with one knee, sits down on the floor and falls back. All of these movements have to be continuous and, again, very relaxed.

When fainting against a wall, the student stands a few inches from the wall and makes a dead-man fall back until he touches the wall. He then slides his back down the wall, bending his knees, and stretching them out after he has reached the floor. The head hangs forward or sideways limply.

Fainting into someone's arms begins with the dead-man fall backwards with the arms spread a bit apart so the person can catch the one falling under the arms.

BEING STABBED

Stabbing may occur in the front or back of the body. If the person is stabbed in front, he grasps the imaginary wound with both hands. His collapse should be sudden, beginning with the head and upper body, and then, after a few seconds, completed by a forward fall.

When stabbed in the back, the actor reaches for the wound and turns, falling to one side, thrusting his feet from under him. The pain that is experienced from the wound should be expressed by facial movements.

DYING ON THE STAGE

Many times, the performer will be required to die on the stage. After the perfect fall, he may spoil the effect if he breathes visibly or holds his arms or legs in an unnatural way. The most important thing to remember is to be relaxed. Breathing exercises are essential, not only for speech and modulation of the voice, but for the breath control necessary to portray the dying person.

The limbs and head must rest on the floor or hang entirely relaxed; the face muscles must also be relaxed.

THE METHOD OF PRACTICE FOR FENCING SCENES

When students have mastered the above exercises, they must combine and elaborate them into fixed successions of movements. The speed and the rhythm of each individual's movements must be coordinated with the others. These routine exercises should be practiced slowly at first, then with increasing speed and complexity, until they are mastered.

The master or director of the show assigns the exercises and has the actors perfect them. After the physical activity is under control, the memorized lines, if any, must be adapted to the fight. For example, in the fencing scene in *Cyrano de Bergerac* almost every line is accompanied by a fencing movement. If there is no background music or text given, the fencers can add extemporaneous battle-cries.

Once the routine exercises are polished, the actors work on the stage to become accustomed to the costumes, scenery, limited space, lights, and other members of the cast. A fencing scene must be practiced many times so that no one is endangered and to make sure the combatants do not step out of view, get entangled in the curtains, knock down stage sets or props, and even, in the fever of the fight, fall off the stage. The sound effects, easily obtained in films, must be emphasized with stamping of feet, lunging heavily on the floor, and beating the blades loud enough so the noise will increase the excitement of the fight. A well-organized fencing scene develops gradually with spectacular movements and speed to the climax of the fight when the wounding or killing of the opponent occurs.

TIMING

Timing is a very important element not only in the routine exercises, but also in the scenes where several pairs or groups of actors fight. Usually limited time or lack of knowledge does not permit the teaching of widely different actions to each pair. However, even though each fight follows the same script, by starting each pair at slightly different times, the audience can be given the feeling that a wide variety of spontaneous actions is occurring.

Finally, the instructor should not forget that the manner of the actor's conduct before, during, and after combat must reflect the character of the person who is being portrayed. This will be illustrated by an example from Molier's *Don Juan* later in this section.

The following scenes from four plays are chosen as examples of theatrical fencing action:

1. Shakespeare's *Hamlet*—the psychological build-up of the fight.

2. Molier's *Don Juan*—The use of fencing to reveal the character.

3. Shakespeare's *Romeo and Juliet*—the use of correct timing in group fencing, and an example of having one person fight more than one combat with different adversaries.

4. Shakespeare's *King Lear*—the use of a variety of weapons and the reflection of knightly manners in the cruel fight between Edgar and Edmund.

Shakespeare used three Italian terms in his plays: passado, stoccata, and punta reversa.

Passado (passata) is a cross-step with one foot placed in front of the other, used in attacks. It was the forerunner of the flèche.

Stoccata is a thrust under the opponent's weapons or arm made with supinated hand.

Punta reversa (punto reverso) is a jabbing attacking thrust made with a dagger from the side or a jabbing defensive thrust made with the rapier from the side.

The Fencing Scene in Hamlet

One of the most popular fencing scenes takes place in Shakespeare's tragedy *Hamlet*. Based partly on the idea in *Buhnenfechtkunst* by I. E. Koch, which gives the best explanation among the many works written about the duel in Hamlet, we are attempting a psychological and practical build-up of the scene. The psychological motives of the fight should be explained on the program or before the last act in order to further the spectators' understanding of the scene.

Shakespeare chose the weapons of his time for the dueling scene because of their greater spectacular value. The weapon of Shakespeare's time was the rapier or rapier and dagger. In order to adhere as much as possible to the story, we have chosen rapier and dagger in our interpretation of the scene. To support the choice, we quote from the play: "What is his weapon?" "Rapier and dagger." If the play is not performed in historical costumes, the épée should be chosen, as is sometimes seen in modern versions.

Because Shakespeare did not give instructions about the fight, there is confusion in most performances of the play regarding the duel. The clash and the exchange of weapons is indicated in the play, but no instructions are given for the execution of the actions. The director of the play has a free hand in arranging the duel according to his own ideas. Many times the staging of the fight is very poor, but in spite of this, this scene is the climax of the play.

The bout is declared to be a friendly one by the king, and for this reason the rapier should be a practice weapon. The points of practice weapons are covered with a safety ball the size of a golf ball, and the edges of the weapons are blunt. The dagger should be real but is only meant to be used for defense (if it is drawn). The practice rapiers are brought to the stage by the attendants; the daggers are attached to the belts of would be duelist as a part of their costumes.

The king bets with Laertes that the latter will not be able to touch Hamlet more than three times out of twelve. Laertes, although acknowledging Hamlet to be the better fencer, assures the king that he will hit Hamlet nine times. In Shakespeare's time usually nine touches decided a match. The limit is raised by the king probably to give Laertes a sure chance to hit Hamlet.

The king and Laertes, however, plot that the practice weapon used by Laertes is to be exchanged for a poisoned one with sharp edges, which will administer the poison into Hamlet's blood by a thrust or a cut. If the blade is sharpened near the point, this is not easily noticeable from a distance. This weapon is kept by the king beside the throne.

Because the doublets (made of heavy velvet or brocade) may give fairly good protection against the strokes, Laertes must try to unbate his weapon for a thrust or hit so hard that the rapier cuts through the doublet.

Hamlet and Laertes assure each other of the friendly spirit of the bout.

We now quote the scene, adding our explanations and comments in upper case letters:

Laertes: I am satisfied in nature,
Whose motive, in this case, should stir me most
To my revenge; but in my terms of honour
I stand aloof; and will no reconcilement,
Till by some elder masters, of known honour,
I have a voice and predecent of peace,
To keep my name ungor'd. But till that time,
I do receive your offered love like love,
And will not wrong it.

Hamlet: I embrace it freely;
And will this brother's wager frankly play.
Give us the foils. Come on.

Laertes: Come, one for me.

Hamlet: I'll be your foil, Laertes; in mine ignorance
Your skill shall like a star i' the darkest night,
Stick fiery off indeed.

Laertes: You mock me, sir.

Hamlet: No, by this hand.

King: Give them the foils, young Osric.
Cousin Hamlet,
You know the wager?

Hamlet: Very well, my lord;
Your Grace hath laid the odds o' the weaker side.

King: I do not fear it; I have seen you both;
But since he's better'd, we have therefore odds.

Laertes: This is too heavy; let me see another. LAERTES THROWS
THE FOIL TO A SERVANT. HAMLET TURNING AWAY FROM
THE KING AND LAERTES, MAKES A FEW PRACTICE LUNGES.

IN THE MEANTIME, THE KING ORDERS THE SERVANT TO HAND THE POISONED RAPIER TO LAERTES.

Hamlet: This likes me well. These foils have all a length?

Osric: Ay, my good lord /They prepare to play./ BOTH SWING THEIR RAPIERS LEFT AND RIGHT AND HAMLET TRIES THE FLEXIBILITY OF THE BLADE BENDING IT IN FRONT OF HIS FACE. LAERTES DOES NOT BEND HIS RAPIER BECAUSE HE DOES NOT WANT TO TOUCH THE POISONED BLADE.

King: Set me the stoups of wine upon that table
If Hamlet gives the first or second hit,
Or quit in answer of the third exchange,
Let all the battlements their ordinance fire;
The king shall drink to Hamlet's better breath;

King (con't): And in the cup a union shall he throw,
Richer than that which four successive kings
In Denmark's crown have worn, Give me the cups;
And let the kettle to the trumpet speak,
The trumpet to the cannoneer without,
The cannons to the heavens, the heavens to earth,
"Now the king drinks to Hamlet." Come, begin;
And you, the judges, bear a wary eye."
BOTH FENCERS KISS THE CROSS OF THE BLADE AND TAKE THE ON GUARD POSITION.

Hamlet: Come on, sir.

Laertes: Come, my lord. /They play/
THEY EXCHANGE BEATS:

Hamlet: 1. Quarte, sixte-beat advance

2. Quarte, sixte-beat advance

Laertes: 3. Rapid quarte-sixte, quarte-sixte beat with two steps forward

Hamlet: 4. Quarte, sixte, quarte-beat thrust

Laertes: 5. Quarte parry-riposte

Hamlet: 6. Quarte parry-riposte

Laertes: 7. Quarte parry-riposte

Hamlet: 8. Quarte parry-riposte (touch)

Hamlet: One.

Laertes: No.

Hamlet: Judgement. THEY GO BACK TO
          UPRIGHT POSITION, AWAITING JUDGEMENT.

Osric: A hit, a very palpable hit.

Laertes: Well; again.

King: Stay; give me drink. Hamlet, this pearl is thine; PUTS
          THE POISON INTO THE CUP. Here's to thy health. Give
          him the cup. GIVES THE CUP TO THE SERVANT.
          /Trumpets sound; and cannon shot off within.

Hamlet: I'll play this bout first; set it by a while. Come. THEY
          TAKE UP THE "ON GUARD" POSITION AGAIN.

Hamlet: 1. Quarte beat disengage
Laertes: 2. Counter-quarte parry, disengage riposte
Hamlet: 3. Quarte counter-quarte parry, disengage riposte
Laertes: 4. Sixte parry, riposte
Hamlet: 5. Octave parry, riposte
Laertes: 6. Quarte parry, riposte
Hamlet: 7. Quarte parry, riposte (touch)

Hamlet (con't): Another hit; what say you?

Laertes: A touch, a touch, I do confess. PAUSE

King: Our son shall win.

Queen: He's faint and scant of breath.
          Here, Hamlet, take my napkin, rub thy brows;
          The queen carouses to thy fortune, Hamlet.
          THE SERVANT TAKES THE CUP TO THE QUEEN.

Hamlet: Good madam!

King: Gertrude, do not drink.

Queen: I will, my lord; I pray you, pardon me. SHE DRINKS.

King: /Aside/ It is the poison'd cup! It is too late.

Hamlet: I dare not drink yet, madam; by and by.

Queen: Come, let me wipe thy face. HAMLET STEPS TO THE
          QUEEN.

Laertes: My lord, I'll hit him now.

King: I do not think't.

Laertes:	REALIZING THAT IF THE POISON STARTS TO WORK HAMLET WILL FIND OUT HIS PERFIDY, AND THAT THIS MEANS THE END FOR HIM. HE MUST THEREFORE WOUND HAMLET NOW. /Aside/ And yet 'tis almost' gainst my conscience. HAMLET IS INDIGNANT BECAUSE HE FEELS LAERTES IS NOT FIGHTING WHOLEHEARTEDLY.
Hamlet:	Come, for the third, Laertes. You but dally. I pray you, pass with your best violence. I am afeard you make a wanton of me.
Laertes:	Say you so? Come on. /They play./ ON GUARD POSITION.
Hamlet:	1. Head-cut, flank-cut
Laertes:	2. Quinte parry, seconde parry, cheek riposte
Hamlet:	3. Tierce parry, chest riposte
Laertes:	4. Prime parry, head riposte
Hamlet:	5. Quinte parry, chest riposte (misses, pause)
Osric:	Nothing, neither way. LAERTES JUMPS BACK, THEN BOTH ATTACK, CLASH TOGETHER AND KEEPING IN CONTACT THEY TURN AROUND, CHANGING PLACE. HAMLET JUMPS BACK PUSHING HIMSELF AWAY FROM LAERTES. LAERTES UNBATES HIS WEAPON WHILE HAMLET IS TURNED AWAY.
Laertes:	Have at you now. LAERTES RUNNING BY HITS HAMLET ON HIS LEFT SHOULDER. PAUSE. HAMLET TEARS THE SLEEVE OF HIS SHIRT, SEES THE WOUND, IS VERY MUCH SURPRISED TO BE WOUNDED BY A PRACTICE WEAPON AND REALIZES THAT SOMETHING IS AMISS WITH LAERTES WEAPON. HE DECIDES TO DISARM HIM AND CHECK HIS BLADE. THEY CLASH IN QUARTE AND WITH A STRONG CHARGE ON LAERTES' BLADE HE DISARMS HIM AND STEPS ON THE FALLEN BLADE. LAERTES BENDS DOWN TO PICK UP THE WEAPON, BUT HAMLET OFFERS HIS OWN RAPIER TO LAERTES. LAERTES IS OBLIGED TO ACCEPT THE OFFER. HAMLET PICKS UP THE OTHER WEAPON, INSPECTS IT AND QUICKLY HE REALIZES WHAT IS GOING ON. HE PULLS OUT HIS DAGGER. LAERTES SEEING THIS, PULLS OUT HIS DAGGER TOO AND TRIES TO TAKE OFF THE BALL OF THE RAPIER BUT HAMLET GIVES HIM NO TIME. HE ATTACKS FURIOUSLY TO HIT

LAERTES. CUTS HIS LEGS. (LAERTES JUMPS) CUTS LEFT AND RIGHT OVER LAERTES' HEAD (LAERTES DUCKS)

King: Part them! They are incens'd.

Hamlet: Nay, come again. LAERTES IS NOT FIGHTING ANY MORE. HIS ONLY THOUGHT IS TO ESCAPE. HAMLET AGAIN CHARGES WILDLY AT THE RETREATING LAERTES.

Hamlet: 1. Head-cut

Laertes: 2. Quinte parry with rapier and dagger, head riposte

Hamlet: 3. Quinte parry with rapier and dagger, rapid head, flank, chest ripostes

Laertes: 4. Quinte, seconde, prime parries (no ripostes)

Laertes: 5. Thrust with the dagger (hoping he can wound Hamlet)

Hamlet: 6. Parries the dagger-thrust with the rapier

Hamlet: 7. Thrust with the dagger

Laertes: 8. Parries the dagger thrust with the rapier (clash, short pause push each other away)

Hamlet: 9. Rapid head, flank, chest cuts

Laertes: 10. Quinte parry but does not parry the flank and chest cuts (touches)

Hamlet (con't): IN RUNNING BACK LAERTES SLIPS ON THE FLOOR, TUMBLES ON HIS KNEE AND AT THIS MOMENT HAMLET HITS HIM AGAIN WITH A THRUST.

/The queen falls/ HAMLET THROWS THE DAGGER TO THE FLOOR. PAUSE.

Osric: Look to the queen there, ho!

Horatio: They bleed on both sides. How is it, my lord?

Osric: How is it, Laertes?

Laertes: Why, as a woodcock to mine own springe, Osric; I am justly kill'd with mine own treachery.

Hamlet: How does the queen?

King: She swoons to see them bleed.

Queen: No, no, the drink, the drink,—O my dear Hamlet! The drink, the drink; I am poison'd. /Dies/

Hamlet: REALIZING THE SITUATION TURNS TO THE KING.
O villany! Ho! let the door be lock'd:
Treachery! seek it out. /Laertes falls/
LAERTES LEANING ON HIS HAND AND KNEE.

Laertes: It is here, Hamlet. Hamlet, thou art slain;
No medicine in the world can do thee good;
In thee there is not half an hour of life;
The treacherous instrument is in thy hand.
Unbated and envenom'd. The foul practice
Hath turn'd itself on me; lo! here I lie,
Never to rise again. Thy mother's poison'd.
I can no more. The king, the king's to blame.

Hamlet: The point envenom'd too!—
Then venom to thy work./ STABS THE KING IN THE STOM-
ACH WITH HIS RAPIER AND THEN THROWS WEAPON TO
THE KING.

Osric & Lords: Treason! treason!

King: O! yet defend me friends; I am but hurt. TUMBLES TO
HIS KNEE.

Hamlet: TAKES THE CUP WITH ONE HAND.
Here, thou incestuous, murderous, damned Dane,
Drink off this potion;—is thy union here?"
HOLDING THE KING'S HEAD WITH THE OTHER HAND, GRAB-
ING HIS HAIR (OR BEARD), POURS THE WINE INTO HIS MOUTH
AND FACE. Follow my mother. /King dies/ FALLING ON
HIS BACK.

Laertes: He is justly serv'd;
It is a poison temper'd by himself.
Exchange forgiveness with me, noble Hamlet;
Mine and my father's death come not upon thee
Nor thine on me! SLIPS FORWARD ON HIS HAND. /Dies/

Molière's Don Juan

The fencing scenes in Moliere's Don Juan are, in the script, il-
lusional off-stage actions and usually not fought on stage. In the

University of California production of March 1963, Professor Robert Goldsby, the director of the play, brought the fights onto the stage, giving the author a chance to elaborate the fight between Don Juan and the outlaws and Don Juan's duel with Don Carlos. Rapiers were chosen as the weapons. Besides contributing more excitement and interest to the play, the action served to delineate more adequately the character of Don Juan. He is pictured as a "passionate, daring, unwise, radical, and doomed" person with disdain of fear who, in spite of his depravity, somehow draws sympathy. Having a superior knowledge of fencing he handles the fights with boundless self-confidence and absolute certainty. Even when seemingly careless in turning away he knows what his opponent's next move will be, suddenly turns back, and with playful insouciance parries the attack. The following actions are intended to portray this character.

As Don Juan is on his way to town, three outlaws attack him simultaneously, thrusting to his chest. Don Juan parries the thrusts with one motion, an elegant sweeping parry from sixte through quarte to seconde. Then, with three quick attacks, he cuts the first's head, the second's flank, and the third's chest. The robbers in turn parry the attacks with quinte, seconde, and prime, respectively. Don Juan grabs the first robber's return thrust with his left hand and with a strong beat of his rapier on the blade disarms the robber, throwing the loose weapon away; with a twisting circular tierce he disarms the second one and parries the third robber's head-cut with quinte and hits with a strong flat chest-cut. When the second robber stoops to regain his weapon, Don Juan hits him on his seat, and then chases the three out of sight like a bunch of pigeons put to flight. Don Carlos' belated appearance to help only makes more credible the robbers' flight.

In the duel with Don Carlos, Don Juan only parries the attacks but does not riposte as he is sure of himself. Don Carlos attacks with repeated head-cut, flank-cut, chest-cut in quick succession and these are parried easily with quinte, seconde, prime, while Don Juan laughs at the unsuccessful attempts. Don Carlos executes a thrust which Don Juan parries with seconde. The thrust is repeated twice and Don Juan parries them with two circle secondes then turns his back to Don Carlos; but, knowing that a head-cut is coming, he turns suddenly back with quinte, parrying and then with a twisting movement disarms Don Carlos, puts the point to Don Carlos' chest to show that he can kill at will.

There are no lines to recite during these fights; the movements can be very rapid and the scenes quite impressive, offering a chance to show Don Juan's character through his fencing as agreed upon with the director of the play.

Romeo and Juliet

Constant references to sword play throughout Shakespeare's *Romeo and Juliet* indicate the importance of fencing in the tragedy. The fights are induced by the hostility between the two houses of Montague and Capulet, the hatred and pride of Tybalt in his feud with Mercutio, the desire for revenge that causes Romeo and Tybalt's combat, and the ironic circumstances that force the fight between Romeo and Paris.

The domestics of the two houses fight to please their masters and are not really fencers. They rather imitate their lords in fighting. Benvolio and Mercutio are good fencers like most gentlemen of the time, while Tybalt is a formidable fencer who loses against Romeo seemingly only because of his quick temper and lack of consideration. Romeo is younger and inexperienced but the desire for revenge gives him the drive to conquer Tybalt, and he kills Paris only in his desperation to get back to the tomb. Paris becomes involved in the fight by chance and forces Romeo into the duel that causes his own death.

The weapons used in the fights vary from the sword and buckler used by the servants to the rapier and dagger used by the gentlemen.

The fights are listed below in order of their occurrence:

ACT I, SCENE 1

Sampson and Gregory of the house of Capulet, Abraham and Balthasar of the house of Montague appear with sword and buckler; Benvolio and Tybalt with rapier.

All four servants fight using the same routine, with the combat of one pair starting a few seconds later than the other.

When all six begin to fight Tybalt and Benvolio delay their duel to salute each other so that the whole staging of this fight should give the impression of disorder and variety.

We now quote the scenes, adding the exercises.

Abraham: You lie.

Sampson: Draw, if you be men. Gregory, remember thy (swashing) blow. (THEY FIGHT)

Sam. Head-cut	Abr. Parry with the buckler
Sam. Cut to Abr.'s right side	Abr. Parry with seconde, return head cut
Sam. Parry with the buckler	Abr. Cut to Sam.'s right side
Sam. Parry with seconde, cut to Abr.'s left side	Abr. Parry with the buckler, head cut
Sam. Parry with quinte, ripostes to head	Abr. Parry with quinte

(Balthasar and Gregory fight the same routine.)

Benvolio: Part fools!

Put up your swords; you know not what you do.

(BEATS DOWN THEIR SWORDS)

ENTER Tybalt.

Tybalt: What, are thou drawn among these heartless hinds? Turn thee, Benvolio, look upon thy death.

Benvolio: I do but keep the peace. Put up thy sword, or manage it to part these men with me.

Tybalt: What, drawn, and talk of peace! I hate the word As I hate hell, all Montagues, and thee.

Have at thee, coward! (THEY FIGHT)

(The servants resume fighting repeating the previous routine.)

(Tybalt and Benvolio salute each other and get into on guard position.)

Tyb. Quarte beat thrust	Ben. Quarte parry, riposte
Tyb. Quarte parry riposte	Ben. Quarte parry head cut, flank cut
Tyb. Quinte parry, seconde parry head cut, flank cut	Ben. Quinte parry, seconde parry

(To lengthen the fight the whole routine of six, may be repeated once or twice to keep up with the lines.)

ENTER THREE OF FOUR CITIZENS (AND OFFICERS), WITH CLUBS OR PARTISANS.

Officer: Clubs, bills, and partisans! Strike! Beat them down! Down with the Capulets! down with the Montagues!

(They break up the fight.)

ACT III, SCENE 1

. . . *Mercutio:* O calm, dishonourable, vile submission! Alla stoccata carries it away.   (DRAWS)
Tybalt, you rat-catcher, will you walk?
Tybalt: What wouldst thou have with me?
Mercutio: Good king of cats, nothing but one of your nine lives; that I mean to make bold withal, and, as you shall use me hereafter, dry-beat the rest of the eight. Will you pluck your sword out of his pilcher by the ears? Make haste, lest mine be about your ears ere it be out.
Tybalt: I am for you.   (DRAWING)
Romeo: Gentle Mercutio, put thy rapier up.
Mercutio: Come, sir, your passado.   (THEY FIGHT)

(Tybalt and Mercutio exchange tapings of the blade moving back and forth.)

Tyb. Quarte beat thrust	Mer. Quarte parry riposte
Tyb. Quarte parry riposte	Mer. Quarte parry head cut, flank cut
Tyb. Quinte parry, seconde parry, head cut, flank cut	
	Mer. Quinte parry, seconde parry, disengage thrust
Tyb. Counter seconde parry	Mer. Repeat thrust
Tyb. Counter seconde parry	

(Both step forward, clash, push each other away and draw dagger.)

| Tyb. Head cut | Mer. Crossing over head, parry with dagger and rapier, riposte head |

Tyb. Head cut

Mer. Crossing over head, parry
with dagger and rapier,
riposte head

Tyb. Crossing over head, parry
with dagger and rapier

(Simultaneous thrusts with rapier, both parried with daggers. They clash and, in close engagement, turn around exchanging places, pushing each other away. Romeo steps in between and puts his hand up to Mercutio's shoulder.)

Romeo: Draw, Benvolio; beat down their weapons.
Gentlemen, for shame, forbear this outrage!
Tybalt, Mercutio, the Prince expressly hath
Forbid this bandying in Verona streets.
Hold, Tybalt! Good Mercutio!
TYBALT UNDER ROMEO'S ARM THRUSTS MERCUTIO, AND FLIES.
(RE-) ENTER Tybalt.

Romeo: (Alive), in triumph. And Mercutio slain!
Away to heaven, respective lenity,
And (fire-eyed) fury be my conduct now!
Now Tybalt, take the "villain" back again
That late thou gav'st me; for Mercutio's soul
Is but a little away above our heads,
Staying for thine to keep him company.
Either thou, or I, or both, must go with him.

Tybalt: Thou, wretched boy, that didst consort him here,
Shalt with him hence.

Romeo: This shall determine that.

(THEY FIGHT)

Rom. Head cut	Tyb. Quinte parry, head riposte
Rom. Quinte parry, chest riposte	Tyb. Prime parry, head riposte
Rom. Quinte parry, head riposte	Tyb. Quinte parry and a wide, angry, chest riposte
Rom. Jump away	Tyb. Missing the chest, a wide head cut
Rom. Passado, thrust	

(TYBALT FALLS)

Romeo: . . . O, be gone!
By heaven, I love thee better than myself,
For I come hither arm'd against myself.
Stay not, be gone; live, and hereafter say
A madman's mercy bid thee run away.
   Paris: I do defy thy (conjurations)
And apprehend thee for a felon here.
   Romeo: Wilt thou provoke me? Then have at thee, boy!
                                                   (THEY FIGHT)

Rom. Head cut	Paris. Quinte parry, head riposte
Rom. Quinte parry, head cut flank cut	Paris. Quinte parry, seconde parry, head cut, flank cut
Rom. Quinte parry, seconde parry, thrust	

Page: O Lord, they fight! I will go call the watch.   (EXIT)
Paris: O, I am slain. (FALLS) If you be merciful,
Open the tomb, lay me with Juliet.   (DIES)

King Lear

In *King Lear* examples are given of the use of long and short swords in the fights. The knights use long swords, the common men short swords (or long daggers). The soldiers are armed with swords and shields and two have two-hand swords. The "Sword of Justice" is always carried, with point up, by the weapon-carrier in the presence of the king. When the king dies, the point is turned down and the sword is held by the blade showing the cross of the sword as the "Sword of Mourning." When the king divides the land between his two daughters, he uses the sword to point the dividing lines on the map.

In the ceremonial fight Edgar and Edmund use long swords but no shields. Edgar is a champion of knights who strictly follows the knightly etiquettes. Edmund is a vicious noble person who is cruel but fair.

We now quote the scenes adding the explanations and comments in upper case letters.

ACT II. SCENE 1

Edgar: . . . I am sure on't a word.
Edmund: I hear my father coming. Pardon me.
  In cunning I must draw my sword upon you.
  Draw, seem to defend yourself.

THEY BOTH DRAW THEIR DAGGERS AND CIRCLING AROUND MAKE THRUSTS TOWARD EACH OTHER. EACH GRABS THE DAGGER-HAND OF THE OTHER WITH HIS FREE HAND AND STRUGGLE FOR A WHILE.

                    now quit you well.
Yield! Come before my father! Light ho here!
Fly, brother. Torches, torches!—So farewell.

ACT II. SCENE 2

Kent: What a brazen-faced varlet are thou to deny thou knowest me! Is it two days since I tripped up thy heels and beet thee befor the King? (*Drawing his sword*) Draw, you rogue, for though it be night, yet the moon shines. I'll make a sop o' th' moonshine of you you whoreson cullionly barbermonger, draw!
Oswald: Away, I have nothing to do with thee.
Kent: Draw, you rascal. You come with letters against the King, and take Vanity the puppet's part against the royalty of her father. Draw you rogue, or I'll so carbonado your shanks. Draw, you rascal. Come your ways!

OSWALD IS NOT WILLING TO FIGHT.

Oswald: Help, ho! Murder! Help!
Kent: Strike, you slave! Stand rogue! Stand you neat slave! Strike! (*Beating him*)

KENT SPANKS OSWALD WITH THE FLAT OF THE SWORD, OSWALD RUNS AROUND.
Oswald: Help, ho! Murder, murder!

(*Enter Edmund, with his rapier drawn, Cornwall Regan, Glou-chester, Servants*)

Edmund: How now? What's the matter? Part!

Kent: With you, goodman boy, if you please! Come I'll flesh ye, come on, young master.

Glouchester: Weapons? Arms? What's the matter here?

FIGHT DOES NOT MATERIALIZE.

ACT II. SCENE 7

First servant: Hold your hand, my lord!
    I have served you ever since I was a child;
    But better service have I never done you
    Than now to bid you hold

Regan: How now, you dog?

First servant: If you did wear a beard upon your chin,
    I'd shake it on this quarrel. What do you mean!

Cornwall: My villain!

(Draw and fight)

CORNWALL WITH LONG, SERVANT WITH SHORT SWORD.

Cornwall. 1. Head-flank cut   Servant. 2. Quinte-seconde parry
          3. Head-flank cut   4. Quinte-seconde parry
          5. Thrust   MISSES

First servant: Nay, then, come on, and take the chance of anger.

WOUNDS CORNWALL IN GUT

Regan: Give me thy sword. A peasant stand up thus?
    (She takes a sword and runs at him behind, kills him.)

ACT IV. SCENE 6

OSWALD, GLOUCHESTER, AND EDGAR ON SCENE. OSWALD TEASINGLY SWINGS THE POINT OF HIS LIGHT SWORD IN THE FRONT OF GLOUCHESTER'S FACE. EDGAR IS DIGUISED, OSWALD DOES NOT RECOGNIZE HIM.

Oswald: Wherefore hold peasant,
    Dar'st thou support a published traitor? Hence!

Lest that th' infection of his fortune take
Like hold on thee. Let go his arm.
Edgar: Chill let not go, zir, without vurther 'casion.
Oswald: Let go, slave, or thou diest!
Edgar: Good gentleman, go your gait, and let poor volk pass. And chud ha'bin zwaggered out of my life 'twould not ha'bin zo long as 'tis by a vortnight. Nay come not near th' old man; keep out, che vor' ye, or I'se try whether your costard or my ballow be the harder: chill be plain with you.
Oswald: Out, dunghill!

(*They fight*)

OSWALD SWINGS HIS SWORD CLOSE TO EDGAR'S FACE.
Edgar: Chill pick your teeth, zir: come; no matter vor your foins.

EDGAR TAKES A HIDDEN DAGGER AND DUCKING UNDER OSWALD'S SWORD,
STABS HIM IN THE STOMACH.

(*Oswald falls*)

ACT V. SCENE 3

EDGAR AND EDMUND'S FIGHT TAKES PLACE ON A HIGH PLATFORM
ABOVE THE STAGE. THEIR SWORDS ARE DRAWN.

Edmund: In wisdom I should ask thy name,
But since thy outside looks so fair and warlike,
And that thy tounge say of breading breathes,
What safe and nicely I might well delay
By rule of knighthood, I disdane and spurn:
Back do I toss these treasons to thy head;
With the hell-hated lie o'erhelm thy heart:
Which for they yet glance by and scarcely bruise
This sword of mine shall give them instant way,
Where they shall rest for ever. Trumpets, speak!

(*Alarums. They fight*)

THEY SALUTE EACH OTHER. BOTH GET INTO ON GUARD POSITION. EDGAR
ADVANCES TAPPING EDMUND'S BLADE ON BOTH SIDES, EDMUND RE-
TREATS. EDMUND TAKES OVER, ADVANCES TAPPING EDGAR'S BLADE ON
BOTH SIDES, EDGAR RETREATS.

Edmund. 1. Head cut

3. Quinte parry,
head riposte

Edgar. 2. Quinte parry,
head riposte

4. Quinte parry

PART. SHORT PAUSE.

Edgar. 1. Head cut

Edmund. 2. Quinte parry,
flank cut

3. Seconde parry,
head cut

4. Quinte parry,
chest cut

5. Prime parry

PART. SHORT PAUSE.

EDMUND MAKES WIDE SWINGING CUTS TO RIGHT AND LEFT, EDGAR STEPS BACK TO AVOID THE CUTS. MOVING IN CIRCLE THEY CHANGE ENDS.

Edmund. 1. Head-flank cuts

Edgar. 2. Quinte-seconde
parries

3. Head-flank cuts

4. Quinte-seconde
parries

REPEAT.

PART. SHORT PAUSE.

THEY ENGAGE THE BLADES. SLIDING ALONG THE BLADE, CLASH. IN LOCK THEY CHANGE ENDS. PUSHING AWAY EACH OTHER WITH THEIR LEFT ARMS, PART.

Edmund. 1. Thrust

3. Repeated thrust

Edgar. 2. Seconde parry

4. Circular seconde parry

PART. SHORT PAUSE.

EDGAR GRABBING HIS SWORD'S HANDLE WITH BOTH HANDS

Edgar. 1. Head cut

Edmund. 2. Quinte parry

3. Chest cut

4. Prime parry

5. Head cut

6. Quinte parry

7. Thrust HIT.

8. LOOSING HIS SWORD FALLS.

EDMUND DRAWS HIS DAGGER TO KILL THE WOUNDED OPPONENT DELIV-
ERING HIM FROM SUFFERING. EDMUND CREEPS TO THE EDGE OF THE
PLATFORM AND ROLLING OVER THE EDGE OF THE PLATFORM FALLS
DOWN TO THE LOWER STAGE.

WITH THE PAUSES THE RHYTHM OF THE FIGHT CAN BE CHANGED. TO
ADD MORE DRAMATICS TO THE FIGHT, BATTLE CRIES SHOULD BE USED
DURING THE ACTIONS.

Appendix

Summary of the Olympic and World Championship Winners According to Nations

Because in sports nations are ranked by the Olympic medals they have received, in this summary modern fencing will be viewed through Olympic results. Only the winners of yearly World Championships are given except where special emphasis is needed or when countries have not won gold medals.

Italy

Olympic results:

1908	London	Saber team	—: *2nd*
1912	Stockholm	Men's foil individual	*1st: N. Nadi*
1920	Antwerp	Men's foil team	—: *1st*
		Épée team	—: *1st*
		Saber team	—: *1st*
		Men's foil individual	*1st: N. Nadi*
		Saber individual	*1st: N. Nadi*
			2nd: A. Nadi
1924	Paris	Épée team	—: *3rd*
		Saber team	—: *1st*
1928	Amsterdam	Men's foil team	—: *1st*
		Épée team	—: *1st*
		Saber team	—: *2nd*
		Men's foil individual	3rd: Gaudini
		Saber individual	3rd: Bini
1932	Los Angeles	Men's foil team	—: *2nd*

		Épée team	—: 2nd
		Saber team	—: 2nd
		Men's foil individual	1st: *Marzi*
			3rd: Gaudini
		Épée individual	1st: *Cornaggia-Medici*
			3rd: Agostoni
		Saber individual	2nd: Gaudini
1936	Berlin	Men's foil team	—: *1st*
		Épée team	—: *1st*
		Saber team	—: 2nd
		Men's foil individual	1st: *Gaudini*
			3rd: Bocchino
		Épée individual	1st: *Riccardi*
			2nd: Ragno
			3rd: Cornaggia-Medici
		Saber individual	2nd: Marzi
1948	London	Men's foil team	—: 2nd
		Épée team	—: 2nd
		Saber team	—: 2nd
		Épée individual	1st: *Cantone*
			3rd: E. Mangiarotti
		Saber individual	2nd: Pinton
1952	Helsinki	Men's foil team	—: 2nd
		Épée team	—: *1st*
		Saber team	—: 2nd
		Men's foil individual	2nd: E. Mangierotti
		Épée individual	1st: *E. Mangierotti*
			2nd: D. Mangierotti
		Ladies' foil individual	1st: *Camber*
1956	Melbourne	Men's foil team	—: *1st*
		Épée team	—: *1st*
		Men's foil individual	2nd: Bergamini
			3rd: Spallino
		Épée individual	1st: *Pavesi*
			2nd: Delfino
			3rd: E. Mangierotti
1960	Rome	Men's foil team	—: 2nd
		Épée team	—: *1st*
		Saber team	—: 3rd
		Ladies' foil team	—: 3rd
		Épée individual	1st: *Delfino*

1964	Tokyo	Saber individual	3rd: Calarese
		Épée Team	—: 2nd
		Saber Team	—: 2nd
		Ladies' foil individual	3rd: Ragno

World Championship results:

1906	Athens	Saber individual	3rd: Ceserano
1926	Budapest	Men's foil individual	*1st: Chiavacci*
1927	Vichy	Men's foil individual	*1st: Puliti*
1929	Naples	Men's foil team	—: 1st
		Men's foil individual	*1st: Puliti*
1930	Liege	Men's foil team	—: 1st
		Men's foil individual	*1st: Gaudini*
1931	Vienna	Men's foil team	—: *1st*
		Épée team	—: *1st*
1933	Budapest	Men's foil team	—: *1st*
		Épée team	—: *1st*
		Men's foil individual	*1st: Guaragna*
1934	Warsaw	Men's foil team	—: *1st*
		Men's foil individual	*1st: Gaudini*
1935	Lausanne	Men's foil team	—: *1st*
1937	Paris	Men's foil team	—: *1st*
		Épée team	—: *1st*
		Men's foil individual	*1st: Marzi*
1938	Piestany	Men's foil team	—: *1st*
		Saber team	—: *1st*
		Men's foil individual	*1st: Guaragna*
		Saber individual	*1st: Montano*
1947	Lisbon	Saber team	—: *1st*
		Saber individual	*1st: Montano*
1949	Cairo	Men's foil team	—: *1st*
		Épée team	—: *1st*
		Saber team	—: *1st*
		Épée individual	*1st: D. Mangierotti*
		Saber individual	*1st: Dare*
1950	Monte Carlo	Men's foil team	—: *1st*
		Épée team	—: *1st*
		Saber team	—: *1st*
		Men's foil individual	*1st: Nostini*
1951	Stockholm	Men's foil individual	*1st: DiRosa*
		Épée individual	*1st: E. Mangiarotti*

1953	Brussels	Épée team	—: *1st*
		Ladies' foil individual	*1st: Camber*
1954	Luxembourg	Men's foil team	—: *1st*
		Épée team	—: *1st*
		Épée individual	*1st: E. Mangierotti*
1955	Rome	Men's foil team	—: *1st*
		Épée team	—: *1st*
		Épée individual	*1st: Anglesio*
1957	Paris	Épée team	—: *1st*
		Ladies' foil team	—: *1st*
1958	Philadelphia	Épée team	—: *1st*
		Men's foil individual	*1st: Bergamini*
1959	Budapest	No Gold Medal	
1961	Turin	No Gold Medal	
1962	Buenos Aires	No Gold Medal	
1963	Gdansk	No Gold Medal	

France

Olympic results:

1896	Athens	Men's foil individual	*1st: Gravelotte*
			2nd: Callot
			3rd: Dankla
1900	Paris	Men's foil individual	*1st: Costa*
			2nd: Masson
			3rd: Boulenger
		Épée individual	2nd: Perrèe
			3rd: Sèe
		Saber individual	*1st: de la Falaise*
			2nd: Thiebaud
1908	London	Épée team	—: *1st*
		Saber team	—: 2nd
		Épée individual	*1st: Alibert*
			2nd: Lippmann
1912	Stockholm	No Medal	
1920	Antwerp	Men's foil team	—: 2nd
		Épée team	—: 3rd
		Saber team	—: 2nd
		Men's foil individual	2nd: Cattiau
		Épée individual	*1st: Massard*
1924	Paris	Men's foil team	—: *1st*

		Épée team	—: *1st*
		Men's foil individual	*1st*: *Ducret*
			2nd: Cattiau
		Épée individual	2nd: Ducret
		Saber individual	2nd: Ducret
1928	Amsterdam	Men's foil team	—: 2nd
		Épée team	—: 2nd
		Men's foil individual	*1st*: *Gaudin*
			2nd: Buchard
1932	Los Angeles	Men's foil team	—: *1st*
		Épée team	—: *1st*
		Épée individual	2nd: Buchard
1936	Berlin	Men's foil team	—: 2nd
		Épée team	—: 3rd
		Men's foil individual	2nd: E. Gardere
1948	London	Men's foil team	—: *1st*
		Épée team	—: *1st*
		Men's foil individual	*1st*: *Buhan*
			2nd: D'Oriola
1952	Helsinki	Men's foil team	—: *1st*
		Saber team	—: 3rd
		Men's foil individual	*1st*: *D'Oriola*
1956	Melbourne	Men's foil team	—: 2nd
		Épée team	—: 3rd
		Men's foil individual	*1st*: *D'Oriola*
		Ladies' foil individual	3rd: Garilhe
1960	Rome	No (1. 2. 3.) Medals	
1964	Tokyo	Men's foil team	—: 3rd
		Épée team	—: 3rd
		Men's foil individual	2nd: Magnan
			3rd: Revenu
		Saber individual	2nd: Arabo

World Championship results:

1906	Athens	Épée team	—: *1st*
		Men's foil individual	*1st*: *Dillon-Cavanagh*
			3rd: d'Hugues
		Épée individual	*1st*: *de la Falaise*
			2nd: Dillon-Cavanagh
1921	Paris	Épée individual	*1st*: *Gaudin*
1925	Ostend	Épée individual	*1st*: *Tainturier*

1927	Vichy	Épée individual	*1st: Buchard*
1929	Naples	Épée individual	*1st: Cattiau*
1930	Liege	Épée individual	*1st: Cattiau*
1931	Vienna	Men's foil individual	*1st: Lemoine*
		Épée individual	*1st: Buchard*
1933	Budapest	Épée individual	*1st: Buchard*
1934	Warsaw	Épée team	*—: 1st*
1935	Lausanne	Épée team	*—: 1st*
		Men's foil individual	*1st: E. Gardere*
1937	Paris	Épée individual	*1st: Shmetz*
1938	Piestany	Épée team	*—: 1st*
		Épée individual	*1st: Pecheux*
1947	Lisbon	Men's foil team	*—: 1st*
		Épée team	*—: 1st*
		Men's foil individual	*1st: D'Oriola*
		Épée individual	*1st: Artigas*
1949	Cairo	Men's foil individual	*1st: D'Oriola*
1950	Monte Carlo	Ladies' foil team	*—: 1st*
		Saber individual	*1st: Levavasseur*
1951	Stockholm	Men's foil team	*—: 1st*
		Épée team	*—: 1st*
		Ladies' foil team	*—: 1st*
1953	Brussels	Men's foil team	*—: 1st*
		Men's foil individual	*1st: D'Oriola*
1954	Luxembourg	Men's foil individual	*1st: D'Oriola*
1955	Rome	No Gold Medal	
1957	Paris	Épée individual	*1st: Mouyal*
1958	Philadelphia	Men's foil team	*—: 1st*
1959	Budapest	No Gold Medal	
1961	Turin	Épée individual	*1st: Guittet*
1962	Buenos Aires	Épée team	*—: 1st*
1963	Gdansk	Men's foil individual	*1st: Magnan*
1965	Paris	Épée team	*—: 1st*
		Men's foil individual	*1st: Magnan*

Hungary

Olympic results:

1908	London	Saber team	*—: 1st*
		Saber individual	*1st: Fuchs*
			2nd: Zulawski
1912	Stockholm	Saber team	*—: 1st*

		Saber individual	1st: Fuchs
			2nd: Békessy
			3rd: Mészáros
1920	Antwerp	No team allowed	
1924	Paris	Men's foil team	—: 3rd
		Saber team	—: 2nd
		Saber individual	1st: Posta
			2nd: Garay
1928	Amsterdam	Saber team	—: 1st
		Saber individual	1st: Tersztianszky
			2nd: Petschauer
1932	Los Angeles	Saber team	—: 1st
		Saber individual	1st: Piller
			3rd: Kabos
		Ladies' individual foil	3rd: Bogáthy
1936	Berlin	Saber team	—: 1st
		Saber individual	1st: Kabos
			3rd: Gerevich
		Ladies' foil individual	1st: I. Elek
1948	London	Saber team	—: 1st
		Men's foil individual	3rd: Maszlay
		Saber individual	1st: Gerevich
			3rd: Kovács
		Ladies' foil individual	1st: I. Elek
1952	Helsinki	Men's foil team	—: 3rd
		Saber team	—: 1st
		Saber individual	1st: Kovács
			2nd: Gerevich
			3rd: Berczelly
1956	Melbourne	Men's foil team	—: 3rd
		Épée team	—: 2nd
		Saber team	—: 1st
		Saber individual	1st: Kárpáti
1960	Rome	Saber team	—: 1st
		Ladies' foil team	—: 2nd
		Saber individual	1st: Kárpáti
			2nd: Horváth
1964	Tokyo	Épée team	—: 1st
		Ladies' foil team	—: 1st
		Saber individual	1st: Pesza
		Ladies' foil individual	1st: Rejtö

World Championship results:

1925	Ostend	Saber individual	*1st*: Garay
1926	Budapest	Saber individual	*1st*: Gombos
1927	Vichy	Saber individual	*1st*: Gombos
1929	Naples	Saber individual	*1st*: Glykais
1930	Liege	Saber team	—: *1st*
		Saber individual	*1st*: Piller
1931	Vienna	Saber team	—: *1st*
		Saber individual	*1st*: Piller
1933	Budapest	Saber team	—: *1st*
		Ladies' foil team	—: *1st*
		Saber individual	*1st*: Kabos
1934	Warsaw	Saber team	—: *1st*
		Ladies' foil team	—: *1st*
		Épée individual	*1st*: Dunay
		Saber individual	*1st*: Kabos
		Ladies' foil individual	*1st*: I. Elek
1935	Lausanne	Saber team	—: *1st*
		Ladies' foil team	—: *1st*
		Saber individual	*1st*: Gerevich
		Ladies' foil individual	*1st*: I. Elek
1937	Paris	Saber team	—: *1st*
		Ladies' foil team	—: *1st*
		Saber individual	*1st*: Kovács
1938	Piestany	Not participating	
1947	Lisbon	Not participating	
1950	Monte Carlo	Not participating	
1951	Stockholm	Saber team	—: *1st*
		Saber individual	*1st*: Gerevich
		Ladies' foil individual	*1st*: I. Elek
1952	Copenhagen	Ladies' foil team	—: *1st*
1953	Brussels	Saber team	—: *1st*
		Ladies' foil team	—: *1st*
		Épée individual	*1st*: Sákovics
		Saber individual	*1st*: Kovács
1954	Luxembourg	Saber team	—: *1st*
		Ladies' foil team	—: *1st*
		Saber individual	*1st*: Kárpáti
1955	Rome	Saber team	—: *1st*
		Ladies' foil team	—: *1st*
		Men's foil individual	*1st*: Gyuricza

		Saber individual	1st: *Gerevich*
		Ladies' foil individual	1st: *Dömölki*
1957	Paris	Men's foil team	—: *1st*
		Saber team	—: *1st*
		Men's foil individual	1st: *Fülöp*
1958	Philadelphia	Saber team	—: *1st*
1959	Budapest	Épée team	—: *1st*
		Ladies' foil team	—: *1st*
		Saber individual	1st: *Kárpáti*
1961	Turin	No Gold Medal	
1962	Buenos Aires	Ladies' foil team	—: *1st*
		Épée individual	1st: *Kausz*
		Saber individual	1st: *Horváth*
1963	Gdansk	Ladies' foil individual	1st: *Rejtö*
1965	Paris	Saber individual	1st: *Nemere*

England

Olympic results:

1896	Athens	Men's foil individual	3rd: Dankla
1908	London	Épée team	—: 2nd
1912	Stockholm	Épée team	—: 2nd
1924	Paris	Ladies' foil individual	2nd: Davis
1928	Amsterdam	Ladies' foil individual	2nd: Freeman
1932	Los Angeles	Ladies' foil individual	2nd: Guiness
1956	Melbourne	Ladies' foil individual	1st: *Sheen*
1960	Rome	Épée team	—: 2nd
		Épée individual	2nd: Jay
1964	Tokyo	Épée individual	2nd: Hoskyns

World Championship results:

1906	Athens	Épée team	—: 2nd
1931	Vienna	Men's foil individual	3rd: Lloyd
1933	Budapest	Men's foil individual	3rd: Lloyd
		Ladies' foil team	—: 2nd
		Ladies' foil individual	1st: *Neligan*
1934	Warsaw	Ladies' foil team	—: 3rd
1950	Monte Carlo	Ladies' foil team	—: 3rd
1955	Rome	Men's foil team	—: 3rd
1957	Paris	Men's foil individual	2nd: Jay
1958	Philadelphia	Épée individual	1st: *Hoskyns*

1959	Budapest	Men's foil individual	*1st: Jay*
		Épée individual	2nd: Jay

Russia

Olympic results:

1956	Melbourne	Saber team	—: 3rd
		Saber individual	3rd: Kouzenetsov
1960	Rome	Men's foil team	—: *1st*
		Épée team	—: 3rd
		Ladies' foil team	—: *1st*
		Men's foil individual	*1st: Jdanovics*
			2nd: Sissikin
		Épée individual	3rd: Khabarov
		Ladies' foil individual	2nd: Rostvorova
1964	Tokyo	Men's foil team	—: *1st*
		Saber team	—: *1st*
		Ladies' foil team	—: 2nd
		Épée individual	*1st: Kriss*
			3rd: Kostava
		Saber individual	2nd: Mavlikhanov
			3rd: Rylsky

World Championship results:

1957	Paris	Ladies' foil individual	*1st: Zabelina*
1958	Philadelphia	Ladies' foil team	—: *1st*
		Saber individual	*1st: Rylsky*
		Ladies' foil individual	*1st: Kiszeleva*
1959	Budapest	Men's foil team	—: *1st*
		Épée individual	*1st: Khabarov*
		Ladies' foil individual	*1st: Efimova*
1961	Turin	Men's foil team	—: *1st*
		Épée team	—: *1st*
		Ladies' foil team	—: *1st*
		Saber individual	*1st: Rylsky*
1962	Buenos Aires	Men's foil team	—: *1st*
		Épée team	—: *1st*
		Men's foil individual	*1st: Sveshnikov*
1963	Gdansk	Men's foil team	—: *1st*
		Ladies' foil team	—: *1st*
		Saber individual	*1st: Rylskii*
1965	Paris	Men's foil team	—: *1st*

Ladies' foil team	—: *1st*
Saber team	—: *1st*
Ladies' foil individual	*1st*: *Gorokhova*

Germany

Olympic results:

1928	Amsterdam	Men's foil individual	2nd: E. Casmir
		Ladies' foil individual	*1st*: *Mayer*
			3rd: Oelkers
1936	Berlin	Men's foil team	—: 3rd
		Saber team	—: 3rd
		Ladies' foil individual	2nd: Mayer
1960	Rome	Men's foil team	—: 3rd
		Ladies' foil individual	*1st*: *Schmid*
1964	Tokyo	Ladies' foil team	—: 3rd
		Ladies' foil individual	2nd: H. Mees

World Championship results:

1906	Athens	Épée team	—: 3rd
		Saber team	—: *1st*
		Men's foil individual	2nd: G. Casmir
1931	Vienna	Ladies' foil individual	*1st*: *Mayer*
1936	San Remo	Ladies' foil team	—: *1st*
1937	Paris	Ladies' foil individual	*1st*: *Mayer*
1961	Turin	Ladies' foil individual	*1st*: *Schmid*

Poland

Olympic results:

1928	Amsterdam	Saber team	—: 3rd
1932	Los Angeles	Saber team	—: 3rd
1956	Melbourne	Saber team	—: 2nd
		Saber individual	2nd: Pawlowski
1960	Rome	Saber team	—: 2nd
1964	Tokyo	Men's foil team	—: 2nd
		Saber team	—: 3rd
		Men's foil individual	*1st*: *Franke*

World Championship results:

| 1957 | Paris | Saber individual | *1st*: *Pawlowski* |
| 1959 | Budapest | Saber team | —: *1st* |

		Men's foil individual	1st: *Parulski*
1962	Buenos Aires	Saber team	—: *1st*
1963	Gdansk	Épée team	—: *1st*
		Saber team	—: *1st*
1965	Paris	Saber individual	1st: *Pawlowski*

United States

Olympic results:

1904	St. Louis	Saber team	—: 2nd
		Men's foil individual	3rd: Tatham
		Épée individual	2nd: Tatham
		Saber individual	2nd: Grebe
1920	Atwerp	Men's foil team	—: 3rd
1928	Amsterdam	Épée individual	3rd: Calnan
1932	Los Angeles	Men's foil team	—: 3rd
		Épée team	—: 3rd
		Men's foil individual	2nd: Levis
1948	London	Saber team	—: 3rd
1960	Rome	Men's foil individual	3rd: Axelrod

The Men's foil team in 1948 and 1956—4th
The Saber team in 1932, 1952, and 1956—4th
Ladies' foil individual 1948, 1952, and 1956—4th

World Championship results: no medals.

The rest of the Olympic and World Championship medals have been divided among other nations whose fencing styles were developed parallel to and influenced by the leading nations in fencing technique.

Belgium

Olympic results:

1908	London	Épée team	—: 3rd
		Épée individual	3rd: Anspach
1912	Stockholm	Épée team	—: *1st*
		Épée individual	1st: *Anspach*
			3rd: deBeaulieu
1920	Antwerp	Épée team	—: 2nd

		Épée individual	3rd: Gevers
1924	Paris	Men's foil individual	3rd: Van Damme
		Épée team	—: 2nd
		Épée individual	*1st*: *Delport*

World Championship results:

		Épée team	—: *1st*
1930	Liège	Ladies' foil individual	*1st*: *Addams*

Denmark

Olympic results:

1896	Athens	Saber individual	3rd: Nielsen
1912	Stockholm	Épée individual	2nd: I. Osiier
1924	Paris	Ladies' foil individual	*1st*: *E. D. Osiier*
			3rd: Heckscher
1948	London	Ladies' foil individual	2nd: Lachmann
1952	Helsinki	Ladies' foil individual	3rd: Lachmann

World Championship results:

1906	Athens	Saber individual	2nd: Vasimir
1932	Copenhagen	Ladies' foil team	—: *1st*
1947	Lisbon	Ladies' foil team	—: *1st*
1948	The Hague	Ladies' foil team	—: *1st*
1950	Monte Carlo	Épée individual	*1st*: *Luchov*
1954	Luxembourg	Ladies' foil individual	*1st*: *Lachmann*

Austria

Olympic results:

1900	Paris	Saber individual	3rd: Flesh
1912	Stockholm	Saber team	—: 2nd
		Men's foil individual	3rd: Verderber
1932	Los Angeles	Ladies' foil individual	*1st*: *Preiss*
1936	Berlin	Ladies' foil individual	3rd: Preiss
1948	London	Ladies' foil individual	3rd: Preiss

World Championship results:

1947	Lisbon	Ladies' foil individual	*1st*: *Preiss*
1949	Cairo	Ladies' foil individual	*1st*: *Preiss*
1950	Monte Carlo	Ladies' foil individual	*1st*: *Preiss*
1963	Gdansk	Épée individual	*1st*: *Losert*

Holland

1912	Stockholm	Saber team	—: 3rd
1920	Antwerp	Saber team	—: 3rd
1924	Paris	Saber team	—: 3rd

World Championship results:

1906	Athens	Épée individual	3rd: Van Blyenburgh
1922	Paris	Saber individual	*1st: deJong*
1923	The Hague	Épée individual	*1st: Brouver*
		Saber individual	*1st: deJong*

Saber team 1938—3rd
Épée individual 1921—3rd, 1923—3rd
Saber individual 1923—3rd
Ladies' foil individual 1929—2nd

Sweden

Olympic results:

1924	Paris	Épée individual	3rd: Hellsten
1936	Berlin	Épée team	—: 2nd
1948	London	Épée team	—: 3rd
1952	Helsinki	Épée team	—: 2nd

World Championship results:

1935	Lousanne	Épée individual	*1st: Drakenberg*

Épée team: 1931—3rd, 1933—3rd, 1934—3rd, 1935—2nd, 1937—3rd, 1938—2nd, 1947—2nd, 1949—2nd, 1950—3rd, 1954—2nd, 1961—3rd, 1962—2nd.
Épée individual: 1934—2nd and 3rd, 1947—2nd, 1950—3rd, 1951—3rd, 1961—2nd.

Czechoslovakia (1908, Bohemia)

Olympic results:

1908	London	Saber team	—: 3rd
		Saber individual	3rd: Gophold v. Lobsdorf

World Championship results:

1938	Piestany	Ladies' foil individual	*1st: Sediva*

| Ladies' foil individual | —: 2nd |
| Men's foil team | —: 3rd |

Switzerland

Olympic results:

| 1948 | London | Épée individual | 2nd: Zapelli |
| 1952 | Helsinki | Épée individual | 3rd: Zapelli |

World Champion results:

| 1953 | Brussels | Épée team | —: 3rd |

Romania

Olympic results:

| 1956 | Melbourne | Ladies' foil individual | 2nd: Orban |
| 1960 | Rome | Ladies' foil individual | 3rd: Vicol |

World Championship results:

| 1961 | Turin | Ladies' foil team | —: 3rd |
| 1962 | Buenos Aires | Ladies' foil individual | *1st: Orban-Szabo* |

Portugal

Olympic results:

| 1928 | Amsterdam | Épée team | —: 3rd |

Argentina

Olympic results:

| 1928 | Amsterdam | Men's foil team | —: 3rd |

Norway

World Championship results:

| 1922 | Paris | Épée individual | *1st: Heide* |

Egypt

World Championship results:

| 1947 | Lisbon | Saber team | —: 3rd |
| 1949 | Cairo | Men's foil team | —: 3rd |

1950	Monte Carlo	Épée team	—: 3rd
		Saber team	—: 3rd
		Men's foil team	—: 3rd
		Saber team	—: 3rd
1951	Stockholm	Men's foil team	—: 3rd

The airplane carrying the Egyptian team and their Hungarian coach, E. Tily, to the 1958 World Championships in Philadelphia crashed into the Mediterranean; there were no survivors.

Greece

Olympic results:

| 1896 | Athens | Saber individual | *1st*: *Giorgiades* |
| | | | 2nd: Karakalos |

World Championship results:

| 1906 | Athens | Saber team | —: 2nd |
| | | Saber individual | *1st*: *Giorgiades* |

Cuba

Olympic results:

1900	Paris	Épée individual	*1st*: *Fonst*
1904	St. Louis	Saber team	—: *1st*
		Men's foil individual	*1st*: *Fonst*
			2nd: Van Zo Post
		Épée individual	*1st*: *Fonst*
			3rd: Van Zo Post
		Saber individual	*1st*: *DeDiaz*
			3rd: Van Zo Post

Grand Total of Olympic and World Championship Gold Medals in Fencing

(Including 1964 Olympics and 1965 World Championships)

Hungary	75	Belgium	5
Italy	69	Cuba	5
France	54	Great Britain	4
Russia	27	Holland	3
Poland	9	Greece	2
Germany	8	Czechoslovakia	1
Denmark	6	Romania	1
Austria	5	Norway	1

Summary of the Olympic Gold Medals in Fencing

(Including 1964)

Nation	Medal		Total
	Team	Individual	
Hungary	11	14	25
Italy	12	11	23
France	8	11	19
Russia	4	2	6
Cuba	1	4	5
Belgium	1	2	3
Germany	—	2	2
Austria	—	1	1
Great Britain	—	1	1
Denmark	—	1	1
Greece	—	1	1
Poland	—	1	1

Summary of the World Championship Gold Medals in Fencing

(Including 1965)

| Nation | Medal | | Total |
	Team	Individual	
Hungary	24	26	50
Italy	27	19	46
France	13	22	35
Russia	12	9	21
Poland	5	3	8
Germany	2	4	6
Denmark	3	2	5
Austria	—	4	4
Great Britain	—	3	3
Holland	—	3	3
Belgium	1	1	2
Sweden	—	1	1
Czechoslovakia	—	1	1
Romania	—	1	1
Norway	—	1	1
Greece	—	1	1

Summary of Olympic Championships in Fencing

Events	Men's foil team	Epee team	Saber team	Ladies' foil team	Men's foil indiv.	Epee individual	Saber individual	Ladies' foil indiv.
1896 Athens	—	—	—	—	Gravelotte/France	—	Giorgiades/Greece	—
1900 Paris	—	—	—	—	Coste/France	Fonst/Cuba	de la Falaise/France	—
1904 St. Louis	—	—	Cuba	—	Fonst/Cuba	Fonst/Cuba	DeDiaz/Cuba	—
1908 London	—	France	Hungary	—	—	Alibert/France	Fuchs/Hungary	—
1912 Stockholm	—	Belgium	Hungary	—	N. Nadi/Italy	Anspach/Belgium	Fuchs/Hungary	—
1920 Antwerp	Italy	Italy	Italy	—	N. Nadi/Italy	Massard/France	—	—
1924 Paris	France	France	Italy	—	Ducret/France	Delport/Belgium	Posta/Hungary	Ossier/Denmark
1928 Amsterdam	Italy	Italy	Hungary	—	Gaudin/France	Gaudin/France	Terstianszky/Hungary	Mayer/Germany
1932 Los Angeles	France	France	Hungary	—	Marzi/Italy	Cornaggia-Medici/Italy	Piller/Hungary	Preiss/Austria
1936 Berlin	Italy	Italy	Hungary	—	Gaudini/Italy	Riccardi/Italy	Kabos/Hungary	I. Elek/Hungary
1948 London	France	France	Hungary	—	Buhan/France	Cantone/Italy	Gerevich/Hungary	I. Elek/Hungary
1952 Helsinki	France	Italy	Hungary	—	D'Oriola/France	E. Mangierotti/Italy	Kovacs/Hungary	Camber/Italy
1956 Melbourne	Italy	Italy	Hungary	—	D'Oriola/France	Pavesi/Italy	Karpati/Hungary	Sheen/Great Britain
1960 Rome	Russia	Italy	Hungary	Russia	Jdanovich/Russia	Delfino/Italy	Karpati/Hungary	Schmid/Germany
1964 Tokyo	Russia	Hungary	Russia	Hungary	Franke/Poland	Kriss/Russia	Pezsa/Hungary	Rejto/Hungary

Summary of World Championships in Fencing

Events	Men's foil team	Epee team	Saber team	Ladies' foil team	Men's foil indiv.	Epee individual	Saber individual	Ladies' foil indiv.
1906 Athens	—	France	Germany	—	Dillon-Cavanagh/France	de la Falaise/France	Giorgiades/Greece	—
1921 Paris	—	—	—	—	—	Gaudin/France	—	—
1922 Paris	—	—	—	—	—	Heide/Norway	deJong/Holland	—
1923 The Hague	—	—	—	—	—	Brouver/Holland	deJong/Holland	—
1925 Ostend	—	—	—	—	—	—	Garay/Hungary	—
1926 Budapest	—	—	—	—	Chiavacci/Italy	Tainturier/France	Gombos/Hungary	—
1927 Vichy	—	—	—	—	Puliti/Italy	Bouchard/France	Gombos/Hungary	—
1929 Naples	Italy	—	—	—	Puliti/Italy	Cattiau/France	Glyckais/Hungary	Mayer/Germany
1930 Liege	Italy	Belgium	Hungary	—	Gaudini/Italy	Cattiau/France	Piller/Hungary	Addams/Belgium
1931 Vienna	Italy	Italy	Hungary	—	Lemoine/France	Bouchard/France	Piller/Hungary	Mayer/Germany
1932 Copenhagen	—	—	—	Denmark	—	—	—	—
1933 Budapest	Italy	Italy	Hungary	Hungary	Guaragna/Italy	Buchard/France	Kabos/Hungary	Neligan/Great Britain
1934 Warsaw	Italy	France	Hungary	Hungary	Gaudini/Italy	Dunay/Hungary	Kabos/Hungary	I. Elek/Hungary
1935 Lausanne	Italy	France	Hungary	Hungary	Cardere/France	Drakenberg/Sweden	Gerevich/Hungary	I. Elek/Hungary
1936 San Remo	—	—	—	Germany	—	—	—	—
1937 Paris	Italy	Italy	Hungary	Hungary	Marzi/Italy	Smetz/France	Kovacs/Hungary	Mayer/Germany
1938 Piestany	Italy	France	Italy	—	Guaragna/Italy	Pecheux/France	Montano/Italy	Sediva/Czechoslovakia

Year / City								
1947 Lisbon	France	France	Italy	Denmark	D'Oriola/France	Artigas/France	Montano/Italy	Preiss/Austria
1948 The Hague	Italy	Italy	Italy	Denmark	D'Oriola/France	D. Mangierotti/Italy	Dare/Italy	Preiss/Austria
1949 Cairo	Italy	Italy	Italy	France	R. Nostini/Italy	Luchow/Denmark	Levavasseur/France	Preiss/Austria
1950 Monte Carlo	France	France	Hungary	France	DiRosa/Italy	E. Mangierotti/Italy	Gerevich/Hungary	—
1951 Stockholm	—	—	—	Hungary	—	—	—	I. Elek/Hungary
1952 Copenhagen	France	Italy	Hungary	—	D'Oriola/France	—	—	—
1953 Brussels	Italy	Italy	Hungary	Hungary	D'Oriola/France	Sakovics/Hungary	Kovacs/Hungary	Camber/Italy
1954 Luxembourg	Italy	Italy	Hungary	Hungary	D'Oriola/France	E. Mangierotti/Italy	Karpati/Hungary	Lachmann/Denmark
1955 Rome	—	—	—	Hungary	Gyuricza/Hungary	Anglesio/Italy	Gerevich/Hungary	Domolki/Hungary
1956 London	Hungary	Hungary	Hungary	Russia	—	—	—	—
1957 Paris	France	Italy	Hungary	Italy	Fulop/Hungary	Mouyal/France	Pawlowski/Poland	Zebelina/Russia
1958 Philadelphia	Russia	Poland	Poland	Russia	Bergamini/Italy	Hoskyns/Great Britain	Rylski/Russia	Kiszeleva/Russia
1959 Budapest	Russia	Russia	Poland	Hungary	Jay/Great Britain	Kabarov/Russia	Karpati/Hungary	Efimova/Russia
1961 Turin	Russia	France	Poland	Russia	Parulski/Poland	Guittet/France	Rylski/Russia	Schmid/Germany
1962 Buenos Aires	Russia	Poland	Poland	Hungary	Sveshnikov/Russia	Kausz/Hungary	Horvath/Hungary	Orban-Szabo/Rumania
1963 Gdansk	Russia	France	Poland	Russia	Magnan/France	Losert/Austria	Rylski/Russia	Rejto/Hungary
1965 Paris	Russia	France	Russia	Russia	Magnan/France	Nemere/Hungary	Pawlowski/Poland	Gorokhova/Russia

References

Emile Merignac: *Histoire de l'escrime*, 1883.

Peccoraro-Pessina: *La scherma di sciabola.*

M. A. Egerton Castle: *Schools and Masters of Fence*, 1893.

A. Hutton: *Sword and the Centuries*, 1901.

Tomanoczy-Gellér: *A vivás kézikönyve*, 1942.

Dr. L. Gerentser: *A Modern Kardvivás*, 1944.

I. E. Koch: *Bühnenfechtkunst*, 1954.

Index

ABSENCE of blades, 87
Actions in time, 94
  in foil fencing, 109–114
  in saber fencing, 162–167
Ambo, 110, 117
Analysis of movement, 39–43
Ancient combat in theatrical fencing, 173, 174
Ancient weapons, 27
Angle thrusts, 121
Apell, 109
Appuntata, 110, 114, 166
Armor
  gothic, 6
  maximilian, 7
Assault-like exercises with master, 70
Attacco simulato, 115
Attack(s)
  compound, in foil fencing, 101–106
  disengage, in foil fencing, 88
  introduced with engagement
    in foil fencing, 96, 97
    in saber fencing, 151
  on blade in foil fencing, 97–99
  with second intention in foil fencing, 112
  with circular movements in saber fencing, 157

BACKSWORDING, 13, 18
Backward roll, 190
Balance, 41
Balestra, 77
Basic fencing rules, 117
Basic positions, 85

Basic routine exercises
  in foil fencing, 90
  in saber fencing, 146, 147
Basic warming-up exercises in theatrical fencing, 189
Battement, 99, 153
Battle of Crècy, 1
Battuta, 99, 153
Bayonet, 15
  in theatrical fencing, 188
Beat
  in épée fencing, 124
  in foil fencing, 99–101
  in saber fencing, 153
Beat-parries, 101
Bind
  in foil fencing, 96
  in saber fencing, 151
Blade
  in line, 87
  of weapons, 69
Blade feeling, 100
Borsody, 21
Botta Scretta, 10
Buckler, 10
  rapier and, in theatrical fencing, 183
  sword and, 13
Bürgerschaft von St. Marcus von Löwenberge, 9
Buttokai, 24
Button, 14

CALCULATED phase of bout, example of, 49
Cane, 31

Cape, 30
Carbohydrates in diet, 58
Cavazione, 88
Cavazione in tempo, 95
Central vision, 45, 46
Check
   in foil fencing, 78
   in saber fencing, 131
      flèche and, 135
Change of engagement
   in foil fencing, 93
   in saber fencing, 152
Changing parries
   in foil fencing, 92, 93
   in saber fencing, 150
Circle parries, 150
Circle quarte, 150
Circle seconde, 150
Circle tierce, 150
Circular-counter-circular-dual feint, 105
Circular-counter-circular feints, 104
Circular parry in foil fencing, 92
Circular passage, 86
Class instruction, 52
Classic flèche attack in saber fencing, 132
Close distance, 87
Close quarters, 87
Cloak, 30
   rapier and, in theatrical fencing, 184, 186
Colpo d'arresto, 110
Combat-like exercises
   in foil fencing, 115
   in saber fencing, 167
Combined exercises
   in épée fencing, 126
   in foil fencing, 92, 101, 105
   in saber fencing, 144, 149, 156, 160
Combined mixed exercises in saber fencing, 156
Combined, progressive and, parry riposte exercises in foil fencing, 107
Competition, 57, 58
Competitive fencing, 63–169. See also épée, foil, and saber.
   general background of, 63, 65
   preparatory and other exercises for, 69, 70

Competitive fencing (Cont.)
   weapons used in, 66
Composite parries
   in foil fencing, 106
   in saber fencing, 158
Compound actions in saber fencing, 155–157
Compound attacks in foil fencing, 101–106
Compound ripostes
   in foil fencing, 107, 108
   in saber fencing, 159
Conditioning the body
   formative stage of, 55
   initial or preparatory stage of, 55
   sustaining stage of, 55
Contra-riposte
   in épée fencing, 113
   in foil fencing, 91
   in saber fencing, 148
Contro-tempo, 113
Copertino, 99
Copoferro, 2
Coquille, 71
Corps à corps, 78
Costumes, 29–31
Coulé, 91, 98, 99
Counter-evasive thrust
   in foil fencing, 95
   in saber fencing, 136
Counter-parry, 92
Counter-riposte in saber fencing, 148
Counter-time
   in foil fencing, 113, 114
   in saber fencing, 167
Coup d'arret, 110
Coup de temps, 110
Coup Droit, 88
Coupé, 95, 104
Coupée, 15
Covered, 88
Croisé, 96
Crossbar, 182
Crossbarred Italian foil, 18
Cudgelling, 18
Cuts in saber fencing
   counter-evasive, 136
   direct, 141–143
   evasive, 136

Cut-over
  in foil fencing, 95, 96
  in saber fencing, 151
    evasive, 136
Cut-over feint, 104

Dagger, 10, 26, 28
  in theatrical fencing, 181
    rapier and, 183, 184
Dead-man backward fall in theatrical
    fencing, 191
Dead-man forward fall in theatrical
    fencing, 190
Defense in foil fencing, 89–101
Degagement, 88
Derobement, 95
Desarmo, 115, 167
Deviamento, 153
Diagonal thrusts, 121
Diet, 58–60
Direct-circular feint, 103
Direct cuts in saber fencing, 141–143
Direct parries
  in foil fencing, 89
  in saber fencing, 144–146
Direct riposte
  in foil fencing, 91
  in saber fencing, 147
Direct thrust
  in foil fencing, 88
  in saber fencing, 141–143
Direct thrust—simple-single feint, 102
Disarmament
  in foil fencing, 115
  in saber fencing, 167
Disengage
  gliding, 97, 98, 104, 151
  sliding, 97, 98, 104
Disengage attack in foil fencing, 88
Disengage-circular feint, 103
Disengage riposte in foil fencing, 93, 94
Disengage-simple-dual feint, 102
Disengage-thrust or cut, 151
Distance, 42
  in foil fencing, 87
  in saber fencing, 87, 141
Doighté, 89
Doppia botta di rimessa, 109

Doubles, 103, 157
Double circulation, 103
Double-step in saber fencing, 131
Dual feints
  in foil fencing, 103
  in saber fencing, 160, 161
Dueling saber, 29
Duels, 36, 37
Dying on stage in theatrical fencing, 193
Dynamics, 40

Early fencing, 2–4
Early middle ages, 4–6
  historical perspective and, 37
Early modern period
  historical perspective and, 38
  theatrical fencing and, 182–187
Eighteenth century, 16–18
  weapons of, 28
Electrum Magicum, 25
Electrical fencing, 117, 118
Engagement(s), 85
  changing, 152
  false, 152
  in foil fencing, 87
  in saber fencing, 150
Engagement direct and indirect thrust
    in foil fencing, 96
Envelopment
  in épée fencing, 122
  in foil fencing, 97
  in saber fencing, 152
Épée, 29, 66, 119–126
  parts of, 119, 120
Épée du combat, 19, 28
Épée fencing, 119–126
  beat in, 124
  footwork in, 120, 121
  hit in, 121
  on guard position in, 120
  other actions in, 122, 124
  parries in, 121, 122
  ripostes in, 121, 122
  target in, 119
Equipment and its proper use, 67–69
Espada, 18
Espadin, 18
Estoc, 5

Evasive cuts in saber fencing, 136, 165
Evasive cut-over in saber fencing, 136
Evasive thrust
  in foil fencing, 95, 101
  in saber fencing, 136, 165
Execution, 48, 49
Exercises
  assault-like, with master, 70
  basic routine
    in foil fencing, 90
    in saber fencing, 146, 147
  combat-like
    in foil fencing, 115
    in saber fencing, 167
  combined
    in épée fencing, 126
    in foil fencing, 92, 101, 105
    in saber fencing, 144, 149, 156,
      160
    progressive and, parry riposte, in
      foil fencing, 107
  combined mixed, in saber fencing,
    156
  for stage movements, 189–195
  free play, 70
  group, in theatrical fencing, 191
  homologous
    in épée fencing, 125
    in saber fencing, 125, 148, 154, 156,
      158
  individual lesson, 70
  miscellaneous, in theatrical fencing,
    191
  mixed, in saber fencing, 143, 154
  mixed progressive, in foil fencing, 106
  progressive
    in foil fencing, 105
    in saber fencing, 161
  progressive combined parry riposte,
    in foil fencing, 108
  reciprocal
    in foil fencing, 116
    in saber fencing, 168
    with partner, 70
  special, in saber fencing, 157, 159
  special foot and hand, 70
  timing, in saber fencing, 163
  warming-up, 69
    in theatrical fencing, 189

Experience, 49–51
Eyes, 43

FAINTING in theatrical fencing, 193
Falling in theatrical fencing, 190, 191
False attacks in foil fencing, 115
False edge, 27
False engagement, 152
False guard, 26
False thrust, 101
Far distance, 87
Fats in diet, 59
Fausse attaques, 115
Fecht Bruderschaft, 9
Feint(s), 98
  against sweeping parries, 104
  circular-counter-circular, 104
  circular-counter-circular-dual, 105
  cut-over, 104
  direct-circular, 103
  disengage-circular, 103
  dual, 103
  in foil fencing, 101–105
  in saber fencing, 155–157
  pressure slide, 103, 104
  simple-dual, 103
  simple-single, 102, 103
  single, 155
Feint in time
  in foil fencing, 113
  in saber fencing, 167
Fencing
  against two or more opponents in
    theatrical fencing, 192
  as a sport, 63, 65
  history of, 1–38
  Molière's definition of, 1
  on stairs in theatrical fencing, 192
  psychology of, 47–51
Fencing jury, 47, 63
Fencing line, 87
Fencing scene
  from Hamlet, 195–202
  from King Lear, 208–213
  from Molière's Don Juan, 202–204
  from Romeo and Juliet, 204–208
Fencing time
  in foil fencing, 94

Fencing time (*Cont.*)
  in saber fencing, 135
Fianconata, 96
Fiefs, 5
Fifteenth century, 7–9
Filo, 98, 99, 152
Filo-feint, 98
Filo riposte, 91
Filo thrust, 99
Finger play, 89
Fingering in saber fencing, 144
Finta, 101, 154
Finta in tempo, 113, 167
Fioretto, 18
First intention attack, 91
First position in foil fencing, 74
Flamberg, 14
Flanconnade in foil fencing, 96
Flèche
  French, 78
  Hungarian, 78
  in épée fencing, 121
  in foil fencing, 78
  in saber fencing, 132–135
Fleuret, 15
Flying parry riposte in saber fencing, 148
Foible of the blade, 27
Foil, 29, 66, 71–118
  parts of, 71
Foil fencing, 71–118
  absence of blades in, 87
  actions in time in, 109–114
  appuntata in, 114
  attacks introduced with engagement
    in, 96, 97
  attacks on blade in, 97–99
  attack with second intention in, 112
  basic routine exercises in, 90
  beat in, 99
  change of engagement in, 93
  changing parry in, 92, 93
  circular parry in, 92
  combined exercises in, 92, 101, 105
  composite parries in, 106
  compound attacks in, 101–106
  compound ripostes in, 107, 108
  contra-riposte in, 91
  counter-evasive thrust in, 95
  counter-time in, 113, 114

Foil fencing (*Cont.*)
  cut-over in, 95, 96
  defense in, 89–101
  direct parry in, 89
  direct riposte in, 91
  direct thrust in, 88
  disarmament in, 115
  disengage attack in, 88
  disengage riposte in, 93, 94
  distances in, 87
  electrical fencing in, 117, 118
  engagement in, 87
  evasive thrust in, 95
  false attacks in, 115
  feint in, 101–105
  feint in time in, 113
  fencing time in, 94
  finger play in, 89
  foot movements in, 75–79
  free play in, 116, 117
  grip in, 71, 73
  hit in, 87
  lines in, 87
  parrying attack on blade in, 101
  parrying attacks with engagement
    in, 97
  passages in, 86
  positions of body in, 74
  positions of weapon in, 81–85
  renewed attacks in, 108, 109
  riposte along blade in, 91
  salute in, 80, 81
  simple actions in, 88, 89
  stop-thrust in, 109
  styles of, 66, 67
  target in, 79, 80
  time-thrust in, 110–112
Foot movements
  in épée fencing, 120, 121
  in foil fencing, 75–79
  in saber fencing, 75–79, 131–136
Force attacks on blade in saber
    fencing, 152
Forced thrust attack along the blade, 99
Formative stage of conditioning the
    body, 55
Forte of the blade, 27
Forward roll, 190
Free play (assault), 70

Free play (assault) (*Cont.*)
  in foil fencing, 116, 117
French flèche, 78
French on guard, 17
French salutation, 32, 33
Froissement, 99, 153
Full mask, 15
Fundamental movements and defi-
    nitions, 86–88

GENERAL advice, theory and, 39–61
General rules of behavior for fencers,
    60, 61
Gladiators, 3, 4
Glide, 97
Gliding disengage
  in foil fencing, 97, 98, 104
  in saber fencing, 151
Glove, 68
Gothic armor, 6
Grand salute, 188
Greek sword, 27
Grip
  foil, 71, 73
  saber, 127
Guard, 10, 26
Guard of Honor, 15

HALBERD
  lance and, 27
  spear and, in theatrical fencing, 179,
    181
Hamlet, fencing scene from, 195–202
Hat, 30
High guard, 10
Hilt, 26
Historical perspective, 37, 38
History of fencing, 1–38
Hit
  in épée fencing, 121
  in foil fencing, 87
  in saber fencing, 141
Hittites, 3
Homologous exercises
  in épée fencing, 125
  in saber fencing, 125, 148, 154, 156,
    158
Hungarian flèche, 78

IMBROCCATA time-thrust, 111
Indirect attacks, 151
Indirect parries, 150
Indirect riposte, 148
Individual lesson, 53, 70
Initial or basic position in foil fencing,
    74
Initial or preparatory stage of condi-
    tioning the body, 55
Inquartata time-thrust, 111, 165
Invitations, 85, 138
Italian on guard, 17

JAPANESE fencing, 24
Jump back, 76
Jump-flèche, 135
Jump forward, 75
Jump-lunge, 77
Jump-step, 131

KENDO fencing, 24
Keresztessy, 19
King Lear, fencing scene from, 208–213
Knights, 5, 7, 9, 34
Knuckle-bow, 26

LA BOESSIERE, 17
La centille, 9
Lance and Halberd, 27
Lanesta, 4
Left-handed fencers, 51
Legion d'Honneur, 21
Letters of privilege, 12
Lines
  in foil fencing, 87
  in saber fencing, 87, 141
Ludi, 4
Lunge, 10, 76–78
  flèche and, 135

MAHABHARATA, 2
Mail gloves, 15
Manners, 33–37, 60, 61
Martial Arts Society, 24
Marxbrüders, 9, 12

Mask, 68
Massage, 56, 57
  types of, 57
Masters of the Noble Science of
    Defense, 13
Maximilian armor, 7
Measure, 110
Medieval weapons, 27
Mensura fencing, 17
Method of practice for fencing scenes
    in theatrical fencing, 194
Middle ages
  historical perspective and, 37
  in theatrical fencing, 175–181
Middle distance, 87
Military sword
  eighteenth century, 28
  nineteenth century, 29
  seventeenth century, 28
  twentieth century, 29
Minerals in diet, 59
Mixed exercises in saber fencing, 143,
    154
Mixed progressive exercises in foil
    fencing, 106
Modern flèche in saber fencing, 132
Modern period
  historical perspective and, 38
  in theatrical fencing, 187–189
Molière's Don Juan, fencing scene from,
    202–204
Moulinets in saber fencing, 136
Movement(s)
  analysis of, 39–43
  fundamental, and definitions, 86–88
Myrmillo gladiators, 3

NET and trident in theatrical fencing,
    174
Nineteenth century, 18–20
  weapons of, 28, 29
Ninus, 2

OCTAVE position, 81, 82
Olympic championships in fencing
  gold medals in, summary of, 231

Olympic championships in fencing
    (Cont.)
  summary of, 233
  world and
    according to nations, summary of,
      215–230
    gold medals in, grand total of, 231
On guard position, 17
  in épée fencing, 120
  in foil fencing, 74
  in saber fencing, 129
One-two feint, 102, 103
One-two-three feint, 103
Oplomachia, 3

PARRY(ies), 43, 44, 85
  changing, 150
  circle, 150
  composite, 106
  direct
    in foil fencing, 89
    in saber fencing, 144–146
    in épée fencing, 121, 122
  indirect, 150
  picco, 89, 101, 118
  semi-circle, 150
  sweeping, 104
Parrying attacks
  on the blade, 101
  with engagement, 97
Pas d'ane, 27, 182
Passado, 12, 195
Passages
  in foil fencing, 86
  in saber fencing, 139, 141
Passata sotto time-thrust, 111, 112, 165
Passe on avant, 78
Passing, 12
Pattinando, 77
Paying the prize, 13
Pecoraro, 20
Peripheral vision, 45, 46
Physical condition, 54–57
Picco-parries, 89, 101, 118
Piste, 47, 63
Point, 14
Point d'arret, 27, 71
Pommel, 26

Position(s)
  first, in foil fencing, 74
  initial or basic, in foil fencing, 74
  of body
    in foil fencing, 74
    in saber fencing, 129
  of foil, 81–85
  of saber, 138–141
  on guard
    in épée fencing, 120
    in foil fencing, 74
  primary, in foil fencing, 81, 82
  secondary, in foil fencing, 81, 85
Practice, 43, 51
Precision, 40
Prehistoric sword, 27
Preliminary analysis, 47, 48
Prelude, 47, 48
Preparation, 48
Preparatory and other exercises for
    competitive fencing, 69, 70
Preparatory or initial stage of condi-
    tioning the body, 55
Pressure, 152
Pressure slide, 97
Pressure slide-feint, 103, 104
Pressure slide-thrust
  in foil fencing, 98, 99
  in saber fencing, 152
Preventive arm-cut in saber fencing, 164
Prima, 138, 182
Prima guardia, 10
Primary positions in foil fencing, 81, 82
Prime position, 10, 81, 85, 138
Progressive combined parry riposte
    exercises in foil fencing, 108
Progressive, combined and, parry riposte
    exercises in foil fencing, 107
Progressive exercises
  in foil fencing, 105
  in saber fencing, 161
Pronation, 81
Proteins in diet, 59
Psychology of fencing, 47–51
Punta reversa, 195

QUARTA, 10, 138, 183
Quarte position, 10, 81, 82, 138

Quillon, 26, 182
Quinte position, 10, 81, 85, 138

RADDOPPIO, 77, 78
Rapier(s)
  history of, 13, 20, 28
  in theatrical fencing, 182, 183
    buckler and, 183
    cloak and, 184, 186
    dagger and, 183, 184
    transition, 186
    two, 186
Reciprocal exercises
  in foil fencing, 116
  in saber fencing, 168
  with partner, 70
Redoublement
  in épée fencing, 124
  in foil fencing, 108, 109
  in saber fencing, 161
Reflex testing and selective responses,
    43–47
Relationship of blades in saber fencing,
    87, 141
Relaxation, 55, 56
  pattern of, 56
Remise
  in épée fencing, 124
  in foil fencing, 108, 109
  in saber fencing, 161, 162
Renaissance, historical perspective and,
    38
Renewed attacks
  in foil fencing, 108, 109
  in saber fencing, 161, 162
Répartée, 109
Repeated-lunge, 77, 78
Reprise d'attaque
  in foil fencing, 109
  in saber fencing, 161, 162
Retiarius gladiators, 3, 174
Retraction, 121
Retreat and flèche in saber fencing, 135
Rhythm, 44
Ricasso, 27, 71
Right-handed fencers, 51
Rimessa, 108, 161
  with raddoppio, 161

Rimessa di filata, 109
Riposte(s)
  along the blade
    in foil fencing, 91
    in saber fencing, 148
  compound
    in foil fencing, 107, 108
    in saber fencing, 159
  contra, 113
  counter, 148
  direct
    in foil fencing, 91
    in saber fencing, 147
  disengage, 93, 94
  flying parry, 148
  in épée fencing, 121, 122
  in foil fencing, 91, 93, 94, 107, 108,
    113
  in saber fencing, 147, 148, 159
  indirect, 148
  simple direct, 147
Ripressa d'attacco, 161
Roman sword, 27
Romeo and Juliet, fencing scene from,
    204–208
Rolling flèche in saber fencing, 135
Rolling in theatrical fencing, 190

SABER, 19, 29, 66, 127–169
  in theatrical fencing, 187
  parts of, 127
  positions of, 138–141
Saber fencing, 127–169
  actions in time in, 162–167
  attacks introduced with engagement
    in, 151
  beat in, 153
  check in, 131
  composite parries in, 158, 159
  compound actions in, 155–157
  compound riposte in, 159
  counter-riposte in, 148
  counter-time in, 167
  direct parries in, 144, 145
  direct riposte in, 147
  disarmament in, 167
  distance in, 87, 141
  double-step in, 131

Saber fencing (Cont.)
  dual feints in, 160, 161
  engagement in, 150
  feint in, 155, 156
  feint in time in, 167
  fencing time in, 135
  fingering in, 144
  flèche in, 132–135
  foot movements in, 75–79, 131–136
  force attacks on blade in, 152
  flying parry riposte in, 148
  grip in, 127
  hit in, 141
  indirect attacks in, 151
  indirect parries in, 150
  indirect riposte in, 148
  jump-step in, 131
  lines in, 87, 141
  moulinets in, 136
  passages in, 139, 141
  position of body in, 129
  preventive arm-cut in, 164
  relationship of blades in, 87, 141
  renewed attacks in, 161, 162
  riposte along blade in, 148
  salute in, 137
  second intention parry riposte in, 166
  simple actions in, 141–154
  slide and check in, 131
  slide in, 131
  styles of, 66, 67
  target in, 137
  timing in, 136
Salutations, 31–33
Salute
  grand, 188
  in foil fencing, 80, 81
  in saber fencing, 137
Samnite gladiators, 3
Samurai, 24
Schlager fencing, 17
Scoring, 63
Second intention attack, 91
Second intention in épée fencing, 122
Second intention parry riposte in saber
    fencing, 166
Second intention remise, 162
Seconda, 10, 138, 183
Seconda intenzione, 112

Secondary positions in foil fencing, 81,
    85
Seconde position, 10, 81, 85, 138
Seconds, 35, 36
Selective responses, reflex testing and,
    43–47
Semi-circular parry, 92
Semi-circular passage, 86
Semi-circle parries, 150
Septime position, 81, 82, 138, 139
Seventeenth century, 14–16
    weapons of, 28
Sforzo, 115, 167
Shield and sword in theatrical fencing,
    173, 174
Shoes, 68
Simple actions
    in foil fencing, 88, 89
    in saber fencing, 141–154
Simple direct riposte, 147
Simple-dual feint, 103
Simple-single feint, 102, 103
Simplicity, 42
Single feint in saber fencing, 155
Singlestick type fencing, 13
Sixte position, 81, 82, 138, 139
Sixteenth century, 9–14
    weapons of, 28
Slide
    check and, 131
    flèche and, 135
    in foil fencing, 97
    in saber fencing, 131, 135
Sliding disengage, 97, 98, 104
Spanish salutation, 31, 32
Spear and halberd in theatrical fencing,
    179, 181
Special exercises
    for foot and hand, 70
    in saber fencing, 157, 159
Speed, 40
St. George, 17
Stabbing in theatrical fencing, 193
Stamp and flèche in saber fencing, 135
Step back in foil fencing, 75
Step-flèche in saber fencing, 135
Step forward in foil fencing, 75
Step-lunge in foil fencing, 77
Stereoscopic vision, 45

Stereoscopic-peripheral vision, 45
Stoccata, 195
Stoccata guard, 10
Stop-hits in foil fencing, 109, 110
Stop-thrust in foil fencing, 110
Strategy, 47–49
Styles of fencing, 66, 67
Supination, 81
Sustaining stage of conditioning the
    body, 55
Sweeping parries, 104
    feints against, 104
Sword(s), 25, 26
    ancient Greek, 3, 27
    ancient Roman, 3, 27
    buckler and, 13
    medieval, 27
    shield and, in theatrical fencing, 173,
        174
    sixteenth century, 28
    small
        eighteenth century, 28
        in theatrical fencing, 187
        nineteenth century, 28
        seventeenth century, 28
    two-hand, 27
        in theatrical fencing, 176–178
Sword-belt, 29, 30
Sword-rapier, 9
Swordsmith's craft, 24, 25

Tactics, 47–49
Tagliata, 95
Tang, 26
Target
    in épée fencing, 119
    in foil fencing, 79, 80
    in saber fencing, 137
Teaching of fencing, 65, 66
Tempo, 109, 162
Tempo comune, 117
Terza, 10, 138, 183
Theatrical fencing, 171–213
    ancient combat and, 173, 174
    bayonet in, 188
    dagger in, 181
    dying on stage in, 193
    early modern period and, 182–187

Theatrical fencing (*Cont.*)
    examples of, 195–213
    fainting in, 193
    falling in, 190, 191
    fencing against two or more oppo-
        nents in, 192
    fencing on stairs in, 192
    introduction to, 171
    method of practice for fencing scenes
        in, 194
    middle ages and, 175–181
    modern period and, 187–189
    net and trident in, 174
    rapier(s) in, 182, 183
        buckler and, 183
        cloak and, 184, 186
        dagger and, 183, 184
        two, 186
    rolling in, 190
    saber in, 187
    spear and halberd in, 179, 181
    stabbing in, 193
    sword in
        shield and, 173, 174
        small, 187
        two-hand, 176–178
    timing in, 194
    transition rapier in, 186
Theory and general advice, 39–61
Thracian gladiators, 3
Three-quarter circle passage, 86
Thrusts
    angle, in épée fencing, 121
    counter-evasive, in saber fencing, 136
    diagonal, 121
    direct
        in foil fencing, 88
        in saber fencing, 141–143
    disengage, 151
    evasive
        in foil fencing, 95, 101
        in saber fencing, 136, 165
    false, 101
    filo, 99
    forced, 99
    pressure slide
        in foil fencing, 98, 99
        in saber fencing, 152
    sliding, in foil fencing, 97, 98

Thrusts (*Cont.*)
    stop, in foil fencing, 110
    time
        in foil fencing, 110
        in saber fencing, 165
Tierce position, 10, 81, 85, 138
Tik-tak parries, 118
Time-hits, 109
Time-thrust
    imbroccata, 111
    in foil fencing, 110–112
    in saber fencing, 165
    inquartata, 111
    passata sotto, 111, 112
Timing, 44, 45
    in foil fencing, 109
    in saber fencing, 136
    in theatrical fencing, 194
Timing exercises in saber fencing, 163
Touches, 63
Training, 51–54
Transfer in foil fencing, 97
Transition rapier in theatrical fencing,
    186
Transporto di ferro, 97, 151
Trial by duel, 34
Trial by ordeal, 5
Trident and net in theatrical fencing,
    174
Triple circulation, 103
Trompement, 101
Twentieth century, 20–24
    weapons of, 29
Two-hand sword, 27
    in theatrical fencing, 176–178
Two rapiers in theatrical fencing, 186

Universal parry, 14

Violent pressure attack
    in foil fencing, 99
    in saber fencing, 153
Vision, 45–47
Vitamins in diet, 59

Warming-up exercises, 69
Waster type fencing, 13

Weapons
    ancient, 27
    description of, 26, 27
    dimensions of, 27–29
    eighteenth century, 28
    in modern fencing, 66
    medieval, 27
    nineteenth century, 28, 29
    prehistoric, 27
    seventeenth century, 28

Weapons (*Cont.*)
    sixteenth century, 28
    twentieth century, 29
World championships in fencing
    gold medals in, summary of, 232
    olympic and
        according to nations, summary of,
          215–230
        gold medals in, grand total of, 231
    summary of, 234, 235